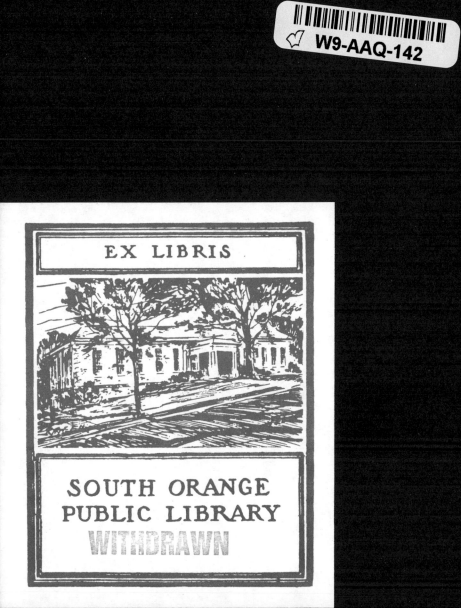

Shamanism in North America

Shamanism
in North America

Norman Bancroft Hunt

FIREFLY BOOKS

A FIREFLY BOOK

Published by Firefly Books (U.S.) Inc. 2003

First printing

Publisher Cataloging-in-Publication Data (U. S.)
Hunt, Norman Bancroft.
Shamanism in North America / Norman Bancroft Hunt.–1st ed.
[232] p. : photos. (some col) ; cm.
Includes bibliographical references and index.
Summary: A study of North American shamanism, history, beliefs, and practices.
ISBN 1-55297-678-5
1. Shamanism—North America. 2. Indians of North America—Religion. I. Title.
291.1/44 21   CIP BL2370.S5S48H86 2003

First published in the United States in 2003 by
Firefly Books (U. S.) Inc.
P. O. Box 1338, Ellicott Station
Buffalo, New York, USA 14205

Published in Canada in 2002 by Key Porter Books Limited

Designed and produced by
Opus Publishing Limited
36 Camden Square, London NW1 9XA

Design: Martin Heller
Cover photographs: Werner Forman

Printed and bound in the Czech Republic

Frontispiece: *Scene of an event which may have involved contact with supernatural powers, in Kitksan (Tsimshian) territory on the Skeena River near Prince Rupert, British Columbia. The petroglyphs include a prominent anthropomorphic head and depictions of precious copper shields, some with crests.*

Contents

Introduction

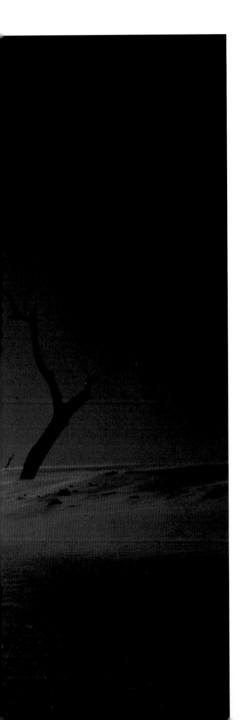

When Europeans first arrived in North America they were amazed by the piety and devotion of the Native people they encountered. Captain Bonneville, who travelled among the Plains tribes of the northwest during the early years of the fur trade, noted that they were 'more like a nation of saints than a horde of savages'. Equally surprising to the Europeans was the fact that while many of the Native beliefs and practices were founded in traditions that appeared quite unlike those of their own organised religions, they shared certain familiar concepts. Tribally recognised ideas about the creation of the world and stories of a great flood were important in indigenous beliefs and were themes to which the Europeans could relate.

Despite these similarities the Europeans nevertheless thought of Native Americans as pagans: people who had only a superstitious outlook and no concept of a higher God. This was partly because Native beliefs were expressed in highly individualistic ways and seemed to lack the formal structures of European religion. Although some tribes – particularly those of the Southeast and Southwest – had priests whose primary function was to conduct rituals for the tribal good, most of them had no apparent system for separating a religious fraternity or priesthood from ordinary people, or for separating people from the animals and spirit beings with whom they shared their world.

Native Americans thought that human beings, animals, spirits, even trees and grasses, as well as the forces of nature, were equal, and that each had its own character, disposition, and form. Because of this different elements were recognised for their individual power

LEFT: *In shamanic thinking all natural forces are considered as sentient beings, capable of thought, motivation, and with individual wills. Native American shamans respond directly to the interplay of elements within their environments, such as the relationship established between sun, sand, sky and trees in this photo from Cumberland Island, Georgia.*

and ability: Bear was noted for his strength; Eagle for his swiftness and ability to travel between earth and sky; Rock for its permanence. But none was better, or worse, than any other, and not even the Creator Gods were omnipotent.

People, however, had one special responsibility. In the distant past recalled in the legends and stories, some people had acted without due regard for the welfare of the rest of creation. The deities therefore decided to make the people responsible for the rituals that would keep the world in harmony and balance. Only people were capable of destroying this balance and only they might restore it. In this way they would always be reminded that they were part of a complex interactive universe which could only be maintained through proper respect for all its different parts.

The manner of showing respect varied from tribe to tribe and from individual to individual depending on their different needs and circumstances. Generally, for a hunter, it was essential to bless the animals he sought and to ask their acquiescence, otherwise they would withdraw and his family would starve. Farmers blessed their fields and seedlings, for failure to do so would result in the deities withholding the rain the crops needed. Failure to follow these customs by anyone was thought to affect the entire community, thus making personal devotions and attitudes matters of public concern.

The degree of power anyone possessed – that is, the ability of an individual to influence events – varied greatly from one person to another. Some people, often as a result of a traumatic experience, were thought capable of achieving a separation of their spirit from their body and to converse directly with other spirits that controlled the various forces of nature in an attempt to solicit their intervention on behalf of the community. These people were the shamans.

The word shaman is a convenient term that has been adopted in anthropological literature in the context of any religious belief that encompasses direct contact with spirit forces. It is derived from 'saman', from a Tungusic language of Siberia, and translates as 'the wise one'. Shamanism itself, however, is a very widespread belief system with an ancient history and continues into the present day. Despite its broad distribution and numerous adherents it is remarkable for its consistency over vast areas and prolonged periods. Similar themes and ideas occur in many parts of the world and modern shamans, although separated both by distance and in time from their ancient counterparts, have been known to recognise and interpret details of shamanic costume and paraphernalia depicted in cave paintings of the Paleolithic period.

OPPOSITE: *Rituals that are intended to appease the deities and ensure favourable outcomes are important in Native American cultures and can be traced back to ancient times. The female figure in this late prehistoric Anasazi wall painting from northern Arizona is holding a bunch of green twigs, which serve as symbols of fertility and growth.*

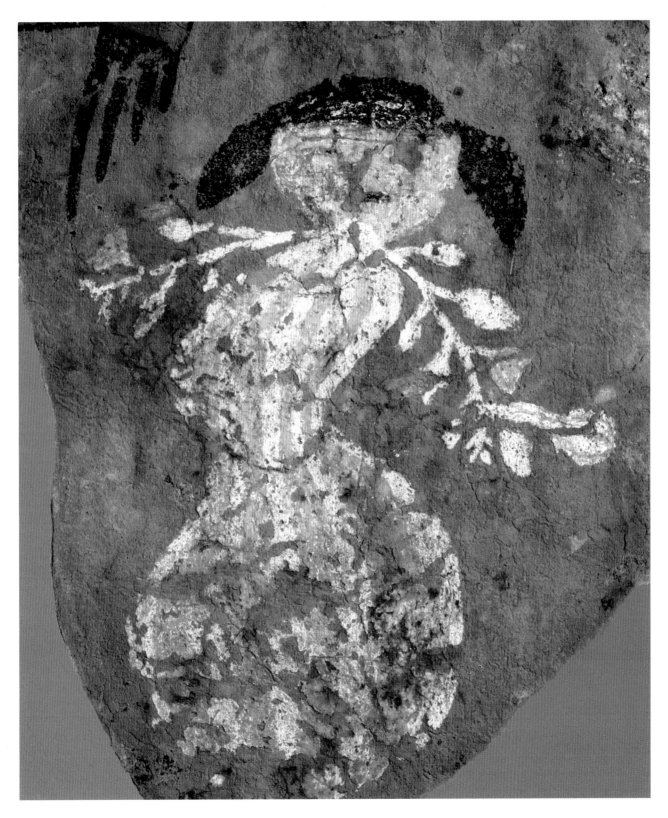

From this it would appear that shamanism originated with the very first hunting-gathering cultures. By performing rituals the shamans attempted to engender a form of spiritual affinity with the animals being hunted, and this notion gave the hunters confidence they would be successful. Yet it is also apparent that even as early as the Paleolithic the shamans were thinking in broader and more abstract terms, since some of the animals depicted are not game animals and others are clearly spirit beings with both human and animal attributes. Shamanism is thus the oldest form of ritual activity, and is the earliest indication we have of human communities developing a sense of non-material existence and an awareness of their place in a broader environment that was not concerned only with the practical realities of everyday survival.

Shamanism in North America also has an ancient origin. Some scholars believe that it can be traced back to early migrations from Asia to the Americas as much as 50,000 years ago; but it is also clear that many distinctive traits have developed since then as a response to widely divergent environmental conditions in different parts of the North American continent. Yet despite these developments there are a number of common elements. These include the fact that shamanism is primarily exercised through the intervention of a small number of highly gifted and sensitive men and women; that it is animistic – that is, founded on a belief that everything possesses a soul or life force; that contact with spirit powers is established through controlled trance; and that shamans attain knowledge and raised consciousness through a series of spiritual journeys, or tests, of increasing difficulty and danger.

Central to the practice of North American shamanism is a concept known as medicine. This comes from the term used by the first French colonists to describe the activities of the shamans. The French used it because they witnessed shamanic healing rituals and observed the shamans using herbal remedies to effect cures. Many of the French pioneers lived in or travelled through areas where there were no European doctors or surgeons and they benefited from and had direct experience of the shamans' skills in treating their various wounds and ailments. Yet despite their reliance on the shamans and the obvious fact that shamanic healing could be effective, the deeply held spiritual beliefs of the shamans were nevertheless seen by the Europeans as no more than pagan ritual.

The ethnic arrogance of the French and other Europeans led them to denigrate the activities of the shamans and to generally deny that there could be any factual base for the shamans' claims that they were able to exercise control or influence in the spirit world. Shamanic activities were consequently often dismissed as witchcraft. We should, nevertheless, remember that at the time of the early contacts European pharmacology and medicine were doctrinaire and narrow. The *Pharmacopœia Londinensis* of 1618, for example, lists mummy dust, human and pigeon excrement, and stag's penis as important European medicines. European priests, too, were likely to respond to shamans' speeches by hurling back exorcisms, and to claim that such verbal attacks proved most efficacious.

Adoption of the term medicine has given rise to a widely held but nonetheless inaccurate understanding of the shamans' principal role as healers or physicians. Native Americans consider shamanic healing as applicable in life-threatening situations, but they interpret the term medicine in a broader sense. Perhaps the closest to the Native meaning is mysterious power, if this is taken to mean a complex set of beliefs, rituals, and paraphernalia that extends far beyond the use of simple remedies. The shaman, who is adept at dealing with the esoteric, may, in addition to possessing healing power, be a prophet or diviner, have power to control or influence natural forces, act as a priest or as tribal leader, and, perhaps most importantly, be the keeper of Native lore and history. Thus the shaman is a medicineman or medicinewoman in the sense that he or she is the controller of mysteries, but only in life-threatening circumstances does he or she act as a physician.

Antagonism toward the shamans, seen as guardians of tradition and the main force opposing the civilisation of Native America, continued well into the nineteenth century. As late as the 1880s it was still generally believed that shamanic practices verged on the ridiculous or satanic, and it was not until the 1940s that the burgeoning science of anthropology demanded an end to prejudice and suggested that the shamans might have something to contribute to human knowledge and understanding of the world in which we live.

More recently, linked with a sense of frustration at materialistic attitudes and an increasing awareness of environmental issues, sympathetic observers have begun to accept, or even to wholeheartedly adopt, a neo-shamanic view. This incorporates much Native American lore and practice, as well as shamanic beliefs from other parts of the world, and fuses these together to create a new shamanism. Shamanic techniques of rhythmic drumming and controlled dreaming enable neo-shamans to connect with higher planes of consciousness that do not exploit natural resources and which are removed from the mundane realities of everyday life.

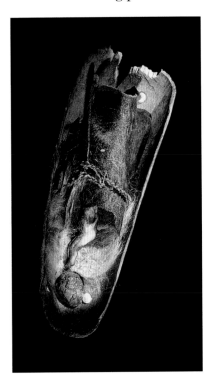

Nearly two thousand years ago an Eskimo shaman relied on the ivory figure and the other objects in this wooden bowl to help him succeed in a healing procedure.

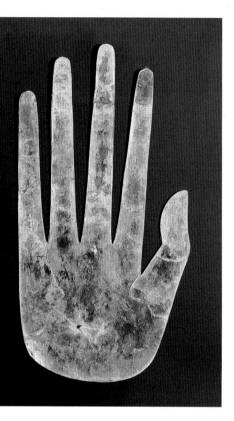

ABOVE: *The larger than life-size (10 in. high) silhouette of a hand cut from a mica sheet was found in an Ohio burial hundreds of miles away from the nearest source of mica. The hand was a powerful shamanistic symbol.*

Neo-shamanism focusses attention on contemporary issues, and as such can distort the views of more traditional adherents. Traditional shamans, such as the *angakoks* of the Eskimo or the *diyi* of the Apache, generally welcome these new approaches but do so advisedly. They take us back to tales of *Sedna* the Eskimo Sea Goddess, of the Twin Brothers of the Apache, or of the Pawnee conception of the Creator, *Tirawahat*, who is also known as Vault of Heaven. They remind us that the world was originally created in harmony and that only people can disrupt this, and point to the evidence contained in tribal mythologies as proof of these ancient laws.

Despite the inroads of neo-shamanic belief and the confusions and distortions of North American history and politics, we should remember that Native American shamans were never narrow in their perceptions. They had a broad concept of power, which enabled them to incorporate Christian beliefs in a monolithic deity, or supreme Godhead: their own creator gods, despite the fact these were often unnamed and only rarely clearly identified, were seen by them as equivalent to the European concept of a universal creator. Christian saints could similarly be equated with the numerous kachinas of the Pueblo tribes.

The shamans felt that Christian beliefs differed in detail rather than principle from the ancient inherited laws, and have left us with a body of knowledge about what these ancient laws entailed. Ironically, given the opposition shown by missionaries to the shamans, much of this was volunteered by the shamans themselves. Under the impact of the Christian church they felt the old ways were dying out or being undermined and wished to preserve a record for future generations.

There is much evidence of the sometimes astonishing accomplishments of shamans, both past and present, many of which have been recorded by observers who initially expressed scepticism but could offer no logical or scientific explanation for the feats they witnessed. Modern Native American shamans believe that in the old days the powers of the shamans were greater than they are today, and quote miraculous cures of people whom conventional medicine had deemed incurable; skills in using controlled dreaming to locate the presence of animals or bring them close to the camps during periods of scarcity; and an ability to predict future events with a high degree of accuracy.

Although there may be a degree of exaggeration in the shamans' statements about the powers possessed by their ancestors, shamanic skills are still in demand in a scientific age. Many people, in fact, claim it is only now that science is beginning to probe some of the mysterious powers the shamans have been able to exert since antiquity. Yet the shaman remains a shadowy figure, hovering on the verge of the incredible. This is partly because shamanism is a practice rather than a theory and is based on a wide range of feelings and impulses which the shaman is able to take to extremes and to reinterpret in terms of his/her own spiritual experiences. Out-of-body flights and the dismemberment of the shaman's physical shell in spirit contacts are beyond the capabilities of ordinary individuals and defy generalisation or categorisation.

The shaman does not distinguish between the worlds of the physical and the imagined, to him/her they are the same and movement between them is readily made. It is through the integration of elements from these different worlds that shamanic power is realised. This does not, however, mean that the Native American shamans must remain forever beyond our comprehension, or that they cannot provide an inspirational source of knowledge and understanding. The world of the shaman is, essentially, an open and unbiased one; but it may bring us into contact with forms of spiritual experience that defy reason and test a demand for scientific proof.

1 *The Half-World of the Eskimo Aleut*

The Far North, home to the Eskimo and Aleut of the Arctic coasts, is a world of illusions. Powder snow driven by the constant winds, and thick fog raised as water vapour crosses frozen land masses, create an environment in which things are seen and half-seen; where they become both tangible and intangible. There is an ephemeral sense to the landscape: great banks of snow standing tall and solid as mountains can shift or disappear overnight with contrary winds.

The Spirits of the Weather - of Storm, Wind, Cloud, Snow, and Cold play capricious tricks. Sometimes they cooperate, and a clear, bright, sunlit morning heralds a day that is good for hunting or travelling; but at other times they compete in elemental battles fierce enough to tear the landscape apart and rearrange it, and when visibility may be reduced to absolute zero. When vision is restored the world is no longer as it had been, and the Eskimo gazes out over unfamiliar vistas. There are few clear points of reference in a world as impermanent as this.

In this land – the most inhospitable region occupied by human communities – the Eskimo and Aleut eke out a precarious existence. They are subject not only to the whims of the Weather Spirits but also to the humours of a host of powerful and often malevolent *tunghat*: mythical beasts whose home is on the moon but who travel widely and which only shamans can see. They control and regulate the supply of fish and game animals, yet have little love for humans whom they consider to be puny creatures who invade their space and hunt and kill the seals, polar bears, Arctic foxes, and other creatures the *tunghat* care for, or who, often inadvertently, cause offence by their improper behaviour. Even the mere presence of humans and

The Eskimo and Aleut live in a world in which the demarcations between water, land, and sky are often obscured by mists and snow. In this half-world of indefinite character dwell numerous spirits who act as helpers to the shamans.

15

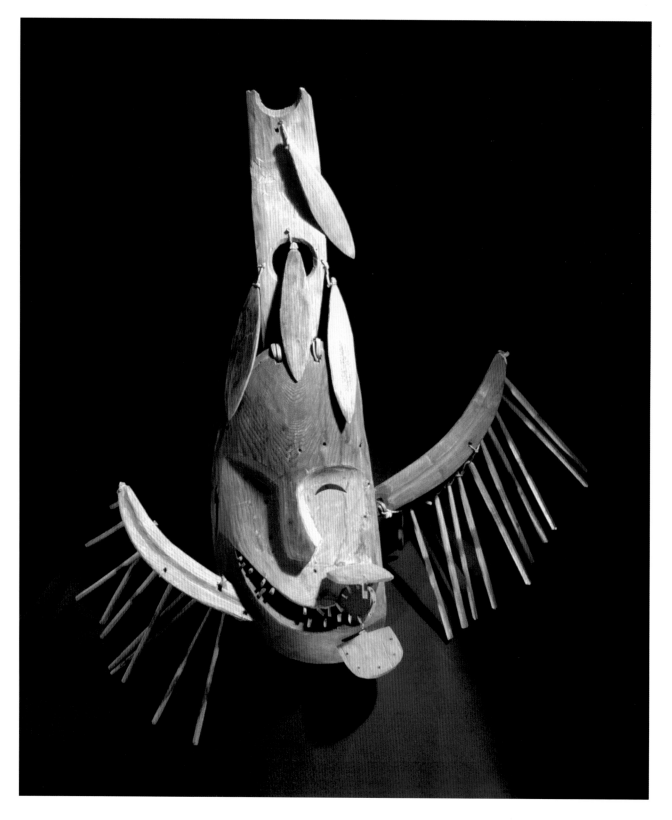

the unintelligible babble of their voices, can drive the *tunghat* into tantrums of uncontrollable rage. Here, too, are lizard-like *palraiyuk*, which leave their secret hiding places with the spring thaws and take up residence in marshes, lakes, and streams, where they are ever ready to pounce on and devour the incautious and unwary.

Against this background of uncertainty, the Eskimo and Aleut live for the moment and make few plans for the future. Daily life centres on the family and the immediate needs of survival. Although most families are also part of loosely organised tribal groups, these meet rarely and then only for a few days when hard packed snow and good visibility make it possible to take out the sleds and dog teams on long journeys, or, in coastal areas, when warmer weather breaks up the winter ice and permits sea travel in tiny one- or two-person skin-covered kayaks, or in larger umiaks capable of transporting entire families.

The unpredictability of the Arctic environment means that every aspect of Eskimo-Aleut life is linked with numerous taboos, conditions, and precautionary measures that are intended to solicit beneficent aid from the spirit world. Many of these proscriptions and conditions are formulated in obscure terms and are subject to very variable individual interpretation: what works for one family and brings hunting success, health, and joy may prove disastrous if attempted by someone else in identical circumstances. Similarly, a formula repeated successfully on several previous occasions may suddenly fail to produce the desired effect. Sometimes the family may simply be unable to find food for a few days and go hungry, or they might find themselves wrapped in an all-enveloping blizzard with wind speeds so high it is impossible to stand against them. Such blizzards can last for days or weeks, with tragic consequences.

Yet the Eskimo-Aleut are a pragmatic people, and if one charm or chant fails they have recourse to countless others. The Eskimo simply say that if one spirit helper is good, then several must be better. 'Memories' of spirit contacts and contracts are carried in the form of small ivory, bone, or wood carvings worn in the hair, attached to bags and containers, or sewn into the lining of wind- and water-proof parkas. It is not unusual for a single individual to have as many as thirty or forty of these talismans secreted somewhere about the person or scattered in his or her belongings, and each of these, to be effective, requires the invoking of its power through special observances and ritual performance. Should its power prove inadequate, the charm is simply tossed away, discarded.

For most people the power inherent in these charms comes indi-

OPPOSITE: For most of the time the spirit beings hover near the edges of encampments and are rarely seen. However, when they appear it is clear from their features that they are non-human. The distorted features of this Twisted Face mask are characteristic of a range of supernatural beings that, despite their frightening appearance, are generally the bearers of good news and act as helpers to the humans.

ABOVE: Eskimo shamans often direct spirit familiars said to reside within their bodies to carry out their instructions. Although tupilaqs usually take the form of small mammals, they sometimes appear in grotesque form such as that shown here.

rectly from the *tunghat* which hover close to the fringes of camps. Their presence is felt rather than seen, or is made manifest through their voices carried on Arctic winds. For this reason, Eskimo carvers listen to the materials they work with and only after hearing the 'voice' of the spirit within them do they carve away any excess ivory, bone, or wood to reveal the essence contained within it.

But some people have greater access to the *tunghat*. These are the *angakoks*, or shamans, who are believed to travel in immaterial form over vast distances – even to the *tunghats'* abode on the moon - and converse directly with the spirit powers. In doing so they enter the half-world of the Eskimo – a world in which nothing is quite what it appears to be. In this world the ordinary reality of the people is turned upside down: day becomes night, and intense cold can be converted into an energy source that the shaman can use. In his spiritual or out-of-body state the shaman is thought to have an immaterial presence which is denied to other people.

In order to function in the spirit world – a domain where human presence is usually unthinkable – the shaman must cloak himself in layers of protective force. To this end he seeks the assistance of strong *tunghat*, perhaps those associated with Raven or Polar Bear, upon whom he relies as protectors and through whose persuasion the other spirit powers might more readily tolerate his presence.

Even so, he remains vulnerable. His own spirit – known to the Eskimo as the *inua*, or soul – separated from the familiar environment of the Eskimo and from the physical body of the shaman to which it gives life, is nervous and frightened yet must show no sign of weakness which could be taken advantage of. Anything untoward, a slight mistake, even a sudden noise, can nevertheless so startle the soul that it flees from the nightmare world of the *tunghat* into an unknowable and unreachable void from which it may never be recovered. Then the shaman's physical shell, deprived of its life-giving *inua*, slowly withers, loses strength, and eventually dies.

Despite having the protection of one or more powerful *tunghat*, the nervousness of the shaman's soul reflects the fact that even the guardians may not be all they seem. Apparently real and clear signs from the spirits have their visible and invisible aspects, which are subject to the shaman's interpretation and thus open to misunderstanding. Shamans are not infallible and may be deceived or misled.

Lieutenant Zagoskin, working for the Russian American Company in the 1840s prior to the sale of Alaska to the United States, was invited to a ceremony conducted by a Yup'ik Eskimo shaman who was influenced by the *tunghat* of Raven. Wearing a

ABOVE: *Shaman's ivory fertility charm in phallic form. Arctic environments are harsh and the dangers to nomadic hunting peoples great. Deaths from hunting accidents or exposure were common, as were still-births and deaths of young children. One of the shaman's concerns was to seek assistance from the deities in ensuring the potency of men and the fecundity of women. Charms such as this one carved from walrus ivory, were thought to assist the shaman in his rituals.*

Raven mask, the shaman imitated the actions of a bird hopping and perching, accompanied by a rhythmic beat from a group of drummers. Zagoskin was impressed with the strength of the performance, and the audience were enthralled by this display of the shaman's power and of his control over supernatural forces; but part way through the shaman began to sing the familiar lament of a man who is unsuccessful in everything he does.

The words of the shaman's song explained that he was accompanied by Raven wherever he went and that it was from Raven he obtained the power to make out-of-body journeys and to predict future events, but

> he is hungry, and he notices that wherever he goes a raven goes with him and gets in his way. If the game he is pursuing is a deer, the raven from some place or other caws, startles the deer, and makes it impossible to creep up within bowshot of it. If the man sets a noose for hare or partridge, the raven tangles it or runs off with it. If he sets a fish-trap for *imagnat*, there too the raven finds a way to do him harm.
>
> 'Who are you?' cries the shaman at last. The spirit in the form of the raven smiles and answers: 'Your evil fate.'
>
> Michael, 1967: 227

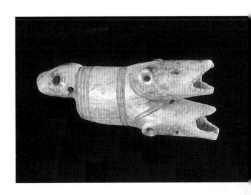

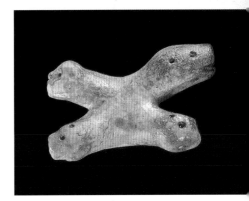

Although deception is part of the character of the *tunghat*, through experience the angakok becomes wiser and more adept at recognising this and exercising his own will; but his journey in gaining the spiritual strength and awareness to do so, as well as the degree of power he may eventually control, begins, like other aspects of Arctic life, in an unpredictable manner. It may be slow, gentle, and subtle; or it can come upon him with unprecedented swiftness and violence. The call to shamanism experienced by two angakoks, both influenced by Seal, demonstrates these extremes.

The first was a middle-aged man of average hunting ability, competent but inconspicuous, whose vocation was indicated by the feather he found in the bottom of his kayak after an unusually successful seal-hunting foray. He carried the feather with him on his next hunting expedition and was again successful. Time after time this happened, while other more experienced hunters returned with little or nothing to show.

Eventually a well-known hunter who had been having a run of bad luck asked to borrow the feather. This was willingly lent, and on his next trip the skilled hunter brought home four seal: enough to

ABOVE: *The draghandle for hauling dead seals with heads of polar bears and a seal served also as a hunter's amulet. Small charms or talismans were thought to embody the powers of the spirit forces, and with the assistance of the shamans this power could be realised in the human realm. In the lower carving the predatory nature of the human hunter and of the polar bear are combined with an image of their common prey, the seal.*

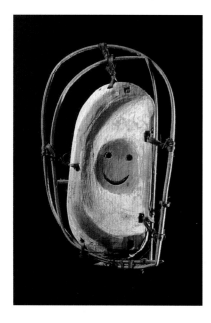

ABOVE: *An Eskimo driftwood mask. Eskimo shamans were believed to be in direct contact with the celestial powers, and through them with all the forces of the cosmos. The central figure bears similarities to Eskimo depictions of the Moon. The stick framework surrounding the central figure is a stylised representation of the different layers of the cosmos through which the shaman travelled during seances to contact the spirits of the other world.*
OPPOSITE: *A dancer's forehead mask made from materials with magical or symbolic character.*

feed the entire community for several days. This went on for some time, and every hunter who carried the feather brought home fresh meat. Eventually the man had a dream in which Seal appeared and explained that the feather had a calming influence: its presence in a kayak ensured smooth waters, which attracted seals within reach of the hunter's harpoon. Seal instructed him to follow certain directions, through which he gained fame not only for his newly-acquired hunting prowess but also for the ability to exert influence over the weather and to calm storms at sea.

The second man, younger and already recognised as one of the most proficient sealers of his band, also gained power from Seal but in a rather different and more dramatic manner. He had been out hunting on a particularly bright, clear morning, and, as usual, had already harpooned two seals long before the other hunters even came in sight of their prey. He had lashed the carcasses to the sides of his kayak, where they were kept buoyant with bladder floats, and was on his way back to the village when he saw a third seal drifting lazily in the water, apparently oblivious of any danger.

His instinct told him to return home, and Eskimo common sense prescribes this as the better course of action: only the most foolhardy pursue further quarry after a catch has been secured, for the drag of the carcasses and bladder floats slows the kayak and limits its manoeuvrability. Yet he felt an irresistible urge to add the third seal to those he had already caught. Despite the fact the seal floated in calm water only a short distance away, harpoon after harpoon failed to strike its target.

The hunter cut loose the attached carcasses and floats and, by now in a raging temper, rammed his kayak against the seal – which glanced up as if mocking him – and then thrust his harpoon downward into the seal's body with all the strength he could muster. On shore he began butchering his kill, when he discovered to his horror that this was no ordinary creature. Its rib cage was human, and its other bones were those of different animals. As he gazed at the monster he had brought ashore he felt a blow at the back of his head and a tug on his parka. A sudden fierce wind dashed snow and ice into his face, blinding him, as he lashed out at his unseen assailants.

Several days later men from the village found the hunter barely alive. White bone protruded from where his leg and arm had been broken, his face was bloodied, and a great gash exposed his weakly beating heart. The snow around was covered in blood from his kill and from the terrific fight that had taken place, yet, search as they might, they found no tracks other than those of the hunter himself.

ABOVE: *Mount Iliamna is one of a series of snow-capped volcanoes of the Alaskan Peninsula and the Aleutian Islands. Although the shamans often presented such geographic features as evidence of the power of the deities and of the natural forces with which the people had to contend, to the shamans themselves they were thought of as gateways to the worlds beyond those in which the people lived.*

He recovered under the care of an old angakok, who made several out-of-body journeys to the moon to plead with the *tunghat* to spare the hunter's life; although his injured arm remained stiff and he was no longer able to throw a harpoon with accuracy. He gave up hunting and instead became the old angakok's assistant, learning the ways of the *tunghat* from him and eventually becoming a famous shaman in his own right.

Other Eskimo-Aleut angakoks receive their initial calls in various ways: through dreams, on recovery from an illness or by long arduous years of tuition and training. Invariably however, they describe the first indication that they are to be given the ability to exercise power as coming upon them unexpectedly in the form of a brilliant blue flash. At this moment their mind and body seem to separate and they experience a clarity of vision that knows no bounds. One describes it as the ability 'to see forever': a piercing vision that can define detail on the moon or under the sea; that looks through and beyond solid objects.

This sudden realisation, despite the traumas the angakoks will have to face in their daily activities, is felt as a sense of euphoria; of great and inexplicable joy. It is a feeling of release, of letting go of everyday concerns and of being absolutely and unreservedly free of any constraints.

The joy expressed by the angakok is a typical Eskimo response to situations of personal or collective crisis. Faced with the terror of an impossible but unavoidable fact, or in the angakok's case with the sudden realisation that future entry into unfamiliar realms containing unknown trials has become possible, the Eskimo-Aleut peoples subdue tension and fear through laughter. Many visitors to Eskimo-Aleut camps are surprised, even shocked, to find them coping with intolerable conditions that threaten their survival through dance, song, games, and pantomime. Even driftwood carvings of the most ferocious and terrifying *tunghat* have twisted faces and distorted grins that give them a comical rather than frightening appearance.

This, too, is part of the half-world that the angakok has access to, for the Eskimo are well aware that appearances can be deceptive and that things in the physical world may be reversed in the world of the spirits. Humour and light-heartedness are simply another aspect of sorrow and fear: they are the twin facets of a single emotional state or condition. It is an Eskimo belief that by employing opposites conditions can be reversed: humour works as the antidote to sorrow, just as fear can be overcome by an outward show of bravery.

This belief in reversals is something with which the angakok will become increasingly familiar and more adept at using as he gains experience in out-of-body journeys and through his contacts with the occupants of the spirit world. He must learn to laugh off threats, to appear confident despite his nervousness, and to shrug off dangers as if they were unimportant. Through his use of tricks and false appearances he can master his weak points and turn them to his advantage.

The *tunghat*, too, as he knows very well, will play tricks on him and often conceal their real intentions. Like the seal that presented itself as a victim in order to 'capture' the hunter's soul, they may make a pretence of friendship to catch the angakok off guard. Or they may approach in a menacing manner even when they intend no harm or are offering protection and help.

The angakok's self-awareness, however, only makes access to the spirit world and influence over the forces contained within a possibility. It gives no clues as to what may actually be found there, nor does it provide any guidelines as to how to react and respond to the unexpected or ambiguous situations with which he may be confronted. At this early stage in his career he is also confused as to his

BELOW: *This carving of a human figure with attached blue beads is drilled so that it can be attached to a cord and worn as a pendant. In Eskimo and Aleut belief blue is thought of as representing a life-force that exists beyond the constraints of the physical body, and the penetrating gaze of shamans that enables them to see beyond the immediate and the obvious is often said to be accompanied by an intense aura of blue light.*

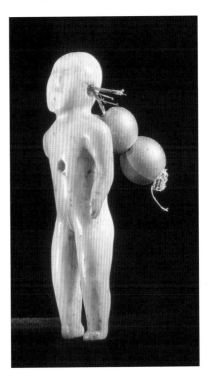

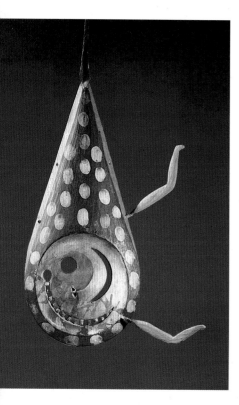

ABOVE: *The distorted features of this mask from southwestern Alaska suggest that a spirit figure is intended; it may have been used by a dancer during rituals at which spirit contact was sought. Only shamans could converse with the spirits, and this mask probably had a shamanic function.*

own identity: his personality is split between his physical needs and those of his mind or spirit.

The most obvious – and the most widely employed – method of gaining power and insight is through tuition or apprenticeship. This may come directly from a guiding *tunghat*, but is more often gained by becoming an assistant to an experienced angakok who is able to provide instruction based on his experiences in the spirit world. He can also request his own protective *tungha*t to extend their favour to the initiate, but is unable to compel them to do so: some will willingly offer help whereas others may refuse, and others still may make a pretence of helpfulness although they really have malicious intent.

The second part of the angakok's journey, his spiritual voyage in search of experience and understanding, is a hazardous one during which he is extremely vulnerable. Any errors or mistakes may lead to death or insanity. It is a journey few undertake willingly, although the angakoks typically describe it as pleasurable or ecstatic.

Under the guidance of his tutor the apprentice learns a number of practical skills. Foremost among these are the construction and use of the unique and highly distinctive tambourine drum, which is used only by shamans, and the ability to communicate in an esoteric language known only to angakoks and the spirits. Although drumming and 'drum dancing' as a form of shamanic communication was banned in Alaska by Moravian missionaries in the 1870s and in Canada by the Canadian Indian Act of 1875, drums continued to be used – especially in isolated areas – and drum lore is still recognised and understood today. The secret language of the shamans has also been kept alive. In a region as vast and remote as the Arctic, religious and governmental edicts and repressive laws that might have undermined the Eskimo/Aleut cultural heritage and destroyed the power of the angakoks have proven difficult or impossible to enforce.

Skill in the use of the shaman's drum and knowledge of the shamanic language are gained through participating in ceremonies conducted by an older angakok, when it is the apprentice's role to continue the chanting after his tutor goes into a trance-like state. During his trance an angakok repeats the words of the spirits and questions his audience to determine whether any taboos have been broken or indiscretions committed, while his assistant interprets the messages he receives for the benefit of the crowd of spectators that has gathered as witness to the events.

Such practical tuition may last many years, and the initiate often fails to pass beyond the stage of being a shaman's assistant and able to make out-of-body journeys on his own behalf. Although able to

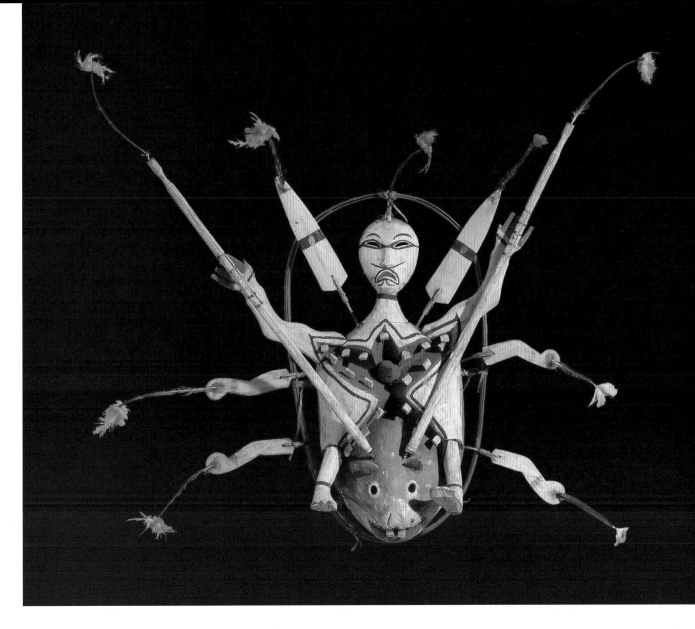

see into and understand much about the spirit world, shaman's assistants lack the ability to separate the physical from the metaphysical and are unable to withstand the hardships that the *inua* must undergo when released from the confines of the body.

In order to become a fully-functioning angakok, the apprentice must seek − or be subjected to − other experiences which enable him to travel freely between the human world and the spirit world. These experiences, which form the third part of his journey, are under the direct control of the *tunghat* and involve the common shamanic theme of dismemberment and reassembly, or of death and rebirth. Through this the initiate becomes 'transparent': a state halfway between that of the solid, physical human presence and the invisible immaterial presence of the spirits. The Eskimo call him a

ABOVE: *The shaman on this mask is riding a beaver armed with paddles and harpoons for spiritual confrontations. The hoop represents the realm dividing the spiritual from the human through which the shaman must pass during his journey.*

'thin man'; although for others to see him in this condition would prove fatal to them and dangerous for the angakok, who may then be unable to return to the human world from his journey into the realm of the spirits.

To become a 'thin man' the apprentice undergoes a terrifying ordeal. He is seized by an irresistible urge to act in bizarre and dangerous ways: he may fling himself upon a harpoon so that its point pierces his body, tear off his clothes and run naked into the snow and ice of an Arctic winter where he can wander aimlessly for days, or he may stand motionless and refuse food or water for hours on end. He may die in these attempts if the *tunghat* do not favour him, since it is they who decide whether he should succumb to the fate of ordinary mortals.

Acceptance of the potential angakok by the *tunghat* will enable him to recover from this test. He is not, however, unchanged. During the test they beset him with frightful abandon: tearing the skin from his limbs, breaking his bones, and ripping out his internal organs. They play with his body, and at times leave cruel evidence of their acts: a shattered or incomplete leg bone, leaving an angakok lame for life, or loss of his power of sight so that he is entirely dependent on the inner vision that came with the initial realisation of his calling.

Even if he emerges physically unscathed he is still dramatically altered, since during the process of reassembling the shattered remains of his physical being the *tunghat* insert power of their own by replacing some of the vital organs. These, usually, are the heart and liver. The Eskimo maintain that in an angakok these are of quartz crystal, which pulsates and vibrates of itself, independently from the body. Quartz is unimpaired when the body deteriorates, and it allows the angakok to gain a measure of immortality denied to others.

In the Eskimo view, the emergent angakok is no longer as he had been prior to his ordeal. The impact of the spirits, emanating from an invisible immaterial realm, makes him different from other people. His gaze no longer rests on solid objects but seems to penetrate them, observing something intangible that lies beyond the immediate and apparent. Shifting landscapes are no surprise to him, since things are never what they seem to be. He is aware of paradox and contradiction and begins to realise that everyday things and ordinary vision may be limited or illusory: that behind the mask of reality lie hidden depths of meaning that can only be accessed at a spiritual level.

The inner vision of the angakoks has led European observers to express their feelings of unease in the presence of these remarkable

ABOVE: *Although the tribal origin of this transformation mask is not completely clear, it is likely to have been carved by the Yupik speaking Chugach of Prince William Sound. The Chugach shared certain cultural traits with the tribes of the Northwest Coast. Among these was a belief in the Otterman, a powerful supernatural. Merely sighting the Otterman would cause the death of a mortal human, but the strongest shamans might seek the Otterman's help to enhance their own invulnerability and power. When closed, the mask represents the sea otter in a characteristic pose floating on its back. On opening the mask the* inua, *or spirit, of the sea otter is revealed in its human form.*

men and women. Even when few words have been exchanged, or when the absence of an interpreter has made conversation impossible, the angakoks seemed able to judge with uncanny accuracy the attitude and sincerity of their visitors. They are dismissive of the sceptical and the insincere and, even though their own lives are shrouded in mystery and spent in activities that defy reason, they respond well to honesty and forthrightness.

The uncanny ability of the angakoks to distinguish truth from falsity, as well as their inclination to protect the unwary from dangerous exposure to the awesome forces with which they are involved, is also felt by the Eskimo themselves. Young boys, who move out of their family homes into the *qasgiq*, or communal men's house, for instruction by the angakoks, often mention the sense of exposure they feel there. Joseph Eriday, a Yup'ik Eskimo from Chevak, recorded in 1978 how he felt when he underwent training as a young boy:

> It was good to hear the admonitions of those in the *qasgiq* who did the speaking there, though we did not always think so. Poor me! Sometimes I thought they could see right through into me, into my life, when they spoke. It was chilling. I tingled all over. How could they know me so well? Their instructions on how to live come up again, and again.
>
> It is true, the *qasgiq* is a place of instruction, the only place where the necessary instructions can be given in full.
> Fitzhugh and Caplan, 1982: 210

Having successfully endured the demanding trials, the angakok is expected not only to instruct people about the conduct of their lives, but in particular to intervene on behalf of the community at

LEFT: *The disc-like markings on this ivory Otterman figure are characteristic of Chugach carving.* OVERLEAF: *The forbidding front of Child's Glacier on Prince William Sound in southern Alaska is stark reminder of the harshness of the Arctic home of the Eskimos.*

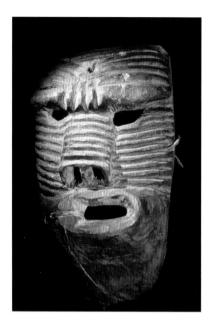

ABOVE: *An essential aspect of Eskimo shamanic practice is the ability to demonstrate self-control in difficult circumstances.*
A consequence of this is the competition during which rival shamans relate ridiculous tales in an attempt to compromise their opponents or force them into uncontrolled laughter. At ridicule contests the opposing shamans wear masks such as this one.
OPPOSITE: *The shadowy spirit figures that are believed to lurk about the fringes of Eskimo encampments are known as* tunghat, *and are thought to possess power that can be used for both good and bad.*
In carvings they are often portrayed as threatening and menacing; their power can, however, be harnessed by the shamans and turned to beneficial purpose.

times of exceptional hardship or crisis; this constitutes the final part of his journey. It immediately introduces another paradox. The angakok's actions do not stem from self-interest. He puts himself in life-threatening situations in order to avert disasters to which he is immune, at least in theory. But to be successful he must commune with the *tunghat* whose motives are self-serving. They care little for the survival of human communities and are thought to be responsible for the difficulties people face. The angakok attracts threats to himself to divert threats from others.

Since threats to human communities are posed by the *tunghats*, the angakok uses the partial immunity granted during his ordeal to travel into the spirit world and confront the spirits in an attempt to persuade them to stop harming the community. His strategy is a combination of appeasement, flattery and trickery; but these are also devices the spirits may use against him in order to exert their will.

The angakok's communication with the spirits takes place within the *qasgiq*, with a large mixed audience in attendance. The audience is essential, both to witness and encourage the angakok and to admit to any transgressions which may have offended the spirits. It is said the angakok is able to detect a dark cloud that is invisible to ordinary people which gathers around a transgressor.

Preparations begin several days before the event, during which the angakok undergoes a period of fasting and meditation and looks for signs indicating what the outcome of his endeavour might be. These signs may be hidden anywhere, and only the angakok knows where to look for them and how to interpret them. They may be promising, or they can spell disaster. Nevertheless, once his intention has been made known, the angakok has no choice but to proceed, regardless of any warnings that his life may be in jeopardy or that his predictions will reveal grave consequences for the entire community. If the signs are ominous, all he can do is exert even greater effort and plead with his guiding helpers to use their benevolent influence to the full.

A characteristic Eskimo shamanic performance was observed by Peter Freuchen, a close friend of the famous Arctic explorer Knud Rasmussen, who was present at a seance held in the early 1900s by the aged angakok Sorqaq. The extended family group in which Sorqaq lived had suffered a series of misfortunes and he was now about to travel through the rock to the Underworld to discover what had gone wrong. Sorqaq was afraid his revelations would bring little comfort, since the signs told him he would predict more deaths.

RIGHT: The Moon is important in Eskimo cosmology, since it is on the moon that the spirits of the game animals reside. In this carving from western Alaska the white board surrounding the face of the moon represents the air, the hoops are the different levels of the universe, and feathers act as symbols of the stars. During out-of-body journeys, shamans travel through these regions to request the spirits to intercede on the people's behalf.

Freuchen left a vivid first-hand description of what took place.

Sorqaq was the last to enter the vast *qasgiq*, which was in the form of a double-igloo that had been specially built for this occasion, and he seemed bewildered at the number of Eskimo men, women, and children who crowded the raised seating platforms about the *qasgiq's* perimeter. His attention, however, focused on Freuchen and his friends. Waving his arm to indicate the presence of such a large audience, he turned to Freuchen and said:

> 'This is nothing for the great white man to look at. I am a big liar, and even if these fools are stupid enough to believe me, I could never deceive you, and your presence will embarrass me. What happens here has nothing to do with the truth.'
>
> 'I should like to listen to your great wisdom.'
>
> 'Naw, naw,' he said. 'That goes to show you that even a white man may be born foolish.'

Krilerneq, Sorqaq's assistant, tied up the old angakok, who had completely undressed, and extinguished all the seal-oil lamps except for one tiny flame. He placed the shaman's drum and drumstick next to Sorqaq, who, Freuchen assures us, after examining the knots in

RIGHT: *This Eskimo shaman from Alaska is shown with a sick boy whom he is treating. In order to effect a cure the shaman must converse with the disease-causing spirits, and he therefore assumes a guise that the spirits will recognise. Exaggerated features, such as the gigantic hands the shaman exhibits in this photograph, indicate that the shaman has passed beyond the 'normal' realm of the people and of human understanding and is prepared to enter the rarefied realm of the spirit beings.*

33

minute detail, was completely immobilised: his arms were secured behind his back with a stout rope above the elbows, his thumbs were lashed together with strips of rawhide, and a rope extending from these wrapped around his ankles so that his feet were drawn up beneath him.

Sorqaq began to sing in his ancient cracked voice while the spectators shouted encouragement and praised him for his great abilities. For a long time Sorqaq chanted, breaking his song every so often with a despairing cry that his *tunghat* had forsaken him and he would be unable to travel through rock and plead with the spirits, or that his power would leave him at the mercy of their tricks and make it impossible for him to return to the people.

Each time he uttered his words of despair the crowd yelled that he could make it, until the *qasgiq* was filled with shouts and cries urging him on. Slowly his chant increased in strength and tempo, while the drum which the Eskimo say 'plays itself' – began to beat faster. The *qasgiq* trembled with the sound of the drumbeats. Sealskins crackled through the air, or could be heard passing through the ground beneath the audience's feet. Krilerneq's voice boomed in accompaniment to Sorqaq's song, which was becoming wilder and wilder, while the audience sang and shouted. Freuchen lost track of how long this 'infernal din' lasted, but recalls that he held on to Krilerneq's arm to make certain he was not party to any trickery on Sorqaq's part.

Finally the angakok's voice became fainter and then stopped. Krilerneq relit the lamps. Sorqaq had disappeared. Only his drum and a sealskin that had been placed over his body remained on the ledge where the angakok had lain, but there was nowhere in the *qasgiq* where he might have hidden himself.

The audience were by now ecstatic:

cheeks swollen, eyes bright and unseeing . . . they swayed back and forth to the rhythm of the song. Krilerneq was writhing and twisting like a dancer, driving the men and women into a higher and higher frenzy.

After some hours everything changed. Krilerneq announced that Sorqaq was trying to come back and urged everyone to return to their places and concentrate on the songs which would help the angakok in his difficult task of swimming through rock as if it were water. It was an anxious time. Sorqaq's journey was not only a hard one, but he had himself predicted that his return might not be pos-

OPPOSITE: *Shaman's mask representing a supernatural spirit. Shamans were credited with the ability to expose their insides and to see into the bodies of others. When they go into trance and undertake spirit journeys, shamans frequently enter this 'half-naked' state and at such times contact with them is charged with supernatural energy.*

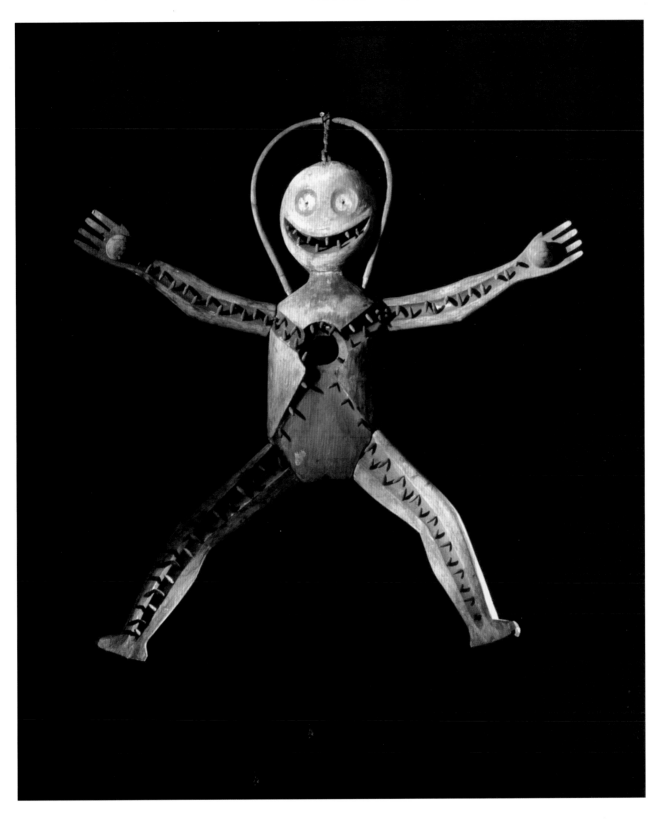

ABOVE: *The sounds of percussive instruments, particularly drums and rattles, were the traditional accompaniment to dances in North America. When used by shamans their rhythms were regulated to emulate the 'voices' of the spirits or to create a lulling, almost hypnotic, effect that aided the shaman's trance or helped put a patient at ease during a curing ritual. The dance gauntlets shown here were used only by the Aleuts and Western Eskimo, and are made from puffin beaks sewn to a sealskin backing. Worn during men's dances, they accompanied the rhythmic beat of the drum.*

sible. Krilerneq extinguished all the lamps, since to travel through rock Sorqaq had to shed his skin and become 'muscle-naked' and anyone seeing him thus would die.

The old angakok's voice was at last heard very faintly in the distance, but as he came closer its sound grew in intensity and the drum beat more furiously until the *qasgiq* again seemed to tremble and sealskins crackled through the air. The sceptical Freuchen reached up to grab at a sealskin he heard whistling just above his head, receiving a blow that almost broke his arm and left him severely bruised for days. As he tells it, 'all hell had broken loose.'

Then it suddenly stopped. Krilerneq begged Sorqaq to reveal what he had learned in the Underworld:

> The Great Spirits are embarrassed by the presence of white men among us and will not reveal the reason for the accidents. Three deaths are still to come. So as to avoid more tragedies, our women must refrain from eating of the female walrus until the winter darkness returns!

The lamps were relit. Sorqaq, untied and exhausted, was again sitting on the ledge. He looked across at Freuchen, smiled, and said: 'Just lies and tricks. The wisdom of our ancestors is not in me. Do not believe in any of it!'

Freuchen's experience reveals a number of features of the angakok's journey. Of particular interest is the angakok's denigration of his own skills and abilities. Rasmussen, too, experienced this when, at the beginning of a seance conducted by the highly respected angakok Sagdlork, he peered through the seal-gut window of Sagd lork's igloo and the old man laughed and said: 'Pure tomfoolery! Stupid faking! A total tissue of lies!'

We must, however, view the angakok's denial of any special ability from other than the purely literal perspective. In many ways it serves to stimulate and encourage the audience in its support of the angakok's efforts. Their help is essential in enabling the angakok to become psychologically prepared to undertake the Journey. As Freuchen noted, Sorqaq was urged on by the exhortations of his audience and their belief in the great power he possessed. During Sorqaq's absence his assistant, Krilerneq, also appealed to the spectators to return to their places and take up the angakok's song to assist him in his return to the human realm.

Audience support serves to focus the angakok's power and reaffirms a belief in the world of the spirits, and by appealing to him as a great adept in spite of his denials they boost his own confidence in his abilities to intercede with the spirits and undertake a journey which he knows to be fraught with difficulty and danger. Despite the angakok's protestations and claims that what he does 'is as nothing', both he and his audience are acutely aware that the powers he comes in contact with can threaten lives and change destinies.

The experienced angakok is, therefore, charged with a tremendous responsibility to safeguard the community or, at least, to accurately predict what the future might hold and to advise the people accordingly. He relies to a great extent on his contacts with the spirits in making these predictions, but is also acutely aware of other signs – such as changes in wind direction or weather patterns – that provide clues of conditions which may affect the community. Other hunters, of course, also possess these latter skills; but in the angakok they are honed to perfection and reinterpreted in accordance with his belief in the guiding advice of his *tunghat*.

The angakoks possess extraordinary spiritual and physical abilities.

LEFT: *Throughout the Arctic regions, the principal means of contact with the spirits was via the shaman's drum. The distinctive tambourine drum was used exclusively by shamans, and its beat was said to echo the 'heartbeat' of the spirit world. Such drums are not thought of as inanimate objects, but are said to possess a life and motivation of their own.*

37

ABOVE: *This carved wooden bowl from southwestern Alaska is painted with the image of a caribou and its spirit counterpart. All animate (as well as some inanimate) beings are thought to possess a spiritual reflection, or 'echo', of their physical selves. Shamanic communion with the spirit-animal world is generally via the 'echo' of the real animal.*

They have the stamina to undergo extreme privation, as well as the courage to venture into forbidden realms. Only the most experienced, however, undertake what is perhaps the angakok's most difficult task: an out-of-body journey to the depths of the oceans; home of the Sea Goddess, Sedna.

Sedna's story is a classic tale of Eskimo survival subject to unpredictable whims and caprice. She was the daughter of a prominent leader, and as a young girl was renowned for her beauty; but she refused all suitors, and her father, fearful that he would have no son-in-law to care for him in old age, decided she must marry the next eligible man to appear at their household.

Soon after, a kayak was pulled ashore by a young man in a dark cloak. Neither Sedna nor her father saw his face since he kept it hidden, but true to his vow the old man let him take Sedna away. They travelled over rough seas for many hours until they finally arrived at a rocky island which was the young man's home. He then revealed himself as Storm Petrel. Sedna was disgusted, because she had nothing to eat except fish and no bed covers other than fish skins.

After some time the old man, feeling lonely and regretting he had forced Sedna to marry against her will, set out to rescue her. His journey to the island was uneventful but on his way home, with Sedna in his kayak, he noticed a black cloud racing behind them. He hid Sedna beneath some furs, but the cloud swirled around his kayak and Storm Petrel called out, demanding the return of his wife. The old man refused, so Storm Petrel dipped his wings in the waves, causing them to froth furiously about the fragile boat and threatening to capsize it.

In his fear and agitation, Sedna's father threw her overboard; yet she hung to the gunwale of the kayak, pleading for her life. With the edge of his paddle he cut off her fingers at the first joint, which dropped into the ocean and became seals. She clung desperately until her father cut off her fingers at the second joint, which became walrus. Unable to hold on any longer Sedna slowly sank beneath the waves.

At the bottom of the sea, Sedna vowed revenge on the people. She became the Sea Goddess, and gathered around her all the fish and sea mammals that the people used for food. Even today, when angry, she calls the sea creatures to her and deprives people of sustenance. For her the starvation of the people is just retribution for her own drowning at the hands of her father.

The *tunghat* who look after the animals on the moon fear Sedna

Right: This shaman's spirit familiar, or tupilaq, *is carved in the form of a half-raven, half-dead-child. Although this example is described as an 'evil spirit', the* tupilaqs *generally respond to the wishes of the shaman and can be used for either good or evil purposes. One of their functions is to seek out and devour the causes of illness, but they can also be sent out on mischievous errands against other shamans with whom their master is in competition.*

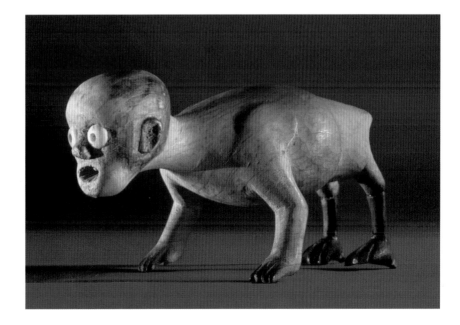

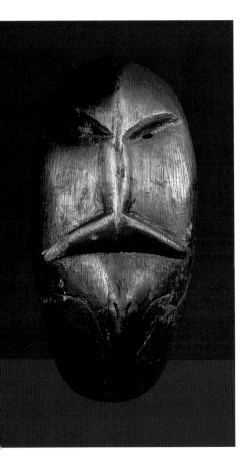

ABOVE: *Features of the hunter's face and moustache are combined with those of the tailfin and flippers of a whale in a mask to promote sympathetic understanding between hunter and his prey. It was used prior to a hunt in shamanic rituals to ensure success and to protect the hunters.*

and are unable to prevent them responding to her call; but it is to her the angakok must go to plead for mercy when famine strikes. Because Sedna is displeased she places obstacles in the angakok's way. As he swims through water she causes it to boil. She turns his path into a maze, confusing him at every turn. And if he finds the right path she guards it with ferocious sea monsters and cannibals against which the angakok's *tunghat* are powerless.

Even if he succeeds in reaching Sedna's home she refuses to speak with him and turns her back. He pleads with her and flatters her, remarking on her power and her beauty. Finally he tries to comb out her long, matted hair, since Sedna is unable to do this for herself with the stumps of her hands. Every tangle and knot represents a transgression on the part of the people, and it is only by removing these that the sins of the people can be mitigated. Sedna, if she is gracious, will reveal the nature of the people's indiscretions to the angakok; the 'combing-out', however, is only completed after the angakok's return, when the people confess their transgressions and do penance according to the instructions the angakok has brought back from the undersea world.

This most difficult of the angakok's tasks summarises Eskimo-Aleut beliefs and responses to the hostile and shifting environment they occupy, in which real physical terrors and hardships are explained through mythological events and countered with methods rooted in the paradoxical world of the *tunghat*. But we should not dismiss the Eskimo half-world as merely an imaginative response. The angakoks have successfully guided their people through centuries of adversity and their methods are proven ones.

The angakok's world is the world of the unknown and, in some senses, the unknowable: only the most experienced angakoks can travel within this realm, and even for them it is difficult and hazardous. For the Eskimo there is no doubt as to the genuineness and reality of the angakok's encounters, yet there are also tangible criteria by which the power wielded by angakoks can be judged. Rasmussen visited the Agiarmiut Eskimo during a terrible snow storm that had lasted for days, when visibility was so poor and wind speeds so high that people became disoriented moving from one igloo to the next. Even the Eskimo sled dogs, although accustomed to the most extreme weather conditions, had been permitted the almost unheard of luxury of admittance to the warmth of the igloo to prevent them freezing to death.

Baleen, a young angakok, was attempting to calm the storm. During his seance he grasped an elderly man, Kigiuna, by the throat

BELOW: *This Eskimo carving from Point Hope, Alaska, depicts a shaman releasing a whale. Much shamanic activity is devoted to ensuring that game animals and other resources are treated with reverence and respect after they are killed or utilised, thereby persuading the collective souls of the species of the people's good intentions. The whale being released here is the 'spirit figure' of the animal, which it is thought will return to its fellow creatures bearing messages of good will.*

with such force that he was starved of oxygen and collapsed unconscious on the floor. Baleen dragged him senseless around the igloo before reviving him, and then 'killed' him twice more. Kigiuna, a powerful angakok, called on his own powers, staggered to his feet, and within seconds forced the younger and stronger Baleen into submission. Although the storm still raged unabated, Kigiuna calmly announced that his helping spirits had met and defeated the evil powers called on by Storm Boy. The morning would be fine. Rasmussen 'in dazzling sunshine and hard-blown drifts' continued his journey next day.

Similar tales of an angakok's intervention having the precise desired effect are legion. They are far too many and too well recorded – even by the most sceptical of observers such as Freuchen – to be mere coincidence. At one level, of course, the angakok fulfills the people's real need of reassurance, as well as providing a safe outlet for confessions of indiscretions that would otherwise rapidly give rise to

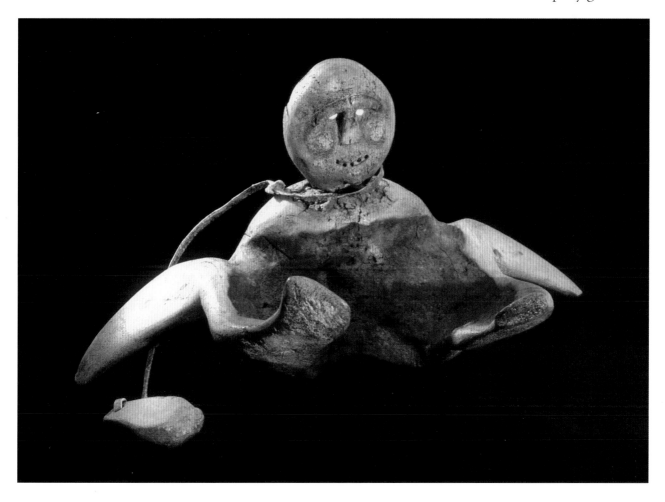

RIGHT: *This mask depicts a flying or swimming shaman during a trance journey. When undertaking such journeys the shaman's physical body is 'reduced to nothing' and the spirit, or soul, of the shaman takes control. The dominance of the soul is indicated here by the face of the spirit that has replaced the shaman's internal organs.*

severe tensions within such close-knit communities. Eskimo survival depends on close cooperation and sharing, and festering tensions would undermine the viability of the group. Without a mechanism for resolving differences, Eskimo communities would become fragmented and vulnerable. At a deeper level, however, the activities of the angakok weld together many streams of Eskimo consciousness and understanding. These relate to the physical as well as the spiritual aspects of existence, and are closely tied to the ephemeral nature of the land.

'Hard proof' simply does not have relevance in a country where nothing is static and where causal relationships are often difficult to determine. The Eskimo-Aleut angakok draws on the timeless and indeterminate nature of the land to discern order in chaos, and uses this to reaffirm and define the people's relationships with each other and with the powerful forces of Nature.

2   *The Power of their Dreams*

SUBARCTIC AND GREAT LAKES

The northern forests of the American Subarctic span a region stretching from Alaska and the coastal mountains of British Columbia across all of Canada to Labrador and Newfoundland, and from south of Hudson Bay north to the Arctic. The region, though vast, is a relatively homogeneous one of coniferous forest and birch with innumerable small streams and lakes, which gives way in the far north to more open tundra. It is marked by extremes of temperature, with long, cold winters and short, mosquito-infested summers.

The Subarctic is harsh and uncompromising, although this harshness is often veiled in a subtle beauty. Meandering streams and rivers overhung with frost- or snow-laden branches set against the sheen of birchbark provide an enchanted landscape; yet their character is one of concealment rather than revelation. The meanders hide but do not lessen the stark realities that threaten survival in this region, and that make it impossible for the area to support anything more than a few scattered bands of hunters and gatherers. Population estimates suggest the maximum density for the region have never exceeded about one person per hundred square miles; but density could be far less in marginal regions such as Labrador.

People nevertheless do live here and have devised stratagems for minimising potential problems. In the western half of the region are Athapascan speaking tribes, known by dialectical variants of Dine, Dina, or Tinne. Their name simply means 'The People' and serves to set them apart and create a human identity separate from that of the

LEFT: *The Subarctic interior is harsh and uncompromising, and shamans adapted to this by adopting strategies that echoed the survival behaviour of local fauna. Among the most important shamanic animal spirits were the wolf and the wolverine. Shamans were believed to travel in the guise of these animals during the hours of darkness. The scene depicted here is just north of the Great Slave Lake in Canada's Northwest Territories, in a region that is home to the Athapascan-speaking Dog-Rib Indians.*

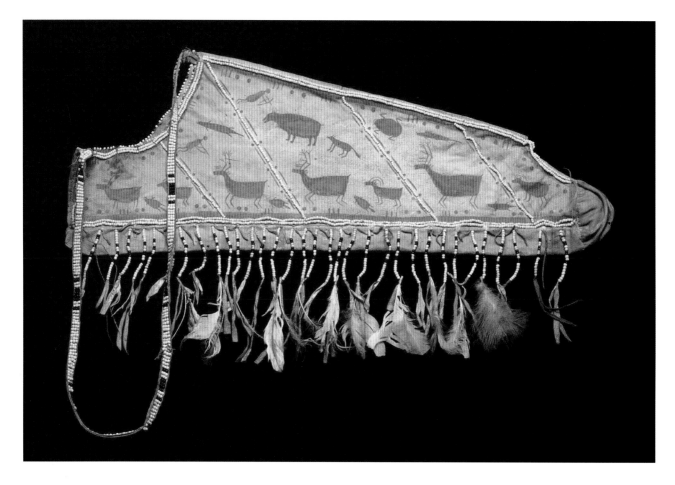

ABOVE: *The difficult conditions of the Subarctic meant that hunters sought to enhance their own human skills by appealing to supernatural forces for assistance. The intercession of the animal spirits on the hunter's behalf was felt to increase the affinity between the hunter and his prey, and thereby to make a successful outcome more probable. The spirit animal at top centre of this Tanaina quiver from southeastern Alaska lent supernatural power to the hunter's arrows.*

other denizens of the forest. The eastern regions are dominated by the Algonquian speaking Cree, with numerous smaller Algonquian tribes such as the Naskapi, Montagnais, and Micmac.

Despite language differences, all the Subarctic tribes share common beliefs that focus specifically on personal initiative and that are dictated by the environment. The year is divided into months, or moons, of seasonal significance such as the 'Moon When Berries Ripen', the 'Moon When Animals Migrate', or the 'Moon When The Rivers Freeze'. The Cree say that early summer, when travel is easy, fishing is good, and game and berries plentiful, is controlled by *Shawanung-nizeo* – the South Wind that has charge of food – and it is the only period when the weather conditions are favourable enough that several families might come together along the shores of lakes and rivers for communal celebrations.

Although such celebrations involve a number of family groups from widely separated regions who may have undertaken difficult journeys over many days to reach the rendezvous, the festivities themselves last only a short while. Summer in the Subarctic is rarely longer than two months. For the rest of the year resources are generally too meagre or spread over too vast an area to support large gatherings, and the people live in small scattered nomadic bands of individuals who are related by marriage and which are dependent for their survival on the experience and knowledge of the band leaders, or family heads, and on the skill of their hunters and trappers in finding game.

Spiritual life reflects the uncertainties and isolation of Subarctic living. There are few organised cults or associations of shamans, and there is little formal training for anyone who wishes to take up shamanism as a vocation. Individuals rely on their own personal spirit contacts, which may come to them in dreams; hunters depend on making offerings to propitiate the souls of the animals and to encourage the game and fish on which they depend to yield willingly to their weapons and traps; healing is usually accomplished with local herbs and placed in the hands of a woman who has an understanding of their curative properties.

Yet, despite the isolation of many of these family groups and the highly individualistic nature of Subarctic social life - which Father Le Jeune noted in 1634 resulted in their 'not enduring in the least those who seem desirous of assuming superiority over others' - the influence of the shamans is apparent in virtually every activity. The woman using healing herbs understands that 'somewhere' these have been tested against the disease-causing spirits by a powerful shaman and are therefore known to be effective. The charms used by the hunter will have been blessed by a shaman, possibly for an ancestor, and they would be useless without a shaman's intervention no matter how far removed in time.

The shaman, by all accounts, exists in the vague and undifferentiated worlds of 'somewhere' or 'sometime'; yet the shaman is also considered to be an immediate and pervasive force. Shamanic help is implicit, for instance, in dream hunting, when the hunter dreams of tracking, cornering, and catching his quarry. Because the chase has been completed successfully with shamanic help in dream-time, it is thought that the hunter will be similarly successful in reality if he follows the pattern given in his dream, since the outcome is already foretold. Other shamanic devices which have their origins in dreams, as well as appeals to the spirits of the animals, are believed to increase the chances of a hunter's success. Thus food which the prey animal is known to enjoy may be placed on the fire as an offering and special rasping sticks or bones used to create a sound which will

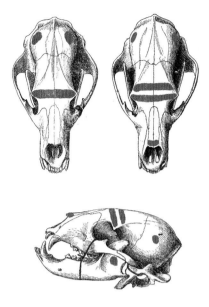

ABOVE: *Although all animals were revered by the Subarctic tribes, the bear was given special acclaim since it was believed to have a close affinity to people and was said to understand human speech. When a bear was killed the carcass was treated with the same respect shown towards an honoured guest, and the skull, after removal of soft tissue and washing, was painted with stripes of vermilion, as shown in these examples from the Eastern Cree. Such painted skulls were preserved in a safe place for three to six months, prior to being carried secretly into the forest where they were hung in the trees.*

attract its attention and draw it closer to the camp.

Even though the power of the shaman permeates everything, the shaman remains mysterious and is often unidentified. No one knows where shamans come from; no one knows the awesome power they may possess; no one is strong enough to appeal directly to them. Any appeals are made through dreams: it is only in dreaming that the spirit can detach itself from the body and enter the realms that are the shamans' domain. Dreaming also releases the mind from Subarctic constraints. In dreams the barriers of distance, weather, and time fall away and become unimportant; and, during periods of privation and hunger, dreams of 'good and excellent things, of heroic deeds and the chase, of bears, and stags, and caribous' promise hope and salvation.

Ordinary people, as well as shamans, draw strength and inspiration from their dreams. Everyday dreams are significant, in that they may dictate a particular course of action. It is not unusual, for example, for a family to discuss their dreams each morning and to base the day's activities on what has been dreamt. Similarly, a hunter who dreams a bad omen immediately before a hunt will stay at home that day and not risk an accident. The underlying importance of dreaming is reflected in the fact that the word for 'dream' is also the word for 'destiny', and that everyone, male and female, seeks a 'dream of life' through which his or her destiny can be controlled.

Tales of what may happen if warnings given in dreams and omens are ignored are legion. The unpredictable and deceptive nature of the Subarctic gives rise to a host of potentially malevolent and dangerous spirit beings who seek opportunities to waylay the incautious and unwary, and any accident or untoward event is blamed on these beings. Pre-eminent among them is the *Windigo* - a strange creature that is rarely seen and whose presence is felt as a suffocating force that is impossible to resist - and its female counterpart, the *Windigokwé*.

The *Windigos* take people beyond the limits of their endurance by leading them endlessly in circles until they become exhausted and hopelessly lost and disoriented. They drive people mad, and anyone who has been possessed by a *Windigo* loses the ability to think clearly. Because of the life-sapping powers of the *Windigo* and *Windigokwé*, the people of the Subarctic think of them as cannibals who sustain themselves by draining the energy and life-force of others. Different malevolent spirits - often appearing in the form of tiny but extremely strong people, and referred to as 'bush men' - are responsible for someone breaking a leg when alone in the forest far

ABOVE: *The most important animal in terms of the economy and survival of the Subarctic tribes was the caribou, which had a significance similar to that of the buffalo to the Plains tribes. Caribou not only provided resources for clothing, shelter, and food, but their migratory habits also dictated the movements of the tribes.*

During the migrations, bands from several tribes would congregate in areas where the caribou were concentrated. Although the caribou did not possess any significant shamanic power, it was nevertheless thought of as a 'life-giver' and its bones were regularly used by shamans in rituals intended to predict the movements of game animals.

from help, for tricking hunters into following false leads, and for springing traps before any game is caught.

Tales such as these focus on the dangers and difficulties of Sub-arctic life, where unforeseen events and chance encounters can spell the difference between success and failure, or between life and death. Dreams provide a recognised method of influencing future events in the dreamer's favour, and taken seriously, dreams and omens warn of impending disasters which prudent action can avoid. It is only when these are ignored that the *Windigo* and the other malevolent spirits can exert their power.

Shamans deal directly with this strange world of dream and real-

49

ity, of truth and superstition. Even when a hunter senses something is wrong and on impulse avoids a potential danger, the warning is believed to come via a shaman, or, at least, through a shaman's animal-familiar: those spirits which, in animal form, communicate with the spirits of the shamans. Although the worlds of the people and of the spirits are thought to be closely related and to interact with each other during dreams, they are nevertheless separate. Threats become real when the invisible boundary between people and the spirit forces is inadvertently crossed, since only the shaman possesses power that enables him or her to cross this divide unscathed.

Although the content of dreams is held to have significance in the daily lives of all Subarctic peoples, it is the shamans who are the dream specialists and dreaming is at the heart of their profession. A distinction has to be made between ordinary dreams which give direction or a warning, and shamanic 'power dreams' which link the shamans with the spirit world of the animal-familiars. Much of the shaman's power and the importance attributed to shamanic dreaming are due to the shaman being considered to be like the spirits and to share common characteristics with them.

He, or she, is usually a shadowy figure that exists at the boundaries of human experience but who can, suddenly and unexpectedly, burst in on people's lives. Unlike ordinary dreams, which affect individuals, those of the shamans may frequently have wider community significance. They can bring blessings such as a good hunt, a happy marriage, or confident and secure band leadership that is of benefit to all; but they can also predict calamities that tear communities apart and set brother against brother in feuds of jealousy and spite. The shaman is often kind and generous; yet can be cruel and angry. Shamans act in dream-time, and events that happened years or generations ago may remain in the shamanic consciousness and be still important long after most people have forgotten them. Thus the dreams of the shamans are thought of as the people's 'collective memory', reminding them they cannot ignore the past and the bearing it may have on the future.

The vagaries of Subarctic existence often demand that the shaman is not identified as such and that the content of shamanic dreams remains a carefully guarded secret. The anonymity of the shaman may further be preserved by the fact that predictive dreams, inspired by the shaman's animal-familiars, may be experienced by someone other than the shaman. Thus events that affect the community may initially be anticipated in the dreams of an impressionable young girl, whose innocence and immaturity make her partic-

OPPOSITE: *The exact function of this Naskapi skin mask is unknown, although it is similar in form to masks from other parts of the Subarctic that were used during shamanic rituals to 'disguise' the identity of the shaman. The red horizontal lines are almost certainly intended to represent animal tracks.*

OPPOSITE: *This type of outer garment made from caribou skin is characteristic of the Naskapi and their close relatives, the Montagnais. The origin of fitted coats of this kind is, controversially, said to have come from the frock coats of the officers serving in the colonial armies. Despite that, the incised and painted markings on the coat bear considerable meaning in terms of Naskapi ideology. They represent the tracks of animals, and by donning the coat the wearer associated himself with their movements as well as with their behavioural characteristics.*

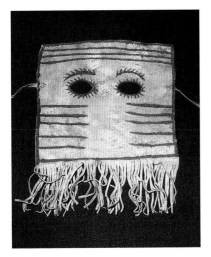

ularly susceptible to the shaman's spirit influence.

Subarctic shamans are both revered and feared, since every shaman has benevolent and harmful power and may exercise these almost indiscriminately. As a consequence of their need to remain unobtrusive, Subarctic shamans are generally indistinguishable from other people. They hunt, fish, and make weapons or clothing, just like any other member of the community; indeed, the Subarctic environment does not allow for 'specialisation', since everyone has to be a capable and productive member of the community to survive.

Initiation as a shaman - or the call to shamanism - is a secret and hidden matter. One simply dreams of power, like anyone else; but dreams that confer shamanic power are not discussed openly or revealed to others. Instead, the shaman is 'taken over' in the dream

by an animal-familiar which invests the shaman with its own abilities. Subarctic shamans are controlled by the animal-spirits that appear in their dreams, which brings the spirits into contact with the human world but in a disguised form.

The most frequent guise of shamanic spirits in the Subarctic is that of the wolf; although they may also appear in other forms, such as the wolverine or spider. These animals are said to have habits akin to those of humans, or to live in close proximity with people. The wolf lives in communities similar to those of the people but avoids human habitation; the wolverine is rarely seen or caught, but its tracks are often found following the people's camps for days on end; and the spider hides in dark corners and eavesdrops on people's conversation so that it can use their confidences and indiscretions to pursue its own ends.

The shamans may assume these disguises at night, when the spirits roam the woodlands and people stay close to their camps. A 'Shaman-as-Wolf' can range freely during darkness and confer with other wolf-spirits, or with the wolverines and spiders. Through this he or she gains knowledge of and influence over a wide area. A calamity befalling a family in one camp which is attributed to some offence they have committed or to the breaking of a taboo which has upset the animal-spirits could have been initiated by the animal-familiar of a shaman living many miles away and lacking any personal knowledge of the family's affairs.

In addition to conferring with other animal-spirit-shamans in disguise, shamanic contact is maintained through dreams and it is often said that shamans consult with one another through dreaming. Their dreaming aptitude enables them to recall dreams as concrete experiences and to act on the messages contained in their dreams, whereas to someone who rarely dreams or whose dreams lack coherent content access to the world of the spirits is barred.

This power of the shamans can be used to advantage, as in the event of a hunter's good dream having been endorsed by an animal-familiar acting through the dream-agency of the shaman. Even though the hunter may not know the shaman, he does expect the favourable aspects of the dream to come true. A bad dream will be taken equally seriously. The dreams therefore provide the space in which the beliefs of the people can find expression and where the powers of the shamans can operate.

Unlike shamans in many other areas, however, those of the Subarctic do not control the content of their dreams or visions. These come unbidden and are entirely at the discretion of the ani-

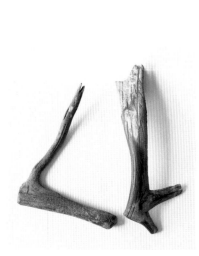

ABOVE: *Subarctic shamans used percussive instruments during their rituals to contact the spirit animals. Among these were the familiar drum and rattle, but extensive use was also made of notched rasping sticks carved from the bone of the animal species it was intended to attract. The caribou bone rasping sticks shown here were made by the Naskapi of central Labrador.*

LEFT: *The Cree were known for their elaborate tattoos, which stood as symbols of ancestral family and clan relationships as well as of status. They were made by pricking the skin with a multi-pronged tool and then rubbing charcoal or gunpowder into the wound to produce a permanently coloured mark. Tattooing was a highly specialised skill and in the hands of an elite group of shamans who were practiced in its techniques and who also knew the rituals and precautions that it was necessary to employ when dealing with the spirits of the ancestors. The pencil and wash drawing shown here is by Karl Bodmer and is a portrait of the Cree chief Mähsette-Kuiuab.*

mal-spirits, so the shaman has no direct influence and is simply the medium through which these are expressed. Yet to dismiss the Subarctic shaman as a mere tool of the spirits would be wrong: he, or she, becomes spirit. 'Shaman-as-Wolf' and 'Wolf-as-Shaman' are interchangeable concepts.

The interchangeability of shaman, spirit, and animal-familiar means that many aspects of ordinary reality in the Subarctic are felt to be imbued with spiritual power or force and are therefore potentially dangerous and need to be regarded with caution. The animal that one hunts may prove to be a shaman's animal-familiar, just as the lone hunter who shuns camp life and duties can be a *Windigo*, or the woman who refuses to marry and does not participate socially a *Windigokwé* in disguise.

Among the Athapascan speaking Carrier of British Columbia this

OVERLEAF: *Power was believed to reside within all the forces of nature and could be utilised by the shamans through the intercession of animal spirit intermediaries. The forces of wind, water, thunder and lightning, as well as of the forests and trees, were all capable of bestowing power.*
Storm clouds and forest are shown here reflected in Muskoka Lake in Huron territory east of Georgian Bay.

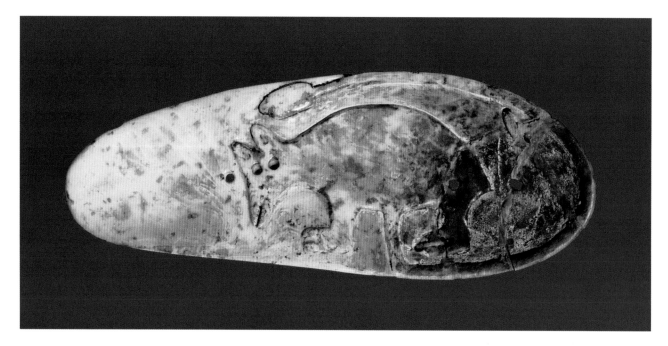

ABOVE: *Preceding and partly contemporary with the great Adena cultures of the northern Woodlands was a little-known cultural complex called Glacial Kame. Its name derives from the kames, or hills, left behind when the glaciers retreated about 1500 BC, and which were used as burial sites. This engraved sandal sole gorget was recovered from one of these burials. It depicts a newborn rodent-like animal with its umbilical cord still attached, perhaps representing the belief that the dead might be reborn in animal form.*

close relationship between people, animals, and spirits is very clearly expressed. They tell us that people, animals, and spirits possess *bini* (mind or intelligence), *bizil* (warmth), and *bitsen* (a shadow, or ghost). Whereas the *bini* and *bizil* always remain with the person, during dreaming the *bitsen* is able to leave the body and travel to the spirit realms where it may be captured by the animals and spirits and remain forever. The captured *bitsen* then gradually drains away the *bini* and *bizil* of the person to join it in the spirit world.

Animals, moreover, have special powers they share with the spirits and which are said to be also characteristic of the shamans. They are able to assume human or animal form at will, can move from place to place almost instantaneously, can become visible or invisible, and are able to pass through solid objects as if they were no obstacle. It is said that the animals, and hence the shamans too, hear every word that is spoken and know every act that takes place in a village or camp.

Although the shamans try to keep their powers secret, and there is genuine apprehension of what a shaman's capabilities may be, in the close-knit communities of Subarctic peoples the shaman's identity tends to become known even if it is not proclaimed. There are, in fact, occasions when a shaman's intercession on someone's behalf is essential and has to be sought, albeit not openly.

Shamanic intercession is, for example, imperative when a person's *bitsen*, or shadow, has been captured. Legend has it that the animals,

LEFT: *To the Subarctic and Great Lakes peoples breath was a sacred symbol of being alive. 'Breath made visible' through the exhalation of smoke from native tobacco and other herbs was seen as a tangible expression of the interconnectedness of human life and the spirit beings who safe-guarded it; elaborate smoking rituals were developed through which such expression could be made. This soapstone pipe bowl dates from the 17th century and was found in a burial in the Huron territories of Ottawa.*

LEFT: *The tribes of the Subarctic and Northern Woodlands felt that everything had a soul or spirit and was, therefore, capable of will and motivation. This pottery bowl was recovered from an Oneida (Iroquois) site in Madison County, N.Y., and is an early example of utilitarian ware, yet includes human effigy figure below each of the four points through which the 'spirit' of the bowl can be expressed.*

in their human form, dwell in houses beneath lakes or inside mountains. The tales tell us that bear, wolf, caribou, even frog, have been known to carry people away during their dreams so they might marry them, and the *bitsen* of such a person is then imprisoned and unable to return to its corporeal body. Without a shaman sending his own *bitsen* to the animal's home, where he can recapture the lost shadow and imprison it inside his own body for later return to its original owner, the 'patient' can suffer delusions, involuntary muscle spasms and paralysis as his or her *bini* (intelligence) is drained. The body will gradually also lose its *bizil* (warmth) and become cold and lifeless. The most violent insanity arises from contact with otter, which, in dreams, takes the form of a girl or youth which lures men or women from their homes and seduces them. Such insanity is incurable, since against otter even the *bitsen* of the most experienced shamans are powerless.

The shaman's help is also directly required when a severely sick person fails to respond to other treatments, since this indicates transgressions on the patient's part which can only be relieved by a full confession of his or her sins. Many of these relate to sexual indiscretions, such as extra-marital affairs or incest, and forced or involuntary participation in the acts does not lessen the burden of guilt placed on the individual. The worst form of sin, however, is for someone to attempt healing without dream sanction, which is considered 'criminal deception' and presents a threat to the entire community because of the offence it causes to the animal-spirits.

In the area considered so far dreaming is very much a personal matter, even when the content of the dream is openly discussed and its significance deemed to have bearing on the lives of others within the community. In the southern areas of the Subarctic and in the region of the Great Lakes however, there are larger permanent settlements based on farming and the gathering of wild rice, and here shamanic dreaming is more publicly expressed through rituals that require the participation, or at least the witness, of other members of the community.

A widespread phenomenon associated with the public demonstration of a shaman's power is the Shaking Tent. This is still practised today in a modified form, but the most dramatic and vivid descriptions come from traders and missionaries among the tribes in the 17th and 18th centuries. The earliest report is from the Jesuit missionary Father Paul Le Jeune, who witnessed the Shaking Tent when he spent the winter of 1633-1634 among the Montagnais. Referring to the shaman as a 'juggler', he wrote:

ABOVE AND OPPOSITE: *The Shaking Tent was a display of shamanic power practised across North America. Once the fettered shaman was placed inside the framework it would be covered by animal hides, blankets or canvas covers. Then he would call his familiar spirits to 'do battle' with opposing spirit forces. The tent would shake violently as the spirit forces entered and left. In the upright structures shown here, typical of the Ojibwa, saplings were bent and lashed together. Elsewhere tribes might construct different frameworks, from dome-shaped bark-covered wigwams in the Subarctic to the conical skin-covered tipi of the Plains and Plateau.*

The juggler, having entered, began to moan softly, as if complaining. He shook the tent, first without violence. Then, becoming animated little by little, he commenced to whistle in a hollow tone, and as if it came from afar; then to talk as if in a bottle, to cry like the owls of these countries; then to howl and sing, constantly varying the tones ... At first he shook this edifice gently; but as he gradually became more animated, he fell into so violent an ecstasy that I thought he would break ... I was astonished at a man having so much strength; for after he had once begun to shake it, he did not stop until the consultation was over, which lasted about three hours.

Father Le Jeune, although a sceptical observer, was impressed by this demonstration of shamanic power. He does not tell us something which we know from numerous other reports which makes the shaman's performance even more striking, namely that the shaman did not simply walk into the tent to begin his performance. He first stripped naked and was securely bound with strong ropes. He was then rolled in a blanket or robe, which was also wrapped round with ropes to the effect that the shaman was totally immobilised and had to be carried into the tent, where he was laid face down on the floor. The only things placed in the tent with him were

ABOVE: *The Medicine Lodge used during meetings of the Midéwiwin was constructed on a framework of bent saplings that were covered with sheets of bark like ordinary dwellings in the region albeit on a larger scale. During rituals the Medicine Lodge became a repository of the power of numerous shamans, and its precincts and the paths leading to it were consecrated and closed to all outsiders.*

59

ABOVE: *Miniature masks like this one were used in the rituals of the Iroquois False Face medicine society as potent charms to help appease the spirits, or False Faces, that caused sickness.*
OPPOSITE: *In common with many of the Woodlands tribes, the Iroquois believe that the forests are the abode of powerful spirit beings whose influence can be used both beneficently and for malign purposes. The False Faces, who hide beneath a façade of distorted features, can bestow tremendous blessings but are also the carriers of disease and paralysis. Traditionally, these masks are carved in situ on a living tree, and when not in use are secluded to prevent any harmful effects that may be caused by the dissipation of their power.*

his drum, medicine pipe, and sacred tobacco.

The Shaking Tent has greater significance than a mere demonstration of shamanic ability, since it is through this ritual that various animal spirits which have revealed themselves in the shaman's dreams are summoned into his presence. Sometimes these are the shamanic animal-familiars, which can be sent out to recover lost items, to locate missing persons, or to predict future events in response to requests made by the witnesses to the event. The shaking of the tent signals their movements into and from the shaman's presence, and the noises the audience hears are said to be the voices of the spirits.

On occasion the spirits of the Shaking Tent come into conflict with one another. The Montagnais describe the calling of three spirits at one Shaking Tent ritual. These were all spirits of major importance: *Mistabeo*, the 'Lord of All Spirits'; *Memegwecio*, the 'Lord of Clawed Animals'; and *Mistacenaku*, the 'Lord of All Water Creatures'. *Mistabeo* was first to arrive and began to tell ribald stories and to make suggestive remarks about relations between the sexes, which caused a great deal of amusement among the audience, but soon thereafter he became angered when *Memegwecio*, the Lord of Clawed Animals, interrupted him by scratching like a bear on the outside of the tent.

During a fight between *Mistabeo* and *Memegwecio* the tent shook so violently that it was lifted a metre into the air and the top bent over so it almost touched the ground. The noise was deafening, as other spirits rallied to the calls of *Mistabeo*, *Memegwecio*, and *Mistacenaku* and arrived to join in the fray in support of their Animal Masters. A European priest who was present, fearing the shaman was summoning devils, fled in panic. Throughout the performance, which lasted several hours, the tent continued to shake, until finally *Mistabeo* defeated his rivals and with loud whistling sounds the spirits left the tent.

Throughout the ritual the Montagnais had shouted cries of encouragement to *Mistabeo*, since only if he won would it be a good year. When the shaking had stopped and the tent was opened, the shaman - the knotted cords with which he had been bound lying beside him - sat calmly in the middle smoking his pipe. Despite the extended strenuous exertions he had just been through, he was completely unruffled and not a bead of sweat showed on his body.

The Shaking Tent is a spectacular example of the individual shaman's power which can be exerted to benefit the community. At times, however, individual shamans bond together in a form of soci-

ety, or group, of shamans which meets regularly; although each responds to the vocation through the power of his own personal dream experiences. Shamans among the Iroquois of northern New York State, for example, are known to combine their collective powers to cure or prevent disease and to combat epidemics or crop failures, as well as in annual rituals intended to promote general health and well-being.

The Iroquois believe that disease, illness, and other calamities arise in dreams and that dreams are closely related to the desires of the shadow, or soul, of the individual. They assert that dreams are an avenue between the conscious behaviour of the patient and the desires of the unconscious, and that any discrepancy between the two must be resolved through the granting and fulfilment of whatever it is the soul wishes. Although unsatisfied desires are thought to cause unhappiness and illness, the desires of the soul are inborn and concealed and only the shamans, who are both dream and thought specialists, are able to identify them. Once known, such desires may be satisfied, subject to the sanction of the community and with its support, and the patient can recover.

The most dramatic instance of Iroquois collective shamanic power and the personification of the spirits that cause disease and

BELOW: *The paraphernalia used by shamans were often highly personal and varied in type and content from one individual to another, yet among the Ojibwa there were shamanic fraternities whose members all used items that were similar in form. These might include a spirit doll or effigy, power beads, invitation sticks, and small rectangular 'spirit cases' containing tokens of supernatural power such as are shown here.*

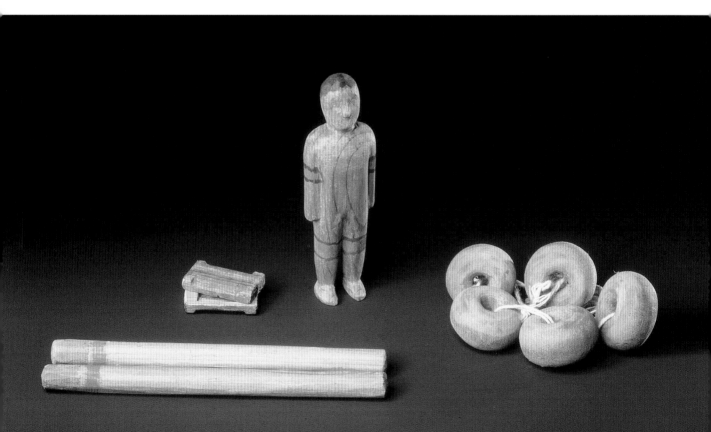

disaster occurs in the False Face Society. The False Face spirits are conceived as disembodied flying heads which appear in dreams. They cause disease but are also able to exert healing power. They can, however, make their presence known at crucial times of the year associated with planting and harvest, when they represent the forces of the forests as opposed to those of cultivation and can bring about disease of epidemic proportion or cause total crop failure. At such times the dreamers of the False Face Society perform publicly, wearing masks which have been carved from a living tree. These masks are said to be 'alive' and are regularly 'fed' with sacred tobacco.

In many senses the False Face spirits represent a dichotomy inherent in Iroquois life. The Iroquois are hunters and farmers and to them the forest abode of the False Face spirits is both the refuge in which game animals are found and a barrier which has to be cleared to grow crops. Because the False Face spirits are forest dwellers, they are resentful of the slash and burn farming techniques used to clear garden plots; hence their desire to strike back at the people at those times of the year when planting and harvesting activities are most intense.

The power of the False Face spirits is immense and directly related to the hunting aspects of Iroquois economy: by protecting their forest domain they also protect the game animals that live there. This power is transferred to the carved masks, which are said to 'become spirit', and is felt to be so strong that non-dreamers need to be protected from it when the masks are not under the calming influence of the False Face Society shamans during their use in rituals. It is also believed that because the mask is 'alive' that its power can become weakened and dissipated through unnecessary exposure. For most of the year the masks are carefully wrapped in clean, white cloth and laid face down so they can 'rest'. Although the use of the False Face masks is exclusive to the society of medicine men, the conception of the False Face spirits is similar to the individual disease-causing powers of other forest spirits.

The illnesses associated with the False Face spirits, the manner in which illness is caused, and curing through shamanic intercession is closely related to the Athapascan belief in theft by the animal-spirits during dreams of a person's *bitsen*, or shadow. Illness is similarly believed by the Iroquois to occur only through dreams; and the False Face spirits are said particularly to cause illnesses of the head and shoulders and to attack a person's ability to think rationally. Paralysis of the facial muscles is one typical symptom of such an affliction. The masks are therefore carved with grotesque distorted features

ABOVE: *Carved spirit figures of various sizes were used during the meetings of the Midéwiwin Society, some as small charms carried by shamans, others as full-size figures in the role of guardians on pathways leading to the sacred lodge. A rectangular recess cut into the figure was used to hold the 'spirit case', similar to that shown opposite.*

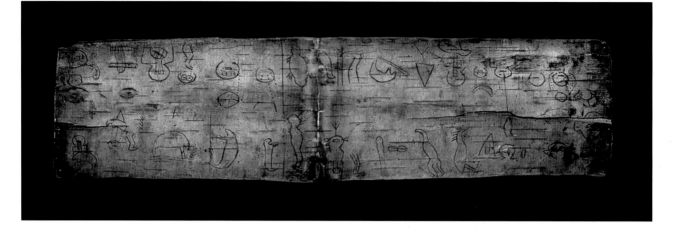

ABOVE: *The rituals of the Midéwiwin Society involved every member of the tribal group, either as direct participants or as witnesses to the events, and necessitated the memorising of complex song systems and seating arrangements. To facilitate this, the Ojibwa prepared long strips of birch bark on which symbols were incised to act as mnemonic devices. The birch bark scroll is 46 cm long and records the sequence of a song.*

that represent the symptoms of the illness.

The mixed hunting-farming economy of the Iroquois also led to the emergence of a shamans' society which drew power from the spirits associated with cultivation, which may be thought of as in opposition to the wild spirits of the forest inspiring the shamans of the False Face Society. Thus the Husk Face Society makes its masks from corn husks and calls on the power of maize to effect cures. The division between the two Societies is further emphasised by the association of the False Faces with *Tawiskaron*, Flint Giant, and of the Husk Faces with *Tharonhiawagon*, or Sapling. In Iroquois thinking flint is associated with hunting, since it is the material from which arrowheads are made; saplings, however, grow on forest tracts that have been cleared for farming. It is significant here that *Tawiskaron* and *Tharonhiawagon* are the Twin Brothers whom the myths credit with creating and shaping Iroquois culture. Both societies, however, have similar functions and may be considered today to bring general blessings, while retaining the function of the shaman as a specialist in utilising non-human powers.

The shift in emphasis from power that is derived from personal dreams and kept secret among the Athapascans, through public demonstrations of individual power in the Shaking Tent, to collective shamanism in the Societies of the Iroquois, reaches its ultimate conclusion among the Iroquois' Algonquian speaking neighbours of the Great Lakes. Here the shamans work cooperatively in the Midéwiwin, or Grand Medicine Society, in which the ability to communicate with the spirit forces is transferred to ordinary members of the community via the shamans' rituals.

It is nevertheless important to think of the Midéwiwin as an extension of traditional Subarctic/Woodlands shamanism which is

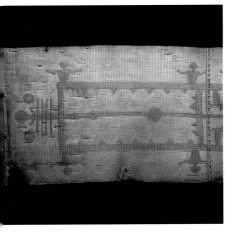

ABOVE: *Part of the seating plan of the Ojibwa Midéwiwin Society on birch bark.*

rooted in the dreams of an individual rather than considering this solely as an organised shamanic cult. The shamans of the Midéwiwin, the Midé priests, function outside the Midé ceremonies as dream interpreters and healers, and it is only during the Midé rituals that any affinity between them is recognised and expressed.

The origins of the Midéwiwin, although following the generalised pattern of Woodlands culture as shown by Iroquois collective endeavour, are obscure. It is not mentioned in the 17th century reports of the Jesuit missionaries, and may therefore be a relatively late phenomenon. Some scholars have nevertheless argued that mention of the Midéwiwin is absent from these records because the rituals were in conflict with the missionary message and were therefore concealed. This, however, is unlikely. Midéwiwin rituals, although their details are kept secret, are highly conspicuous. They include the building of the *midéwigan*, or Grand Medicine Lodge, and the closure of all trails leading to the lodge, as well as the erection of carved wooden spirit figures which guard the trails. Even if the missionaries were not permitted to witness the ceremony, they can hardly have been unaware of the preparations made for it.

A more likely explanation for the origin of the Midéwiwin is that it occurred as a reaction against the social, religious, and cultural upheavals of the late 17th and 18th centuries. At this time tribes such as the Ojibwa, for whom the Midéwiwin is most widely recorded, were embroiled in the territorial disputes of the English and French during the French and Indian Wars, were subject to rapidly changing economies related to the fur trade and the introduction of European trade goods, and were also under intense pressure from missionaries anxious to convert them to Christianity.

The shamans were at the centre of these changes, not only because their beliefs were in conflict with those of the missionaries but also because they were seen as hostile traditionalists. Indeed, much of the Native resistance to Europeans was led by so-called 'prophets', or shamans. A bonding together of the shamans through the Midéwiwin would have strengthened their position as well as acting as a unifying force for traditional beliefs.

Legend has it that the Midéwiwin was founded by the Great Spirit, *Gitche Manido* or *Manitou*, who travelled around the world to unite the people and asked the culture hero, *Manabozho*, to instruct the shamans in the rites of the Midéwiwin. *Manabozho* gave the shamans the plans for the *midéwigan*, the Grand Medicine Lodge, which he said represented the Native cosmos, and also instructed them to record this in pictographs drawn on birchbark scrolls so that

his instructions could be passed on to future generations. The use of the Midéwiwin as a unifying factor that is inter-tribally recognised is therefore endorsed in the legend, and its widespread distribution is not evidence of antiquity - as has been suggested - but of a collective response to a situation of crisis.

Although its details are made known only to those who have undergone elaborate initiations into the Grand Medicine Society, the general structure of the Midéwiwin ceremonies is well known. They begin with the building of the *midéwigan* under the direction of the *midéwiwinini*, a highly ranked shaman who acts as the presiding priest during the annual Midéwiwin rites. He also presides over the carving and erection of the wooden spirit figures, draped with brightly coloured cloth and other articles as offerings to *Manido*,

LEFT: *As a mark of their high status and its attendant responsibilities, the shamans and other leading figures among the Sauk and Fox of the Great Lakes region wore otterskin turbans such as that depicted here. Otter, as the 'chief of the animals', was considered to hold a similar position and status within the animal kingdom as the shamans and chiefs held among the people.*

During ritual and ceremonial performances, the main participants wore costumes that provided a tangible link to the spirit-animal powers that influenced events and assisted the people. Feathers from birds of prey, as those used in this gustoweh headdress from the Seneca, were thought to connect the wearer with the swift approach and hunting prowess of these birds.

which are used to guard the trails leading to the *midéwigan* and are said to prevent the intrusion of any disruptive forces.

The purpose of the Midéwiwin is to initiate candidates into the Mystic Society of Animals - a community of spirit-animals said to have been represented at the founding of the original Grand Medicine Lodge - through a succession of annual rites, usually four, by which they are gradually empowered. The nature of this power is clearly shamanic, since at the end of the initiations the candidate is believed to be able to fly, to change him or herself into an animal, to become clairvoyant and to prophesy, to find lost objects, to resist fire, walk through solid objects, and effect cures.

Although initiation was formerly open only to those who had received sanction through a dream experience, in which their right

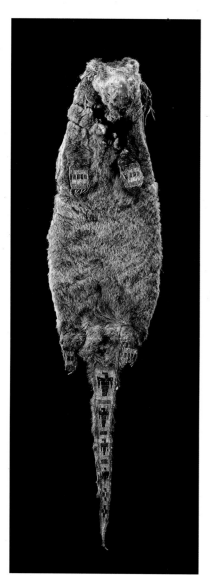

ABOVE: *Among the Midé priests of the Great Lakes tribes, ritual paraphernalia were kept in a medicine bag when not in use. Different degrees of shamanic power were reflected in the animal skin used for the bag, in this case an otterskin, and power was transferred to an initiate during the ritual by pointing or touching the initiate with the medicine bag.*

to participate had been given by an animal-spirit, this has been superseded by initiation through the offering of gifts to *Manido* and by sponsorship of the Midéwiwin feasts. The four stages of initiation in modern Midéwiwin rites are not, however, dissimilar from those that were previously practised. They begin as much as a year in advance, during which the invited candidate is taught the songs and prayers of the Midé and instructed in the uses of various herbs that have curative properties. It is also during this period that family and relatives gather the various offerings and gifts that will be required, which at the higher levels of initiation can be considerable.

Four days before initiation the candidate retires to an isolated hut and fasts and thirsts in order to be cleansed. Sweat baths, in which water is dropped on to hot stones in an enclosed space to produce a cleansing vapour scented with sage or cedar, rid the body of human odours that the spirits find offensive. During this period he or she meditates on the ceremony that is about to be performed. Absolute concentration is required, as not a single mistake is permitted in the Medicine Lodge. On the appointed day, the candidate is brought by his or her mentor to the Medicine Lodge which has been blessed and purified by the *midéwiwinini* and other senior shamans. Each shaman, as well as other members of the Midé Society, carries a medicine bag as insignia of rank. The medicine bags connect the Midé members with the spirit powers of the animal world, such as weasel, mink, wildcat, bear, owl, hawk, or rattlesnake, and each contains a *migis*, or sacred shell, through which power is transferred to the candidate.

The culmination of the Midé ceremony is the 'shooting' of the candidate with the *migis* by pointing at or touching his or her body with the medicine bag. The power contained in the *migis* is said to stun the candidate into unconsciousness. He or she falls down 'as if dead', and in this catatonic state receives a dream or revelation from the animal powers. The candidate is later revived by being again touched with the medicine bag, and on recovery spits the *migis* onto a cloth-covered boulder in the centre of the *midéwigan*. The Midé priest will later collect these *migis* and place them in medicine bags given to the candidates as evidence of their status as Midé members.

Each of the four stages of initiation into the Midéwiwin, although similar in procedure, has a quite distinct meaning. At the first the candidate 'dies' and is 'reborn'. Through this he or she becomes a transformed person - a spiritual being who is in contact with the animal powers. These powers are enhanced at the second stage, for the candidate is now said to be able to see further than the

RIGHT: *The tribes of the Iroquois League spoke of the Lenape, or Delaware, as Grandfathers, to honour them as ancient occupants of the area, and many Delaware beliefs were adopted into Iroquois ideology. The wooden face mask and bear skin costume probably represents Mesingw, the Keeper of Game and the Patron of Hunting.*

eye and to hear beyond the range of the ear. With the third initiation the candidate becomes a *yeesekeewinini* who is capable of invoking the spirits and communicating with the other world. Such a person has the power of a *Jessakid*, the 'conjuror' of the early reports who responds to the spirits' presence by moving and shaking things. The fourth, highest, stage gives power to awaken the potential in others and to instruct new Midé members. Even the most exalted members must, however, return to the Midé lodge each year and perform the ceremonies in order to refresh and sustain their powers.

The basic premise of the Midéwiwin is that moderation in speech, manner, and action will bring good and prolong life. Gentleness, patience, and courtesy are therefore expected of Midé members. Yet the roots of the Midéwiwin in individual shamanic practice highlights a curious paradox. The legends do not distinguish between good and evil, and Midé priests may be either *Jessakid* (conjuror) or *Wabano* (healer), or both. There is an underlying assumption that the animal powers can kill as well as cure. The erection of guardian effigies on the trails to the *midéwigan* prevents the intrusion, but does not deny the existence of the conflicting forces present in the spirit world and the ambivalent nature of Subarctic and Great Lakes shamanism.

This ambivalence in summed up in the creation myths of the Micmac, in which twin brothers with shamanic powers are responsible for the manner in which the forces of nature are divided. The brothers, *Gluskap* and *Malsum*, are total opposites; yet it is also clear they are inseparable and represent the opposing forces that influence and are influenced by the shamans. Thus the well-meaning *Gluskap* brings about good weather whereas *Malsum* makes the world cold and desolate. While *Malsum* sleeps, *Gluskap* creates edible plants; but when *Gluskap* rests, *Malsum* makes them poisonous. *Gluskap*, too, is credited with creating animals that people use for food; but *Malsum* gives them teeth and claws with which they are able to fight and kill.

Gluskap and *Malsum* embody powers that conflict with each other, and their antagonism is foreshadowed in the manner of their birth. *Gluskap* was born normally but *Malsum* burst forth from his mother's armpit in an unnatural birth which killed her. When *Gluskap* eventually defeated and killed his twin brother, the dead *Malsum* became a wolf - the habitual animal-familiar of Subarctic shamans, described in the tales as being cruel and vindictive. *Gluskap*, however, travelled far to the north in a stone canoe where, though living, he resides in a village of dead souls and spends his time making arrows. It is said that when his home is full of arrows

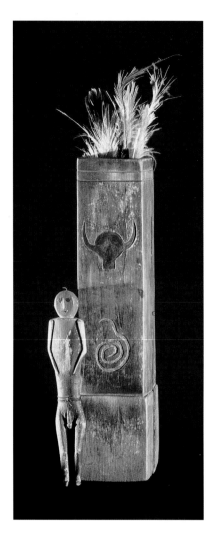

ABOVE: *Carved spirit figure and bark headdress box of the Midéwiwin Society. Their spirit figures and other paraphernalia were only in use for a short time each year, during the initiation of new members. Normally they were carefully stored so that their power could be contained and conserved. They remained potent but latent forces, and disregard or lack of respect could unleash these powers with disastrous consequences.*

he will return to the people and again give them his protection.

Subarctic and Great Lakes shamanism embodies these aspects of the Twin Brothers. The shamans cross the divides between the living and the dead, between good and evil, past and future, and between dream and reality. The shaman as spirit and the animal-familiar as shaman evidence the contrast and the connection between people and the supernatural and between nature and anti-nature, while at the same time providing proof that the worlds of the people and the spirits are both separate yet inseparable.

3 *The North End of the World*

NORTHWEST COAST SHAMANISM

The Northwest Coast is a narrow coastal strip of land stretching from northern California through British Columbia into Alaska, and separated from the interior by the Rocky Mountains. The Gulf Stream runs close off-shore and drives moisture-laden clouds inland which blanket the coast with frequent and heavy mists, dense fog, and rain. The high precipitation transforms the forest: mosses and lichens cover the ground and grow high into the trees, creating a fantastic world of strange and surreal shapes and forms

Despite the high latitude of the northern parts of the region, temperatures here rarely fall below freezing point: the warm waters of the Gulf Stream ensure high air temperatures on the coast, and the coastal mountains provide a buffer against the extremes of the interior. At the same time the coastal mountains tend to isolate the coast. Only the Nass and Skeena Rivers in the central and northern areas and the Columbia River in the south provide access to the interior.

This isolation has benefits for the coast. The warmth of the forest attracts game animals: bear, moose, deer, mountain sheep, and numerous smaller animals are abundant. Off-shore, the warm waters of the Gulf Stream support plankton which attracts whales and makes this one of the major whale habitats in the world. Seals and sea-lions have established major colonies here, as have sea otters. In shallow waters there are vast resources of clams and mussels. Sea birds are literally uncountable.

Most important, however, is salmon. Salmon return to the rivers each year on their annual migrations in numbers so large that this

LEFT: *The high humidity of the Northwest Coast's temperate rainforest created a forbidding interior of tangled moss-covered trees and rotting undergrowth. Shamans sought power in these dangerous regions, and would spend days isolated in the forests, fasting and performing rites intended to appease the animal spirits and mythical beings that lived there.*

73

ABOVE: *This 3,000 year old stone figurine bowl was found in the Fraser River Valley in the territories of the Interior Salish tribes. Although the exact use of these particular bowls is unknown they are similar in form to those used by shamans in the historic period during the performance of rituals. The humanoid figure represents the shaman's guardian spirit.*

fish is the staple food of the Northwest Coast tribes. Eaten fresh, or preserved by smoking and drying, salmon provide a surplus of food, and the rich marine resources of the area mean that the tribes living here rarely suffer from want or privation. Without pressure to expend excessive energy in securing basic needs they are able to form strong settled communities based on ownership of river and beach fronts which provide access to food sources, with a hierarchy of influential and competitive leaders with inherited social rank and status.

The abundance of salmon and other resources means that rituals to propitiate the spirits of the food animals are relatively unimportant, and shamanic intervention to avoid crises due to failure of food supplies is virtually unknown. Fish and animal species are blessed by the fishermen and hunters when they are procured: the carcass of a bear, for instance, is frequently shown all the respect due an honoured guest. The only food-related celebration of major tribal significance is the First Salmon Rite, when the bones of the first salmon caught during the season are returned to the river as an offering of thanks to appease the spirit of the fish and ensure bountiful future supplies. These rituals nevertheless remain under clan, rather than shamanic, control, and the right to perform the rituals is considered to be clan property.

Ownership of, and consequently access to, the richest food gathering areas is the exclusive and jealously guarded right of individual clans, ruled over by wealthy clan chiefs. Wealth itself might even be considered a prerogative granted to prominent families by Property Woman and her child. Various other deities granted these same families the right to sponsor and officiate at rituals, as well as the ownership of dance costumes and songs. Control of the economic and religious life of Northwest Coast peoples is therefore restricted and confined to those in privileged positions, and is outside the direct influence of the shamans.

By inheritance, members of the clan leader's immediate family form an aristocratic group which is supported economically and ritually by other members of the clan without claim to status. The nobles' ownership and control of privileges and rights is publicly proclaimed through elaborately carved and painted lineage crests depicting mythical events in the clan history, which feature most prominently on massive cedar totem poles erected in front of the leading clan house, and by initiation into the ranked positions of secret societies.

The numerous tribes of the Northwest Coast can be grouped

according to language similarity. From north to south the tribes speak various dialects of Tlingit, Tsimshian, Haida, Kwakiutl, Nootka, and Salish; but a social system based on status and wealth is common throughout the area, and the competitiveness of Northwest Coast social order and the importance of the clan structure means the tribes, even when they share a common language, rarely act together as cohesive units. In the past, clan rivalry led to extensive intra-tribal feuding that could last for several generations.

The focus of Northwest Coast economic life has always been maritime, and only occasional recourse was made to food products of the land. Apart from berrying grounds close to the villages, property ownership does not extend to the forests. These are the domain of *Bokwus* and *Tsonoqa*, the Kwakiutl names for the Wild Man and Wild Woman of the Woods. Both are terrifying spirits who dwell in invisible houses deep in the forest and subsist on grubs and rotten

BELOW: *Although all aspects of the environment were thought to contain supernatural power, this force was concentrated in greater intensity at some locales. Such places might be marked as 'different' or 'special' through the use of rock carvings and paintings. The example shown here is carved on rock near Sproat Lake, Vancouver Island, in an area occupied by the Nootka.*

BELOW: *The numerous islands and inlets of the Northwest Coast are the remains of an ancient mountain chain that was flooded at the close of the Ice Age. The contrast between land and sea allowed shamans access to the spirits of both regions, and their ability in creating a harmonious juxtaposition of these opposite forces was a measure of their ability to mobilise supernatural forces. The view shown here is near Skedans, a Haida village on the Queen Charlotte Islands.*

wood. The skeletal *Bokwus* offers what appears to be dried salmon to anyone who chances upon him, but it is really rotted bark and by tasting this the person is changed into a ghost and becomes his servant. *Tsonoqa* is equally feared, since she is known for eating children and carries a large sack on her back in which she places her victims. Although often asleep and rarely seen, *Tsonoqa's* presence can always be detected by the sound of her breathing made as the wind rustles through the tree tops.

Bokwus and *Tsonoqa* are 'outsiders' in the pantheon of Northwest Coast spirits. They do not consort with the other spirits and avoid the rivers and sea where most of them have their abode, and the food they eat - rotted bark, grubs, and the corpses of children - is considered to be that of tormented ghosts who have been unable to find rest and peace. In fact, although extremely powerful, they live far from the source of supernatural power which is conceived to lie

RIGHT: *This Tlingit canoe prow ornament represents an owl with outstretched wings. The owl was thought of as the spirit animal representation of dead people who had been unable to find rest, and who, in the form of ghosts, haunted the graveyards near the villages and the grave houses of deceased shamans. As a potent destructive force their presence on the prows of war canoes was an appropriate one, and their power was eagerly sought by the shamans who led Tlingit war parties. The carving shown here was one of the crests used by the Raven division at Klukwan, the largest of the Chilkat Tlingit villages.*

in the north at the head of a mighty river which supplies water to 'the Pacific Ocean and is the home of *Baxbakualanuxsiwae*, the Cannibal-at-the-North-End-of-the-World.

The attitude and behaviour of *Bokwus* and *Tsonoqa* sets them apart from people and from the other spirits. As outsiders they behave and act like the shamans of the Northwest Coast, who share many of their characteristics and are also considered to be different from others and beyond the normal restrictions of social conventions. Tlingit shamans live alone in a hut outside the village, do not exercise clan privileges, refrain from fishing and hunting and are believed to subsist entirely on 'ghost food' – grubs and rotted bark – or on offerings that are given to them. They are said not to decompose after death but to remain active in a world between that of the people and the ghosts and in contact with both.

The shamans do not inherit their position from the ancestral spirits that determine rank and privilege. Instead they derive their power from the spirits that others avoid, and often spend long periods in the forest where they fast and meditate in order to increase their power. They actively consort with Land Otter, a shamanic creature of awesome strength contact with whom normally results in instant death. Land Otter is, for instance, held to be responsible for over-turning canoes and drowning their occupants in the turbulent whirlpools of offshore waters. The Tlingit state that all shamanic power is called *Kucda* (land otter) and resides in the Land Otter's tongue. By 'cutting the tongue' – a secretive rite in which thin slices are cut from an otter's tongue, wrapped in herbs, and then hidden in a place where water cannot penetrate – a shaman acquires the Land Otter's power and can speak with the voice of the spirit.

Shamanic separation from other members of the community is apparent from the beginning of their call to the profession. They suf-fer 'shamanic sickness' which results in violent vomiting, strange dreams, irrational and anti-social behaviour, foaming at the mouth, and, ultimately, coma. They are said to 'die', and in this condition are transported to the world of the spirits from which they derive power. Unlike ordinary people whose souls are lost and who become ghosts when they journey to the spirit lands, the shamans are able to return unharmed to the world of the living.

During their initial separation, novice shamans lead solitary

BELOW: For the Tlingit the Land Otter Man was the most powerful and the most feared of all the shamanic spirits. The significance of Land Otter Man is reflected in the fact that all shamanic power was referred to by the generic term Kucda (land otter). Land Otter Man is shown below in the form of a canoe prow ornament that ensured the safe passage of canoes through the turbulent waters of the Tlingit area. In this case the Land Otter Man gave directions to the shaman, who lay face down in the canoe and relied on the messages he received from his spirit helpers.

OPPOSITE: *Land Otter Man posed a threat to people, both at sea and in the forests. Someone coming across the spirit unexpectedly while in the forest would be transformed into one of Land Otter Man's helpers. This transformation process resulted in the person losing human form and gaining that of the land otter.*
RIGHT: *Death by drowning if a canoe capsized was attributed to the Land Otter Man and is depicted in this Northern Tlingit shaman's mask.*

secluded lives in the forest, often for months at a time. Occasionally they may have an assistant or helper, someone who will later become the shaman's spy in the villages and covertly gather information which the shaman can claim to have been revealed to him by the spirits in a dream or vision. The helper gathers herbs and plants under the shaman's direction, and is there to protect him if he loses his senses in trance and is at risk of injuring himself. During his seclusion the shaman begins to engage in erratic behaviour characteristic of the shamans and to gain skill in working with the spirit forces. He acquires power from animals, which he is said to be able to kill simply by pointing his finger at them.

LEFT: *To distinguish themselves from ordinary members of the community, Tlingit shamans allowed their hair to grow to extraordinary lengths. From the time of their initiation it remained uncut and was rolled into thick braids that were never combed out or washed. Krause, reporting on Tlingit shamanic practice in the 1880s, noted that the shaman's hair 'had a life of its own' and that during rituals 'it twisted and writhed like so many serpents, independent of the shaman's volition'.*

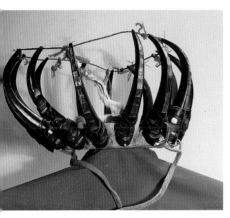

ABOVE: *During curing rituals Tsimshian shamans wore headdresses or 'crowns' made from the horns of mountain goats. These served as a 'badge of office', but also linked the shaman with the mountain goat and with that animal's tenacious grip on life. Mountain goats had a reputation, in fact and myth, for being difficult to kill and able to cross narrow mountain ledges that proved an insurmountable barrier to other creatures. The mountain goat's hold on life and ability to overcome obstacles were characteristics the shaman sought to call to his aid when performing a healing ritual.*

When the novice shamans return from the forest they are different from other members of their community. Their thoughts are no longer focussed on ordinary reality and they may be unable to communicate with other people. Some lose the power of speech, and at first can only utter meaningless phrases. Others spit blood, or stand in contorted postures for hours on end. In this state they are fully possessed by spirit power and unable to act of their own volition. At night they become dogs or owls and haunt the graves of the recently deceased, or they wander far from the village to the grave huts of previous shamans or other places of the dead that are feared and avoided by everyone else.

Slowly, perhaps with the help of an established shaman, they recover their senses; but they can never be like ordinary people and begin to adopt behaviour characteristic of those who have become possessed. Tsimshian and Kwakiutl shamans let their hair grow long as an indication of their calling and leave it uncut and uncombed until it becomes tangled and matted, while the Tlingit shamans never trim their fingernails, which become long and curved. Haida shamans formerly demonstrated they were different from normal people by biting a piece of flesh from the arm of the first woman they met. This flesh was believed to be poisonous to anyone other than those who had gained spirit power.

All of them will later return frequently to the forest and spend long periods of solitude in order to gain additional or greater spiritual strength. This is done by meeting a spirit, often in animal form, which they ritually kill and thereby gain the animal's power. During their periods of 'journeying for power' in the forest, the shamans eat devil's club – a strong emetic and purgative – bathe in ice-cold water, and scourge their bodies with nettles until blood flows freely and the scent of humans, which is offensive to the spirits, is washed away.

The ordeals the shamans put themselves through are physically and emotionally exhausting. Some Tlingit shamans, as a consequence of the violent extremes to which they subject themselves, become so weak they are no longer able to stand or walk and have to be carried by their helper. The helper is protected from harm by the shaman's spirit power and, by association with the shaman, begins to acquire power of his own. The initiation of the shaman, whether assisted or not, is the familiar shamanic theme of death and rebirth. By experiencing and recovering from death the shaman gains access to visionary realms beyond normal comprehension.

On returning to the real world, the shaman must proclaim his newly acquired identity by declaring the name the spirits have given

ABOVE: *Frogs feature conspicuously in the myths and tales of the northern Northwest Coast tribes, where they are often credited with bestowing shamanic power on an ancestor. This Tsimshian Flying Frog helmet refers to an ancestress of the Frog clan who disappeared and was later seen emerging from a lake surrounded by flying frogs.*
It was the shaman's responsibility to establish communion with the ancestral spirit animals and induce them to act beneficially on behalf of the clan members.

him and through a distribution of goods to validate his new name. If he feels strong enough he may make a tribal declaration, but most inexperienced shamans demonstrate their abilities first to close relatives, who, although they may be in awe and fearful of someone who has returned from the other world, can nevertheless be expected to show some sympathy and support. Among the Tlingit, however, a tribal declaration is expected, since a shaman's powers are said to be ineffective for people to whom he is related by blood or clan.

A tribal declaration can nevertheless result in immediate demands from established shamans that the novice 'proves' his or her power through competitive challenges, or who may attempt to drain power away from the inexperienced shaman in order to enhance their own prestige. Shamanic power is elusive and the spirits are likely to favour those through whom they can become most effective, so the neophyte, who has incomplete control of the powers by which he or she is influenced, is always at a disadvantage.

Experienced shamans will recognise from the novice's behaviour the general group of spirits that influence him or her, since different spirits bestow different kinds of power 'and engender particular modes of conduct. The *sqelam* shamans 'of the Coast Salish, for instance, become *siyaikutl* (doctors), *siwin* (seers), or *senwa* (witches) The first two are 'invariably men, although the *senwa* witches are often women and 'are especially feared. Similarly, according to the *Ichta* 'shamans of the Tlingit, all spirits are *Jek*, but can be 'further subdivided into *Kijek*, the spirits of the upper world; *Takijek*, those of the land; and *Tekijek*, who live in the waters.

The *Kijek* are warriors who have been killed in battle, and whose souls have gone to live in the north in the place where supernatural power originates. The *Takijek* are the souls of those who have died an ordinary death and been transformed into land animals. They, too, live in the north, 'but at a place called *Takanku*. The *Tekijek*, or Water Spirits, are the souls of sea mammals. Each of these can bestow shamanic power, and each has its own costume and typical movement. The water spirits glide in undulating waves, as though moving through the sea; whereas the land spirits adopt the characteristic motions of their namesakes. Bear moves ponderously, but powerfully; Rabbit darts quickly and stands motionless at times; Mountain Goat displays extreme agility. The *Kijek* souls of dead warriors are fearsome and agitated, since in death they battle continuously with the souls of their enemies.

From such signs, and through the agency of their own spirit helpers, the established shamans are often able to identify the specific

RIGHT: *A carved wooden figure of a Tlingit shaman dressed for a ceremonial performance, wearing characteristic paraphernalia that define his vocation and also act as a repository of shamanic power. Note particularly the robe painted with representations of spirit helpers, the fringed shamanic apron as well as the necklace and 'scratching sticks' he wears around his neck. Note, too, the woven and painted clan hat. The symbols on this represent the power granted to the clan by ancestral spirits, which the shaman can access through his family membership in addition to the personal powers depicted on other items of his clothing.*

spirit power by which the novice has been possessed. They may then be able to entice this away from the new shaman and claim it for their own. In this way their own power and their prestige increase, and with it the fees the shaman can demand for his or her services.

The shamans are acutely aware that power on the Northwest Coast has to be repeatedly demonstrated through successful cures, magic acts, and other ritual performances, and that these are tested by their peers. The more spirit helpers an individual shaman has, the stronger the likelihood he will be successful in these tests and the greater his ability to retaliate if challenged. Pressure to challenge and defeat an opponent, and thereby lay claim to that shaman's powers in addition to one's own, is therefore intense and such testing is

RIGHT: *Although identified only as a 'mythical beast', the stylised sucker-covered tentacles make it certain that the painting on this shaman's drum represents an octopus or other cephalopod. The octopus, as a powerful Underwater Spirit, was thought to possess tremendous shamanic abilities. Octopi and other related species were believed to live in rocky inlets as well as in deep inland pools. Such places were generally avoided because of the danger they presented to the unprepared; however, shamans would regularly bathe there to test their immunity and to regenerate their powers or acquire new ones.*

almost invariably hostile. The shamans search for faults or mistakes in the performance by which they may damage another's reputation; yet the tests are important if the shaman is to retain credibility.

The untrained shaman is extremely vulnerable during the period of his first testing, and may seek protection from or apprenticeship to an established shaman. The power of the latter can then be used to protect the novice, although the heavy fees demanded for the older shaman's help mean it is available only to those whose relatives are willing and able to support the novice. Even apprenticeship, however, is not always a safe route into shamanic practice, since the mature shaman might attempt to steal for himself the power that the novice has access to.

The Haisla (Northern Kwakiutl) even use apprenticeship as a form of social control. The clan leaders, working in collusion with an adult shaman, might tell a wealthy commoner that his son is destined to become a shaman and must go into training. In the past, the father's refusal to accept such a mandate resulted in the boy's death. Training, however, consists of continual feasts and distributions of property to validate the boy's gradual acquisition of power, and often serves as a useful means of relieving rich commoners of their wealth and reducing their influence in the community.

Whether claiming genuine spirit contact, using shamanism as a means to gain status, or being forced into the role, Northwest Coast shamans separate themselves from other members of the community by breaking socially accepted codes of conduct and status. Thus, although many of them are extremely influential and may at times enjoy positions of authority that rival those of the prominent clan leaders, they remain outside the élite and do not usually inherit any status or privilege.

Among the Tlingit, where a shaman's successor was often a close relative, there is some indication of inherited rights; but for other groups, such as the Kwakiutl, the only avenue by which a non-ranking commoner can gain a position of influence is through shamanism. In these cases the shaman is said to be initiated by the supernatural spirits rather than by the ancestral spirits that determine clan rank and position. The Coast Salish, however, claim that in common with people the spirits have different rank and status, and that a person possessed by a highly ranked spirit power will be automatically elevated to a high social position regardless of his previous status.

The high regard for shamans is also evident among the *saagga* shamans of the Haida. Although their powers are non-hereditary, they usually outrank the chiefs and can override decisions of clan leaders and household heads. Only chiefs and shamans have the right to wear headdresses decorated with sea lion bristles as a sign of their authority, and in the past only the shamans were able to declare war. Similarly, in certain circumstances Tlingit shamans exercised greater' authority than the chiefs; particularly in matters relating to conflict with other Tlingit sub-groups or with other tribes.

The Tlingit shamans not only declared war, but also trained the warriors and led the war party. It was believed they could divine the presence of an enemy, so when the massive dugout war canoes set out, the shaman lay face down in the prow of the leading canoe, directing the path of the party by his thoughts. Warfare among the Tlingit was often decided by shamanic contest rather than in actual conflict, since the shamans of the opposing parties would harangue each other until one conceded that his power was inferior to that of his rival. The losing shaman would then abandon his cause by recognising the superior power of his opponent, and would withdraw to seek additional power so the status quo could be re-established.

Yet although in these competitive wealth- and status-oriented societies shamanism is an accepted route to social standing and authority, contact with the powers granting shamanic ability is rarely sought voluntarily. Contact with the shamanic spirits, such as Land

ABOVE: *A Haida shaman's rattle made to represent an octopus.*

85

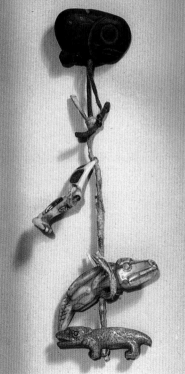

Northwest Coast shamans relied on the efficacy of animal claws, bones, horns and fangs as well as the roots of certain plants. These served as links to the world of the spirits, enabling the shaman to establish communion with his spirit helpers. The Haida neckrings (TOP) consist mainly of bone and ivory pendants, the longer of which were used as 'scratching sticks' since the shaman's hands were the agents through which supernatural power was worked and should not touch his body during a possessed state. The Tsimshian linked charms (LEFT) include a human leg and two marine animals that represent the shaman's spirit helpers. Various roots were

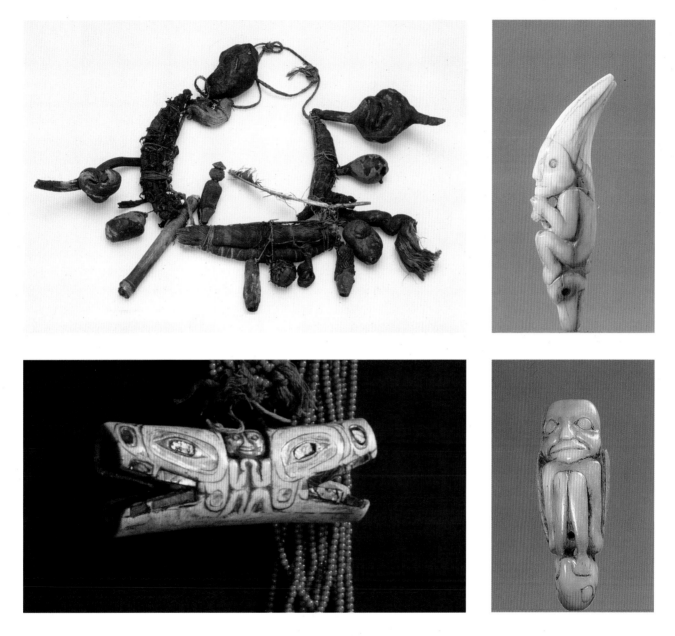

considered to have a protective function, either as medicines or by being burnt to create a purifying aromatic smoke; they are shown here attached to a Tlingit shaman's necklace (TOP LEFT). The two-headed carving (BOTTOM LEFT) is known as a 'soul catcher'. During dreams a patient's soul might wander and become lost, but, if soul loss was diagnosed in time, the shaman could recapture the soul and enclose it in the soul catcher for return to the patient. The shaman's belief in death and rebirth with heightened senses is featured in the two Tsimshian fang carvings showing human figures in the foetal position (RIGHT).

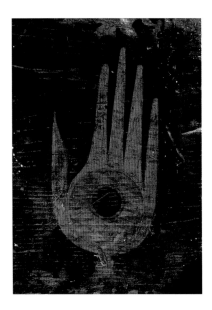

ABOVE: *The hand is a potent symbol of possession and ownership, and is shown here painted on a wooden chest that contained a Tsimshian shaman's ritual paraphernalia. Such chests were believed to have power of their own, which was increased by the supernatural qualities of the items stored within them.*

Otter, is considered to be highly dangerous, and can result in the shaman gaining power which may be used adversely. Previously, shamans held their positions through fear of their power rather than out of respect. The wealth they accumulated came from excessive fees charged for cures and other services they performed and which were paid to avoid giving offence to the shaman and the spirits he could summon. At the same time the shaman was always in fear for his life. Any untoward event or an illness with no evident cause are invariably attributed to a curse made by a shaman, the Bella Coola tribe even claiming that all deaths and illness are caused by magic. One of the methods of curing is to identify a bewitching shaman or sorcerer and to pay a rival shaman to 'capture' the disease-causing agency and redirect it back to the sorcerer with fatal consequences.

Wounds, fractures, breaks, or any other injury or disease that has an obvious cause do not, generally, merit shamanic attention; but it is a commonly held belief that the shamans are able to cure any illness that has a 'mysterious' origin, and that as 'masters of mystery' they are able to cause or cure illness at will. It follows, however, that a failure to effect a cure can be attributed to only one of two possible reasons. Either the power of the shaman causing the illness is greater than that of the shaman who is trying to cure it; or the shaman is deliberately failing in his endeavours. In the latter case this could be because he is himself the instigator of the illness, that he has been bribed by the enemies of the patient to let him or her die, or he is prolonging treatment to increase the fee he can charge.

In either case failure is likely to cause extreme difficulty for the shaman concerned. In the first he is seen as the weaker of two competing shamans and is publicly humiliated by his rival. He is said to 'die of shame': that is, his credibility is brought into doubt and he may be accused of making fraudulent claims as to the powers he says he possesses. The ridicule heaped on him by his rival effectively curtails his ability to function as a shaman. This parallels the competition between rival clan leaders, who validate their positions through lavish distributions of wealth during *potlatches* when they attempt to raise their own status by giving away more than their rival can afford. The loser then finds himself in the embarrassing position of a 'poor man' who lost face and his standing in the community. The shamans challenge each other with the amount of spirit power they can summon in much the same way as the clan leaders establish their positions by challenges through property.

The second eventuality is even more serious. In the past a shaman who was exposed as a sorcerer or who had accepted bribes to con-

RIGHT: *The hours of darkness were considered a time of potential danger, since souls might wander during sleep when they were freed, through dreams, from the confines of the human body. It was also a time when the ghosts of the dead were abroad, often appearing in the form of owls that haunted graveyards. Shamans had recourse to powerful spirits of the night to assist them in their endeavours to counteract such influences. Prominent among these beneficial helpers was Moon, shown here carved on a Tsimshian shaman's storage chest.*

ceal another sorcerer's identity would be put to death. Such shamans were rarely able to depend on family or relatives for protection or deterrence by threatening revenge, since this would be condemned by the community as collusion with the shaman in his evil intent. Only the most powerful shamans enjoyed any immunity by warning the people that harm done to them would be avenged by the spirits they were in contact with: mountains would move and destroy entire villages, Land Otter would cause their fishing fleets to capsize, their women would become barren, or the salmon would refuse to return to the rivers and the people would starve.

Few shamans were thought capable of summoning such awesome retribution, and even as recently as the late 1880s witchcraft hunts were common among the Tlingit. Two women, accused of making spells against their neighbours, were dragged from their beds and taken to the beach front, where they were held under water until they nearly drowned. They were then stripped and held naked on the glowing coals of a recent fire. One died from her ordeal, the other was rescued by a local missionary but had to spend the rest of her life in exile. Only a few years prior to this, shortly before the sale of Alaska by Russia to the United States, two shamans who were held responsible for the death of a man in a nearby village were arrested by local police in the township of Archangel. Their uncombed hair, the symbol of their vocation and considered to be the 'seat' of their power, was cut by the authorities. The hair was put on display in the local church as evidence that the power of these shamans had been neutralised. In neither case did the family or clan of the accused make any direct attempt to intervene.

Male and female shamans were always open to accusations of malpractice. It was believed that even the weaker shamans had power to 'think' a person to death, and most people suspected the shamans of harbouring grudges against other members of the community who were younger, stronger, more virile, or who had greater wealth than they. Among the Bella Coola, a shaman would often substitute his rival's name for food, saying: "I am eating [rival's name] with my soup". The rival, who was made aware of the ploy, was said to grow gradually weaker and to die within a year.

Northwest Coast shamans are also in fear of each other. Apart from frequent accusations of sorcery and attempts made to deprive them of power, which can only be dealt with by demonstrating that one is stronger than the challenger, the competitive nature of the coastal groups means that shamans constantly vie with one another. There are no shamanic societies or organisations and little cooperation between shamans. Instead they use secret methods of identifying, and then attacking, each other's weaknesses and vulnerabilities.

A legendary tale of shamanic competition recorded by Franz Boas in the 1890s refers to a great Tsimshian *halaait* shaman named Only One. He was often called upon in cases of bewitchment, and in one instance detected an arrowhead inside the body of a chief's son which had been placed there by another *halaait* in the pay of a rival family who were jealous of the chief's wealth. Only One found that *haldaogyet*, black magic, had been used and named the *halaait* who was responsible. This man had made an image of the boy, and each day pushed a thorn deeper into the image. Only One saw that the thorn was moving dangerously close to the boy's heart, but was able to tell the chief where the image had been hidden. As soon as the thorn was removed the boy recovered his health and vitality.

The other *halaait*, furious at Only One's intervention but afraid of his power, decided to ask the assistance of other shamans. His intention was that they should combine all their efforts in an attempt to kill Only One. They sent a message saying another shaman was ill and requested Only One's help, then laid secret traps along the route he would need to take to reach his patient's home. These included an invisible magic net in which he would become entangled and an

OPPOSITE: *Tlingit shamans spent much of their lives living in isolated huts away from the villages, where they shunned the company of other people. When their presence in the village was required to perform a cure or other ritual, they donned special garments both as a mark of distinction and as a means of establishing contact with their spirit helpers. The two dance aprons featured here show the exaggerated forms of shamanic spirit beings. Note particularly the painting on the top apron, which was collected on the Admiralty Islands in 1890, where the central figure is shown with exposed ribs. Shamans were often thought to abandon their physical shell when travelling to the spirit world in a possessed state, and at such times their bodies were said to become transparent so that the inner organs and skeletal structure were made visible.*

LEFT: *An essential part of the Northwest Coast shaman's practice was his ability to perform magical acts in front of a critical audience during public ceremonies. Although most shamans acknowledged that these were mere tricks of their trade, they also claimed that the ability to perform them convincingly was granted by the spirits and that the tricks were necessary to convince the audience of their power. The Tsimshian shaman's doll shown here was attached to strings and manipulated by the shaman's helper from his hiding place on the roof of the house. The controlling strings were invisible in the half-light and smoke of the ceremonial fires, so that the puppet seemed to acquire a life of its own and would dance or fly through the air at the shaman's command.*

invisible ditch into which he would fall. Because ordinary people were unable to see these they could do them no harm, and had been especially laid for Only One. He, however, managed to detect and evade them, and discovered the source of illness had been caused by placing some of the patient's excrement in contact with the corpse of a shaman who had recently died. When the witchcraft bundle was removed from the presence of the corpse, the sick shaman recovered.

More furious still, the other shamans invited Only One to a feast at which they intended to poison him. Only One's spirit helpers,

OPPOSITE: *This carved figure from the Bella Coola probably served a similar function as a representation of a shamanic spirit as the shaman's doll on the left. However, the lack of articulated limbs means that it was unlikely to have been used during displays of magic.*

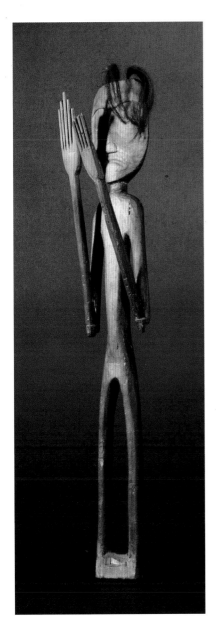

Such rigid dolls might be placed as 'guardians' of the sacred fires in the ceremonial longhouses, or displayed with other shamanic paraphernalia near to the partitioned chamber in which the shaman made his preparations.

who had been informed by the shaman whose life he had saved, foresaw this danger, so when Only One was offered human flesh instead of meat he cut open his stomach and, without being noticed, extracted the flesh from his abdomen before it could do him any harm. His spirit helpers then secretly placed the flesh in the food of the other *halaaits*, who after consuming it complained of stomach pains, went into convulsions, and died. Thus Only One demonstrated his great power and superiority over his rivals.

Tales of famous shamans such as Only One serve to fix the concept of shamanic power in people's memories. They remember what the shamans of the past were able to do and the extraordinary magical powers they had at their command. Contemporary shamans say their own power is less potent than that of their predecessors because in modern times the link between people and the spirits has been weakened; yet there is still an underlying assumption that the tremendous magical power of the old-time shamans is extant and may reappear in the future in a new generation of shamans. This power was, and is, generally expressed through healing rites and demonstrations of power; sorcery and the shamanic competitions are more frequently secret affairs that are conducted away from the public gaze and which only become known after a shaman is convinced that his rival has been defeated and that he no longer has to fear retaliation. The cures and other public displays are, by contrast, spectacular theatrical performances which attract large audiences.

Often the shaman will perform a set of masked dances, each representing one of the spirit powers with whom he is in contact. These take place during *tsetseka*, the sacred winter season when the spirits are thought to stay near to the villages, and are held in large plank longhouses which have had all their effects removed and have been ritually cleansed and prepared by the shaman and his assistants.

Unlike ordinary non-shamanic dance displays, which can be graceful and fluent, the shamans' dances are marked by bursts of frenzied and irregular motion, after which the shamans hold a contorted pose for long periods. During the active part of his dance the shaman is surrounded by men with drawn knives apparently trying to catch and 'tame' him, and at the end of each display he retires behind a partition to a secret room in which his shamanic paraphernalia have been hidden.

The most dramatic parts of the display are the shaman's tricks. Some juggle with glowing coals which they sometimes swallow, or which they may throw into the assembled audience. This can be done with careless abandon and the burning down of the house due

to a shaman's indulgence in his fire-handling routines used to be a very real possibility. Others walk on fire, swallow long, pointed sticks, or consume prodigious quantities of food or liquid; meanwhile they challenge any rivals who may be watching to outdo them. Others may miraculously cause their rivals to faint or collapse.

Such spectacular shows of magic are common. At the turn of the century the Kwakiutl shaman Good-all-over-the-Earth had a carved wooden Raven rattle which he used to bring to life and make it bite his hand until the blood flowed, while another had a stuffed squirrel which he made run up his arm and then finally fly to the rafters of the house. Good-all-over-the-Earth and his rival were defeated and 'made common' when other shamans detected the means whereby these tricks were achieved. Both are said to have given up

ABOVE: *According to legend these islands were created when the world was still covered with water. Tired from flying, Raven needed a place to rest and to this end created the islands by splashing the water and transforming the spray into rock.*

Raven's legendary transformative powers made him a favourite of the shamans, who were themselves claiming to undergo transformation during their journeys into the other world; Raven appears frequently on shamanic objects such as the rattle shown overleaf.

practising shamanism and to have 'died of shame' shortly thereafter.

Franz Boas witnessed another remarkable display of shamanic trickery. Before the shaman even made an appearance his voice was heard singing from the centre of the fire that had been built in the middle of the room. When the shaman finally emerged he appeared dazed and confused, dancing hesitantly as if unsure of himself. Each time he tried to return to his refuge behind the partition it seemed as if some force were dragging him back towards the central fire. Despite his struggles he was drawn closer to the flames, until suddenly he uttered a terrifying scream and was pulled headfirst into the ground until only his legs were showing. In this condition he was pulled violently around the floor of the longhouse, his body ploughing up great furrows of earth as the unseen force dragged him along.

95

Finally his assistants managed to grab his legs and pull him out of the ground, but he was clearly distressed and in such a weakened condition that he was unable to stand and had to be carried off to rest.

This shaman later revealed the secrets of his performance to Boas. During the ritual cleansing and preparation of the long-house the shaman and his helpers had laid hollow kelp stems beneath the floor leading from behind the partition to the fire. By singing into the stems from his concealment behind the partition the shaman's voice appeared to emanate from the fire. They had also dug a deep and rather tortuous trench in the floor, at the bottom of which they had buried a stout rope and covered this with loose earth. The shaman had simply to grasp the rope with both hands and then pull himself along it to give the impression he was being dragged along.

Extraordinary magic abilities were also shown in cures, especially those involving 'soul loss'. It was thought that the souls of people were able to travel away from the body, particularly during sleep, but would generally return. They could, however, be enticed away from the person, often through the actions of a shaman and his spirit assistants. This 'parallels the legend of *Baxbakualanuxsiwae*, the Cannibal-at-the-North-End-of-the-World, whose companion, a beautiful young woman named *Kinqala*, danced naked before *Baxbakualanux-siwae's* house and lured the unwary inside where a monstrous bird called *Hoxhok* consumed their brains and left their corpses as food for *Baxbakualanuxisae* and *Kinqala*.

If a soul has been enticed away, then only a shaman can recover it. He has to do this before the soul tastes any of the food or pleasures of the Ghost World, since it then becomes attached to the other world and is irrecoverable. The journey to the other world often involves an arduous underwater passage. The shaman, with a long rope tied about his waist, wades into the sea and disappears, often for considerable periods of time, while his assistants hold the rope to

BELOW: *This ceremonial club was collected among the Nootka by Captain Cook in the 18th century. It was used during the Wolf Dance, when the Wolves carried off uninitiated children in their teeth. During a period of seclusion, corresponding to their captivity by the Wolves, the children were taught the secrets of the spirit world. These ceremonies were conducted by experienced shamans, who would select from the initiates those who showed any disposition for the shamanic profession.*

ensure he can find his way back.

One shaman from Sitka had himself wrapped in a cedar bark mat which was tightly bound with a strap of Otter, his protective spirit, and then let himself be lowered into the sea. He dropped to the bottom of the ocean 'faster than a stone and faster than a whale which had been shot', while the free end of the line to which he was attached was kept buoyant on the surface by a float made from the bladder of Land Otter. After several hours his companions, assuming he had drowned, returned to the village; but they returned to the spot on successive days to find the Land Otter float exactly as they had left it.

On the fourth day, although the position of the float was unchanged, they heard the sound of a shaman's drum. Following the sound, they discovered the shaman hanging face down on the side of a steep cliff, his face streaming with blood. The cliff was so high and the shaman's position so precarious that his companions faced extreme difficulty in reaching the body, but eventually they were able to secure a rope around it and lower it into their boat. As soon as his body touched the boat the shaman recovered consciousness and began to sing a spirit song he had learned while he was 'dead'.

This tale from Sitka is typical of the shamanic underwater journey, since visiting the Ghost World is fraught with difficulty and can

ABOVE: *Two views of a Tlingit Raven Rattle. Raven is a powerful shamanic figure and often appears in contexts where the shaman is attempting to undergo change; in this case the Raven Rattle is shaken with a peculiar but regular motion, unique to shamanic performances, that is said to induce a trance-like state. The figure of a shaman reclining on the raven's back holds the tongue of his spirit helper in his mouth, since the tongue was considered to be a conduit of power.*

take a shaman hours or days to complete. Evidence of his trials are the blood streaming from his face, and his semi-conscious condition, when he returns. If he has been successful in rescuing the errant soul, he carries it carefully in a hollow bone tube, or soul-catcher, which is stoppered with bungs of sacred red cedar bark. Upon retrieval of the soul the patient recovers from the lethargy that has afflicted him since the soul was enticed away; but if retrieval has been impossible his condition deteriorates and he dies.

Among the Coast Salish, where the shamans tend to cooperate more than in other parts of the Northwest Coast, the visit to the other world is carried out as a pantomime journey. Ten shamans, under the guidance of the one who actually recovers the soul, build a 'spirit canoe' in which they make paddling motions and act out a journey across the River of the Dead. The canoe is constructed from carved 'spirit boards', which are painted and tied with shredded cedar bark when in use. Such boards are said to be animate and powerful, and to move of their own volition.

The journey itself is dangerous. The River of the Dead becomes a raging torrent, and when the shaman crosses it he is faced on its opposite shore by a fearsome guardian who refuses to let him land and enter the Ghost World. If he manages to subdue the guardian, he is confronted by a host of spirits who throw flaming torches at him. In the pantomime journey, this danger is emphatically stated as real torches are thrown at the shamans by the young boys of the tribe. Having overcome these obstacles and recaptured the patient's soul, the shaman is then responsible for closing the door to the spirit world. If he fails in this part of his test, malevolent spirits could be released and cause havoc in the human worl

In the legends of the coastal tribes the Ghost World is often an inverted version of the real world. Some of these tales describe the shaman being met at the river by a ghost in a stone canoe, or in a burial canoe that has had holes drilled through the bottom to allow water to drain off. At the bank of the real world the canoe appears to be empty except for a handful of bones in the bottom, but these become animated when the canoe reaches the opposite shore. When it is low tide in the people's world, it is high tide in the world of the ghosts.

Other inversions include the ghosts' deafness to shouts although they can hear yawns and whispers; their habit to sleep in the day, which is their night, and to act at night in the human world when they haunt graveyards; and, of course, feeding on bark and rotted material. Their lives, however, are thought to be much like those of

ABOVE: *Unlike the northern tribes, where shamans would set off alone to recapture an errant soul, Coast Salish shamans had recourse to the Recovery Rite, in which a group of shamans sharing similar powers mimed a Spirit Canoe journey to the Land of the Dead. During this journey Spirit Boards, or Power Boards, were set up to delineate the outline of the canoe and to provide protection to the shamans. This photograph is a reconstruction of such a journey, using boards that are 2/3 the size of the originals; it was taken in 1920 at Tolt (Carnation), Washington, by J. D. Leechman.*

the people, except for the fact that they do not age and cannot die. They spend their time in the Ghost World playing games and gambling, travelling, hunting and fishing, and participating in dances and celebrations.

Yet although the ghosts behave as if they were people it is nevertheless dangerous for anyone other than a shaman to contact them. The Bella Coola say that ghosts can whistle but not speak, and that on chancing upon a ghost a degree of protection can be obtained by whistling before the ghost does. In this way the person will become seriously ill, but, with a shaman's help, can recover. If the ghost whistles first, then the person's soul will be entrapped and he will die and go to the Ghost World.

Occasionally the ghosts show a kinder face. In a Haida tale a young boy dreamed he had visited the Ghost World. He had vivid memories of the journey and of meeting people who told him they were his deceased relatives and invited the boy to join them. A matronly woman, his dead aunt, showed special affection for him, and a girl his own age invited him to play. He recalled how kindly everyone was, and that if they had not told him they were dead people he would never have known they were ghosts. The chief, however, forbade the boy to touch any of the food they offered and asked if his mother knew he was there. When the boy said she did not, the chief told him he was not yet ready to die and should go back to his mother. On waking, the boy was told he had been in a death-like coma for four days, and that it was only the intercession of a powerful shaman which had persuaded the Chief of the Ghosts to send the boy back, thus saving his life.

The shamans state that they can move between the worlds of the people and the ghosts with impunity, but just how real and effective the powers of the shamans may be has often been called into question. This is because of the indisputable evidence of trickery in their public demonstrations, as well as the accusations of cheating that the shamans make against each other. Yet despite this, and despite missionary activity in the area which has led to the conversion of most Native people, many shamans still profess to be in contact with powers that are inaccessible to White doctors or priests, which cannot be subjected to scientific scrutiny, and which are impossible to explain other than in metaphysical terms.

The first anthropological investigation of the claims of Kwakiutl shamans came at the turn of the century, when George Hunt, a well educated Native man of Tsimshian-Kwakiutl parentage who was raised among the Kwakiutl, became fieldwork assistant to Franz Boas. Hunt was sceptical of the boasts made by the shamans, and, with Boas's encouragement, schemed to have himself initiated as a shaman in order to expose what he called 'their fraudulent practice'.

During his initiation he was taught many of the shamans' tricks: Boas's information on burying hollow kelp stems and digging trenches during the ritual preparation of the longhouse came to him via George Hunt, who was also shown how to make lifeless dolls become animated by the use of attached strings. All of this, and much more, he duly reported as evidence that the shamans were tricksters and frauds.

As part of his initiation, George Hunt was required to perform a cure. He was instructed to show a blood-covered ball of eagle down to represent the illness he pretended to suck out of the patient. To Hunt's surprise his patient suddenly recovered, as did subsequent patients he treated. Gradually his fame as a successful healer grew. He was asked to treat more serious illness, and was always successful. Although at this stage he was convinced that all he did was to display trickery that fooled gullible individuals, he acquired an enviable

ABOVE: *Two views of an Oyster Catcher Rattle. Tlingit shamans held the oyster catcher in high respect and, although less common than the Raven Rattle, a number of examples of this type are known to exist. The figures on the back of the oyster catcher are those of a shaman and the witch he is tormenting by twisting her hair in an attempt to make her confess. The witch's helping spirit, a bear, is shown in diminutive form in comparison with the mountain goat helper of the shaman. Note, too, the extended tongue of the mountain goat, through which the shaman's power is being activated.*

reputation as a powerful shaman. Clan chiefs paid large fees whenever he treated ailing members of their families, so that in addition to fame he acquired wealth - which, incidentally, appeared to embarrass him considerably since he felt it had been gained through fraud. But demands on his healing powers were such that he could not stop.

Gradually, his opinion of the shamans and their activities began to change. Although he always maintained that everything he showed to his patients or during public displays of his power was false, he nevertheless started to feel there was more to it than this and that his success could not be solely attributable to luck. He noted that when he showed blood-stained eagle down, this was not the actual disease-causing object but a tangible representation of it. The disease itself was said to be invisible to anyone other than a shaman, but the blood-soaked down provided a focus for the patient. Although Hunt did not claim he was able to 'see' the disease, he did note: 'At least I offer my patients something to believe in; unlike those shamans who claim to cure but have nothing to show.'

Eventually George Hunt came to believe in his own ability as a healing shaman, but at the same time remaining dubious that it derived from the assistance of supernatural spirits. He claimed simply to have been taught all he knew about the trickery employed by the shamans, and was at a loss to give any more plausible reason for the fact that his patients recovered from their illnesses. He became increasingly convinced his own power was genuine, even if it could not be fully explained, but he continued to deride the false claims of others.

Perhaps unintentionally, George Hunt falls into the characteristic pattern of Northwest Coast shamanism. It is typical for shamans to claim that others are only pretenders, and to knowingly employ tricks to convince a patient or audience of their powers. While these tricks are false in Hunt's definition of the term, many shamans claim such tricks are sanctioned by the spirits and provide public evidence or proof of their abilities. Indeed, the shamans' awareness of trickery is so acute that, as we have seen, much of their time is spent in detecting the tricks employed by their rivals. Magic and sleight-of-hand are a means by which shamans publicly demonstrate their power; but they are also the evidence by which the shamans expose and attempt to defeat rival practitioners.

Despite the tricks of the public performances, there is a genuine belief in the powers that the Northwest Coast shamans claim to possess. Cures by the shamans are often effective when recourse to more conventional methods of treatment have failed; although the shamans also say they are unable to treat certain disorders and problems which arise from the adoption of White values and customs which have been introduced by Whites and were previously unknown.

This latter statement is a significant one in the practice of contemporary Northwest Coast shamanism. A resurgence of faith in shamanic power is a comparatively recent phenomenon, since the shamans lost most of their status and authority during smallpox and measles epidemics in the late 1800s. These killed a very large percentage of the Native population, led to the abandonment of villages, and severely disrupted social and economic life; but it was the shamans who lost their credibility by failing to prevent the spread of the epidemics, which they considered to be 'foreign diseases'. They tried hard to slow the rapidly rising death rates, even, unusually, working cooperatively to throw 'protective shields' around villages.

Yet it was obvious that those villages under shamanic protection suffered heavy losses, whereas the people who had fled to new villages established by the Christian priests, and where the populations had been inoculated, experienced only slight outbreaks. The priests,

OPPOSITE: *Tsimshian carvers were renowned throughout the Northwest Coast for the quality and refinement of their work, and were often 'commissioned' to produce carvings for other tribes such as the Tlingit. The skill of the Tsimshian carver is admirably presented here in this portrait mask of a deceased ancestor, death being symbolised by the upturned and half-closed eyes. Such masks served as permanent reminders of the deceased and were believed to contain power that could be reactivated through their display.*

exploiting the competitive nature of Northwest Coast shamanism, encouraged the people to believe this was because their spirits were stronger than those of the shamans. The shamans were therefore defeated, they 'died of shame' and became 'common'. The claim of modern shamans to be effective only in the treatment of indigenous sickness is, in part, a reaction to historical events such as the epidemics, but it has to be taken into account that shamanic cures did not traditionally cover the entire spectrum of disease and injury. The cause of the disease or injury was often a determining factor in whether or not it would respond to shamanic intervention. Only among a few tribes, such as the Bella Coola, was there a belief that all misfortune was attributable to magic and the supernatural and could be dealt with by shamanic cure.

Modern shamans, like their predecessors, are effective in treating what they refer to as 'mysterious' illnesses. An exact definition of these is difficult: they include illnesses that do not have an immediately apparent cause, but also encompass such things as a sudden loss of energy, lethargy, laziness, unexplained headaches and dizziness, frequent bad dreams and nightmares, or even a failure to follow traditional beliefs and ideas. The shamans are able to 'bring focus' back into the lives of anyone afflicted in these ways, by providing cultural security and demonstrating support for those whose aims in life are unclear and uncertain. Many Northwest Coast people now feel the benefits of having recourse to both modern hospitals and traditional shamanic help, as well as an extensive knowledge of local healing herbs and plants which can be used at home for treating minor injuries and sickness.

The shamans today function at the interface between physical illnesses and injuries and those which, in modern terms, affect an individual's mental health. Soul loss, the domain of the old-time shamans, has been reinterpreted to mean a loss of cultural tradition and identity and the problems associated with this. Coast Salish shamans who are active in 'the *sulia* dances, or 'dramatisations of dreams', are, for instance, highly effective in their treatment of disoriented and alienated members of the community.

Wolfgang Jilek, a psychologist who spent several years working among the Salish of the Upper Stalo region in the late 1960s and early 1970s, noted that Coast Salish shamans were 80% effective in dealing with cases of anomic depression - which results in a lack of purpose and identity - compared with the 30% success rate achieved in the modern hospital in Victoria. Jilek stated that the shamans gave people a sense of worth, of belonging to a community, and also wrote that this was provided not only in the form of local support through sponsorship of or participation in the associated feasts and dances, but made the individual the focus of community and inter-tribal attention. The patients became important, and therefore worthwhile, members of the community at inter-tribal events, where they were seen as exemplars of a return to traditional belief; hence previous depressive acts on their part - including drug and alcohol abuse - could be forgiven.

But we need to remember that Northwest Coast shamans always function at the edge of reality. They obtain their powers by travelling to the North-End-of-the-World, the home of *Baxbakualanuxsiwae*, or through contact with the fearsome Land Otter. In this sense they are exceptional individuals, vital to Northwest Coast cultural survival. Their trials and ordeals are not self-imposed - most reports, early and current, say the shamans are unable to avoid their obligations - but are a response to the pressing concerns of societies struggling to come to terms with outside influence. This influence in the past came from the supernatural world of 'outsider' spirits such as *Bokwus* and *Tsonoqa*; today it stems from 'foreign' government legislation and the alien values of a White society. The shamans, even when their powers are disputed, are at the forefront of this assertion of Native rights and belief. The shamans who previously led war parties now lead communities in their attempts to reassert traditional beliefs and solidarity.

4 *The Encircled Mountain*

SOUTHWEST SHAMANISM

When the Holy People created the world they gave it a metaphysical centre, the Encircled Mountain, which reached down into the depths of space and time to the First World, the Red World, which was without light and without people. The deities of this world were twelve black insects and the bats. In the Second, Blue, World the blue birds, swallows and jays, ruled. In the Third, Yellow, World the grasshoppers were in charge. Only in the present Fourth, or White, World was there light and people, as well as the colours of the preceding worlds.

To protect Encircled Mountain the Holy People placed White Shell Mountain to the east, Turquoise Mountain to the south, Abalone or Corn Mountain to the west, and Jet Mountain in the north, and on each of the mountains they placed a Talking God to listen to the prayers of the people. The Navaho, adopting and adapting beliefs from the Pueblo tribes who were descendants of the Anasazi, the Ancient Ones, thought of Encircled Mountain as the Mountain Around Which Moving is Done. Thus Encircled Mountain came to be the centre of a cosmic world, symbolised by colour, around which all aspects of the Fourth World were created and placed in order.

The different worlds made by the Holy People are located in what we now call the Southwest: New Mexico and Arizona, parts of Utah and Colorado, and extending south into the northern

LEFT: *Southwest shamanism echoes the colours and contrasts apparent in the environment. Rock strata were thought to be reflections of the colours woven into Navaho blankets, which were themselves expressions of the people's relation to the land. In spite of its apparently inhospitable aspect, Petrified Forest supports a great variety of wildlife while ruined pueblos and petroglyphs attest to early human presence. Among the many relics in theis area are some of the earliest American examples of Sun symbolism and solar alignments.*

ABOVE: *A buffalo hide mask or shield representing the Sun. It was probably worn as a back shield during ceremonial dances.*
BELOW: *The prominent symbol of fertility painted on the front and repeated on the back of this effigy of a Hemis Kachina present him in the role of the god of procreation.*

provinces of Mexico. It is a harsh but enchanting land whose physical characteristics reflect the grand scheme of the Holy People. Encircled Mountain is too vast and too powerful to be visible; it spans eons of time and is itself endless and ageless, reaching down to the very beginning and stretching upwards into the unimaginable and unknowable worlds of the future.

The Holy Mountains of the east, south, west, and north mark the physical boundaries of the Southwest. To the east is Blanca Peak in Colorado; south is Mount Taylor in New Mexico; the San Francisco Peaks of Arizona mark the western limits; and in the north are the majestic peaks of the La Plata range. Enclosed within the Holy Mountains is a country of deep canyons and high mesas, of semi-arid desert; a country of sudden and startling contrasts, of brilliant sun and deep shadow; of indescribable stillness and sudden, explosive, motion. At its core lies the Grand Canyon, or Mountain Upside Down, at which the world is inverted and connects back to its ancient past. The Grand Canyon stands as permanent symbol and witness of the passage of time and as a means of connecting with the Ancient Ones. It is sometimes spoken of as the Navel of the Earth, and is said to be located at the waist of the great Earth Mother herself; but it is also a holy *sipapu*, or Place of Emergence, from the Red, Blue, and Yellow Worlds to the present White World.

The Native occupants of the White World come from two very different traditions, and their ritual and ceremonial practices reflect their diverse origins. Some of them, the Pueblo tribes, Zuni, and the Pima and Papago, are direct descendants of the Anasazi and other prehistoric peoples - the Hohokam and Mogollon - who tamed the deserts, constructed massive irrigation canals fed by melt-water from the mountains, and built multi-story village complexes of adobe. Their ancestors, early hunter-gatherers who lived in round brush-covered pit shelters, have left a tangible legacy of their presence in the circular and semi-subterranean ceremonial *kivas* of the Pueblo tribes. Each *kiva* is a symbolic representation of the previous worlds and it is here that the most sacred aspects of Pueblo ritual take place; significantly, each contains a small depression at its centre as a symbolic *sipapu*, or Place of Emergence which links the contemporary world of the Pueblo peoples to the past.

Surrounding the sedentary Pueblo farmers are more recent arrivals: the Athapascan-speaking Apache and Navaho. They came here only shortly before the Spanish incursions of the fifteenth century, bringing with them a body of beliefs derived from their ancient homelands far to the north in Subarctic Canada. Unlike the Pueblo

peoples, with their steady rhythms and agricultural patterns going back to time immemorial, the Apachean tribes were hunters and warriors living a nomadic life. Their life was opportunistic, subject to sudden change and rapid movement, and demanding instant decisions. While the Pueblo priests relied on repetitive formulaic chants which were tied to the natural cycles of the agricultural year, the Apache and Navaho responded to the moment, embracing everything around them and adapting this to their nomadic hunting lifestyle.

Yet, despite vast differences, both the Pueblo tribes and the Apache and Navaho are products of the Southwest. Both look back to and connect with the powers brought into being by the activities of the Holy Ones and entrusted to the guardianship of the Talking Gods, and both consider their homelands to be enclosed within the boundaries marked by the Four Holy Mountains that symbolise the Four Directions and which serve as the foundations, or pillars, of world order.

It is nevertheless to the world of the Pueblos, the original occu-

ABOVE: *The Kachinas, or Rainmakers, were thought of as ancient deities, but included among their number the souls of ancestors who were reincarnated as gods that controlled the the agricultural year. The link between the earth and planting, and the sky, cloud, and rain is made clear in this photograph of Abalone Shell Mountain in the San Francisco Peaks. This, the western home of the Kachinas, was one of four sacred mountains where the Hopi believed the Kachinas dwelt for six months before returning to the Pueblos for the annual ceremonial cycle.*

ABOVE: *Rock drawings in the Rio Grande area. Shamans frequently marked sites of special importance by painting symbols of the deities or of shamans representing deities onto them. Characteristic of such 'deified shamans' in the Southwest pictographs and petroglyps are horned figures such as that shown here.*

OPPOSITE TOP: *One of several ceremonial dancers depicted on an early potsherd found on the Hohokam site at Snaketown on the Gila River. and dating from c. 1000 AD. The wing-like appendages on this shaman's arms suggest transformation, while the spiked hairstyle or headdress is characteristic of Hohokam stylisation in depicting deified or semi-deified figures.*

OPPOSITE BELOW: *Masked dancers on a pottery bowl from the same site as above. They may represent either paired male and female deities of the Twin Gods.*

pants of the Southwest, that we must first turn to gain a glimpse of this land and of the lives of its peoples. According to the Hopi Indians the First World was called *Tokpela*. This, however, was no ordinary world. The Hopi name translates as Endless Space, and the First World is conceived as having no beginning and no end, no shape, no time, no form. It exists solely in the mind of *Taiowa*, the Creator or Infinite Power; yet, simply because this is in the mind of *Taiowa*, it also pervades everything in nature and every aspect of Hopi life. Life without *Taiowa's* creative genius is unthinkable and unimaginable.

Taiowa, wishing to establish order in Endless Space, created two beings to assist him. These were *Sotuknang*, the Transformer, and *Kokyangwuti*, Spider Woman. They were the parents of the First Twins, *Poqanghoya* and *Palongawhoya*. *Poqanghoya's* duty was to solidify the world and keep it in order, whereas *Palongawhoya* was charged with responsibility for generating and maintaining energy in the world. His voice echoed that of *Taiowa* and through his call he created vibrationary centres along the world's axis; thus, in English, he is sometimes known as Echo and it is through sound that is in tune with the earth's vibrations that the Hopi people communicate with *Palongawhoya* and, through him, with *Taiowa*.

Spider Woman, pleased with the work of the First Twins, created trees, plants, and flowers, seed- and nut-bearers, and all forms of animal and human life by covering earth with her White Shell Cape of Creativity and Wisdom. Each part of this creation, though separate and distinct from every other part, contained within itself the wisdom of *Taiowa* and the essence of rhythmic balance. She brought these things into existence through the Song of Creation in which the people were enjoined to:

> Make a joyful sound throughout the land
> A joyful echo resounding everywhere.
> The perfect one laid out the perfect plan
> And gave to us a long span of life,
> Creating song to implant joy in life.
> The songs resound back from our Creator with joy,
> And we of the earth repeat it to our Creator.
> Repeats and repeats again the joyful echo,
> Sounds and resounds for times to come.

The activities of the Creator, of the Transformer and Spider Woman, and of the Twin Gods set the parameters for the ritual and

RIGHT: *Shamans and mountain sheep in a petroglyph from Glen Canyon. Mountain sheep, due to their great agility, were featured in shamanic art as a means of gaining some control over these wary animals. The section shown here was salvaged before the flooding of the Colorado River.*

ceremonial life of the Hopi and other Pueblo peoples. They are based, as the Creation Song makes clear, on patterns of harmonious sound and repetition. It is clear, too, that the nature of these powers can never be separate or seen as different from everyday life. All Pueblo activity, no matter how mundane it may appear to the outsider, is imbued with this sense of oneness with creation, and each and every individual or collective act is part of the process of reaffirming identification with the essential rhythmic harmonies of the world.

This sense of rhythm and harmony, of an underlying stability, is endemic to agricultural communities such as those of the Pueblos. It is essential in the semi-arid conditions of the Southwest that the Rain Gods return each year to nurture the crops of corn, beans, and squash; and it is just as necessary that the staple crop - corn - is treated with reverence. Corn is not only a food crop but also the Corn Mother, and is sometimes identified as a personification of the Earth Mother herself. Yet without rain the corn will perish, so ceremonies are conducted to ensure the Male Rain God will return regularly to fertilise the Female Corn Mother.

The steady pace of Pueblo life means there is no place for the individual ecstatic experiences and personal revelations of shamans, since these would be disruptive of routine. Individualism, indeed any form of deviation from the 'right way' or of excess, is alien to Pueblo concepts of moderation and conservatism which demand repetition and adherence to established form. Although overlaid with a veneer of Catholicism imposed by Europeans, Pueblo ceremonial life today is little changed from that recorded in the Spanish Chronicles of the fifteenth and sixteenth centuries.

The absence of the individual shamanic vision among Pueblo tribes has led some students of Native American culture to claim that 'The Pueblos have no shamans; they have only priests.' Yet it is clear, despite the absence of the sanctioning vision found elsewhere in North America, that the Pueblo priests fulfil the role of shaman, including that of healer, which is expressed elsewhere in more individualistic terms.

This needs to be understood in terms of Pueblo social organisation, which is based on communal needs and shared obligations. Among them every individual belongs to a clan, a group of people claiming a specific relationship to a particular ancestral figure and to which membership is usually inherited through the mother's lineage. A man marries into and lives with and supports the clan relatives of his wife's family, who are from a different clan than his own, and it is to them that he owes allegiance in any economic aspects of Pueblo life. His ritual or ceremonial commitments, however, are to the clan of his birth, and his ceremonial leader - or 'clan chief' - is the priest of the sacred *kiva* descended through his mother's line. Thus, every Pueblo man has material ties to his wife's clan but ceremonial ties to the clan he is born into and which are inherited through his mother's lineage.

The *kiva* leaders, or shaman-priests, inherit position in much the same way as any other Pueblo man except insofar as their families

OPPOSITE: *These two figures from a 10th century burial site at Mimbre, New Mexico, may represent male and female figures. Highly decorated Mimbres pottery was made almost exclusively for funerary purposes and of the many examples that have been found few show signs of practical use. The hole punched in the base of the bowl was intended to release their spirits.*

 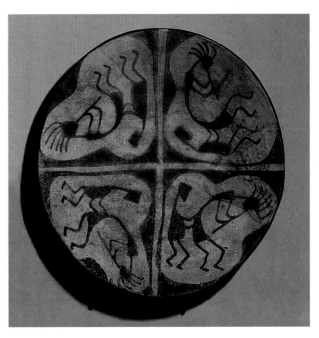

have possession of powerful masks and rituals which can be used for communal benefit and which can be shared through *kiva* rituals with other clan relatives, and, ultimately, with all members of the Pueblo community. It is through knowledge and experience of the esoteric *kiva* rituals that an individual rises to the position of clan leader, or *kiva* priest, and he holds this position, providing he uses his knowledge and power for public good, until his memory fails. His role is defined by tradition, gained through knowledge and experience, and endorsed by all members of his kiva group.

As a trained individual and a member of a specific religious community he is quite different from the highly individualistic ecstatic shamans we have encountered elsewhere. Yet, like them, he obtains his power and position through connection with ancestral spirits and deities: in Hopi thinking, he provides a direct link link back to the Ancient Ones and to *Taiowa*, the original Creator Being. Like the individualistic shamans, too, he possesses power to ward off danger or heal the consequences of contact with malignant forces. Hopi Snake priest-shamans, for instance, not only conduct rituals associated with snakes to bring rain and fertility, but can also use their power to cure people bitten by rattlesnakes or afflicted by other ailments and illnesses, such as paralysis, which the Hopi believe are caused by Lightning, the messenger of Snake, or which are said to be be caused by other elements or spirits over which the snakes are believed to exercise control.

ABOVE: *Kokopelli, the humpbacked flute player, appears on much of the Hohokam and Mimbres pottery around the 11th century AD as well as on pottery from northern New Mexico of much later date. As a symbol of fertility he and his wife were often the subject of explicitly erotic Hopi impersonations.*

ABOVE: *Spider Woman wove blankets out of sunbeams from the top of Spider Rock, in Canyon de Chelly, the location of nearly 400 Anasazi settlements. Spider Woman was also believed to be the creator of the Twin Gods and is revered in the Southwest as a wise old woman. Priests maintain shrines to her in every Hopi village.*

Their most important function, however, is to safeguard the seasonal changes that ensure the regularity of the Pueblo's agricultural year, and it is to this end that the sacred, and often secret, kiva rituals are primarily directed. The Hopi, as one of the most ancient and most conservative of the Pueblo tribes, can provide us with an example of how the ritual year is organised.

The Hopi year begins in November with a ceremony known as *Wuwuchim*. This is the time when *Masau* makes his reappearance. He is a terrifying Black God who wears a mask covered with blood; he is both the God of the Earth and the God of Death. Yet it was *Masau* who first showed benevolence to the people and enabled them to emerge from the underground to the present world via the *sipapu*, by asking Shrike to act as an intermediary and break a hole large enough for the ancestors of the people to pass through. He gave them permission to live in this world and marked off the territories they were to occupy. The *kiva* priests know and identify with *Masau*, since it is through him that new fire is kindled annually in the *kivas* and carried to every home in the village. *Wuwuchim* is so sacred that no one other than a Hopi is permitted to witness it, and all we know is that it re-enacts the Emergence from the Underworld.

Wuwuchim takes us back to the beginning, to the worlds that existed before the present. The priest-shamans bring us into contact with *Masau*, the First Person, the Originator, who was the only Being to exist in the present world before the people entered it via the sipapu, the Place of Emergence enshrined in every kiva, and via this ritual the world is 'made over' each year to enable the annual cycle to repeat.

BELOW LEFT: *Mesa Verde is a complex of canyons containing numerous cliff dwellings. The largest is Cliff Palace, which probably served as a ceremonial centre for a number of smaller village sites located within the region. Cliff Palace contains 23 kivas, circular underground chambers that were used as clan houses and had important ceremonial functions that were associated with both the ritual and secular activities of the people who lived there.*

RIGHT: *Spruce Tree House, also in Mesa Verde, has had some of its kivas reconstructed so they appear today much as they woould have done before the village was abandoned following the great drought of 1276-1298. The kivas seen in the plaza of Spruce Tree House are roofed and access is provided via a ladder reaching down into the kiva from a roof opening. Many of the activities conducted within the kivas were sacred to the men's societies and clans who controlled the ritual year, and were known in detail only to the clan membership.*

Soon after *Wuwuchim* the *Soyal* begins. This is a winter solstice ceremony held in December, to bring the Sun back from its north-ward journey, for purification and blessing, and to mark the rebirth of a new year. *Soyal* is the first appearance of the *Kachinas*. These magical figures, the spirits of ancestors who return to the pueblo each year to help the people, are Rain Makers, and are therefore essential to the growth of Pueblo crops. They also bring the people back into contact with dearly remembered departed ones, since every Hopi who has led a good life becomes a Rain Maker. The *Soyal Kachina* enters the pueblo, walking unsteadily as if just awakened from a deep winter's sleep and singing in a quiet voice redolent of the Pueblo sense of moderation. In recognition of his appearance the shaman-priests reopen the kivas and plant pahos (sacred prayer sticks) on the roads leading into the pueblo to safeguard the people.

Through *Wuwuchim* and *Soyal*, and by their planting of pahos, the shaman-priests throw a protective ring around the pueblo to prevent the intrusion of any adverse influences. Roads into the pueblo are closed so that it is shut off from the outside world, and the pueblo itself becomes a sacred enclosure devoted to religious activities.

Kachinas appear in three different forms among the Hopi. As actual deities they live for six monhs of the year in their mountain homes, they then appear in the villages where they are impersonated by masked dancers, and seen in the form of small cottonwood dolls that are given to children during the ritual performances. To the Hopi, each of these three forms is a manifestation of the deity itself. The doll ABOVE LEFT *is an early form of the Kachina Mana (Kachina Mother), also seen* ABOVE *in a more elaborate costume that includes a tablita (headdress) bearing symbols of rain and fertility. In the* CENTRE *is a Shalako*

Mana (or Maiden) who accompanies the male Shalako dancers. During performances in the pueblo the three female Kachinas shown on page 116 accompany the male Kachinas such as those shown ABOVE. *Although many of the Kachinas appear regularly, others are seen less frequently and in many varied forms. Ahote,* ABOVE LEFT, *is named after the characteristic sound he makes while singing. Among the most popular Kachinas are the Hand Kachinas, or Runner Kachinas, above right, who challenge children to races and reward them if they are successful. Over 250 Kachinas are recognised by the Hopi.*

Throughout January the Pueblo people reaffirm their ties to the Creator and their shared heritage. Butterfly Dancers appear in the plazas to encourage the return of the spring rains, since the Butterfly is the helper of Buffalo who brings snow necessary for successful spring planting and has control over spring weather. Buffalo Dancers may also appear, and may even travel between the Pueblos so their blessings can be shared.

Throughout this period the *Kachinas* dance only in the kivas, under the direction of the shaman-priests. Their seclusion is an indication of the fact they are nervous. In the distant past they used to live permanently among the people, but after some time the people became complacent and began to disregard the strict code of behaviour that the *Kachina*s demanded. Their impious conduct and disrespect drove the *Kachinas* out of the pueblos and now they live for six months of the year in their mountain retreats and only return in December when their presence as Rain Makers is needed and after the shaman-priests have made the pueblos holy and safe.

The *Kachinas*, despite their nervousness and awareness of the people's past irreverence, are benevolent. During their secret ceremonies they plant bean sprouts, which are blessed by themselves and the priests so they may grow tall and strong, and at *Powamu*, which usually takes place in February and is the first major public ceremony of the *Kachina* year, they suddenly emerge from the *kivas* to grant their blessings and purify the pueblos. Their arrival in the open plazas of the pueblos is spectacular. They are led by the *Mong*, or Chief Kachinas; impressive figures over ten feet tall whose dignity and calm reflects the Pueblo sense of belonging. With them come the Butterfly Maidens, the Buffalo Dancers, and a host of other minor figures.

All the *Kachinas* remind the people of their past, of the days before Emergence and of their ancestral links; they bring back memories, and thus reinforce the ancient stories. But they also remind people of the present. Black Gods, reminiscent of *Masau*, and Whipper Kachinas challenge the children to races: if a child wins he or she can chastise the *Kachina*. The *Kachinas* are wise as well as being powerful and benevolent, and, although they could easily win these races if they wished to do so, they usually let the children win and reward them with gifts of decorated plaques, carved *Kachina* dolls, bows and arrows, and mocassins. They then distribute the bean sprouts which have been nurtured in the *kivas*, so each family can partake in the good feelings they engender.

Once every four years the *Kachinas* present a more terrifying aspect. This happens at *Pachavu*, a ceremony held in February, when hundreds of *Kachinas* may appear in the plazas. They dance in rhythmic lines, each *Kachina* repeating the steps of the previous one. Such performances can last for hours, and their cumulative effect is hypnotic. The shaman-priests, with their repetitive drumming and chants, enforce the ideal of a regular rhythm: the heartbeat of Mother Earth, of the Corn Mother herself. But, without warning, *Hu* the Whipper Kachinas, or *Soyoko*, suddenly break free. These Kachinas go to the homes of wayward parents and naughty children; they carry saws which they rasp against the walls of the houses, demanding entrance, and once inside they break the pots the parents use then carry the screaming children away to warn them of the dire consequences that will follow if their behaviour does not improve. But, later the children are brought back to the *kivas*, where they learn that the *Kachinas* are only human impersonators. Boys and girls are shown *Kachina* masks, so they can see through the eyes of the deities and realise these are helpful gods which demand respect, but also so they can be initiated into the *kiva* rituals.

All *Kachina* dances are assertions of the Pueblo past, a repetition of the old stories of emergence and stability and a means whereby

ABOVE: *The return of the Kachinas to the pueblos is heralded by the appearance of the Heheya Kachinas, shown in this photograph from 1879. The Heheyas always appear in pairs and are said to clear a path through the village for the re-emergence of the other Kachinas who follow them. The masked dancer in the background represents a Kachin Mana, or Butterfly Maiden, who wears a white cloak as a symbol of her chastity.*

the annual cycle can be renewed. The shaman-priests are charged with responsibility for ensuring these cycles continue. From December, when the *Kachinas* arrive in the *kivas*, until July, when the *Niman*, or Home Dance, marks their departure, the shaman-priests must repeat the ancient songs which the *Kachinas* recognise.

The three major ceremonials of the winter cycle, *Wuwuchim*, *Soyal*, and *Powamu*, mark special events in the Pueblo calendars and particular phases of the Pueblo past. *Wuwuchim* is the Emergence, the Dawn of Life and the Kindling of New Fire; *Soyal* makes the pueblo holy and enables the Kachinas to return; *Powamu* enables the *Kachinas* to assert their power in public. From time to time following *Powamu* the *Kachinas* leave the kivas and dance in the plazas of the different pueblos; their steady movements reach the vibration centres of the earth and bring the Pueblo people back into contact with *Palongawhoya*, Echo, whose voice is that of the Creator, *Taiowa*.

From December until July the pueblos are sacred places, shrines to the deities, and this is marked by the presence of the *Kachinas*; but in the Other World, the home of the *Kachinas*, order is reversed. Thus, in July, they must leave the people and return to their own homes to perform the dances there. It is at *Niman*, the Home Dance, that the *Kachinas* make their final appearance before leaving the people. *Niman* is a dramatic ceremony that lasts for sixteen days. Any of almost 600 different *Kachinas* may dance during this period, but the preferred one is the *Hemis Kachina*. His name translates as Far-Away, and he presents a sad aspect because the *Kachinas* are reluctant to leave the people.

Niman coincides with the early harvest, and corn, melons, and other Native foods are distributed to the villagers and spectators. In many ways it is a solemn occasion because the *Kachinas* are leaving, having completed their work among the people. Even *Hu*, the Whipper Kachina, seems quiet and subdued, and the performances of the *Hemis Kachinas* are marked by even greater restraint and dignity. Yet between the *Hemis* dancers the *Koshare* or *Koyemsi* appear. They are clowns who make a mockery of all around them. They tumble about and make fun even of the most powerful *Kachinas*. White people, parents who have neglected their duties, and naughty children are all objects of their attention and may find themselves captured, stripped naked, and smeared with mud. Sometimes the *Koshare* and *Koyemsi* are quite obscene, and if they become aware of any illicit affairs in a close-knit pueblo community, they don't hesitate to make them public in the most graphic manner imaginable.

We must, however, consider the antics of the *Koshare* and *Koyemsi*

ABOVE: *Heheya mask worn by dancers at the inauguration of the bean-planting season when the Kachinas returned to the pueblo.*

ABOVE: *The plain 'crown' of this early Gan headdress will have been worn by the boy acting the clown who accompanied the dancers, as in the photo overleaf. His antics reminded the people that even the gods were fallible.*

ABOVE: *Always appearing in groups of four, the Gan dancers represent the Four World Directions, re-enacting the emergence myth of the Apache. The dancers who impersonate the Gans are thought to be imbued with sacred power which could become harmful if misdirected. They are therefore accompanied by a young boy, on the left in this photograph, who acts the part of a clown and by mimicking the actions of the dancers reminds the audience that the dancers are, after all, human.*

in the context of *Niman* as a way of bringing the sacred *Kachina* season to an end. Until now the pueblos have been closed to visitors and all roads leading into them have been guarded by the sacred *pahos*. The clowns break the solemnity and exactness of *Kachina* dances by their levity, and thereby reintroduce elements of a secular rather than sacred character. By mocking it, the clowns also publicly acknowledge the sacred power of the *Kachinas* which is now to be taken out of the pueblos until the following December when *Soyal* returns from his long sojourn and another *Kachina* season is inaugurated.

The Pueblo ceremonial year had already been established in the distant past, among such groups as the ancient Anasazi inhabitants of the area, but in the late 1300s to early 1400s a new force entered the Southwest with the arrival of the Athapascan-speaking Apache and Navaho. These small bands of nomadic hunters had migrated south from their original homelands in Subarctic Canada and Alaska, and brought with them many new ideas and beliefs.

By adopting some Pueblo beliefs and adapting them to fit their own ideas of movement and migration, the Apache and Navaho created a rich mythology of their own in which shamans have a vital

120

function. Among them there is a blending of the symbolism of the Pueblos with the highly individualistic and charismatic concept of shamanism inspired by dreams and visions that is characteristic of the Subarctic.

When the Apache arrived in the Southwest they believed that the creator of their world was *Ysun*, the Maker of All Things. Like *Taiowa* of the Pueblos, the Apache thought of *Ysun* not as a physical character but as an indeterminate presence in every animate or inanimate thing in existence, each of which was imbued with its spiritual force. *Ysun*, too, had helpers: the most important was White Painted Woman, who was assisted by the Twin Gods, Child of Water and Killer of Enemies. Other helpers include the *Gans*, who are sometimes called Mountain Spirits or Fire Dancers and are in some respects similar to the Pueblo *Kachinas*. They, again, once lived among the people but fled to their mountain fastnesses to enjoy eternal life; although, according to the Apache, it was not so much the misdeeds of the people that caused them to flee but rather the mischievous introduction of death, lying, gluttony, thievery, and adultery by the trickster Coyote.

Yet despite having a well-established cosmology with clear links to Pueblo ideals, the Apache place great emphasis on individualistic shamanism. To perform as a *Gan* dancer does not require an inherited right, as among the Pueblos, but a revelatory vision that enables one to do so. Similarly, to become a *diyi*, or shaman, one has to 'have the gift' and be in 'possession of an intense spirituality', rather than being able to claim the established privileges or accept the responsibilities of the Pueblo *kiva*-priests.

John G Bourke, who was responsible for US-Apache relations in the 1880s, wrote:

> '...there is no such thing as settled dogma among these medicine men. Each follows the dictates of his own inclinations, consulting such spirits and powers as are most amenable to his supplications and charms; but no two seem to rely upon identically the same influences.'

Bourke may have misread some aspects of Apache thought, since it is clear that all *diyi* share a common belief and heritage; but his emphasis on individual inclination is very pertinent. This may, indeed, be carried to an extreme where the *diyi* uses a vocabulary which was imparted to him/her alone through a dream-vision. Bourke called this 'gibberish'; but the *diyi* say that words are potentially dangerous and that sanction by the spirits is required to use

ABOVE: *The Apache Gan dancers were, in some respects, equivalent to the Kachinas of the Hopi and the Yeis of the Navaho. They are sometimes referred to as Mountain Spirits, since they dwell in the mountains that mark the boundaries of the Apache world, but they return regularly to the people where they are impersonated by dancers wearing 'crown' headdresses.*

ABOVE: *The Koyemsi, or Mud-Heads, appeared in the Hopi plazas during periods when the Kachina dancers were resting. Like the clowns accompanying the Gan dancers of the Apache, they acted as clowns who purported to protect the pueblo inhabitants from the surfeit of power that accompanied the presence of the Kachinas. Theu tended to deal with ludicrous problems, such as attempting to swim in mud, and would engage in crude and sometimes erotic pantomime performances that depicted the failings of respected pueblo members.*

language that refers to sacred matters. To travel to *chidin-bi-kungua*, the House of the Spirits, or to communicate with the *Gans* is fraught with difficulty, and it would be irresponsible for the *diyi* to use words that might endanger unsanctioned, and therefore vulnerable, people.

The activities and abilities of the *diyi*, although not centred on the regular cycles of the Pueblo agricultural year, are as important to Apache life as the incantations and prayers of *kiva*-priests. Here, however, they are allied with the needs of the Apache as a nomadic hunting people. In hunting communities, long periods of waiting, what Bourke called 'indolence', culminate in a few moments of intense activity. This is the world of the *diyi*, in which ritual preparation extending over several days is rewarded or thwarted in seconds. Immediate decisions have to be made. Unlike the Pueblo *kiva*-priests, who achieve desired results by strict adherence to established form, the *diyi* relies entirely on his own ability to react effectively in any situation without relying on prescribed formulae.

The individualistic nature of Apache life means that most *diyi* act independently, without reference to others. In the past they protected people by giving them an early warning of approaching enemies or by guarding the paths along which the war parties travelled, or they guided the hunters to where game animals might be found. Their role today is different, but no less significant, and the services of the shamans are called on both in healing and in order to bestow blessings and perform ritual acts.

In healing, the patient's relatives approach the *diyi* and offer a gift, which may be something as paltry as a single cigarette. Acceptance of the gift indicates the *diyi's* willingness to perform a four-day rite which has the dual purpose of diagnosing the illness and, on the fourth day, of attempting to remove any malignant elements that are believed to be lodged in the patient's body. Throughout the cure the *diyi's* body and that of the patient are marked with pollen which, although adopted from the Pueblos, has come to be taken by the Apache as symbolic of the Life-Bringer.

In ordinary cures the contract is between the *diyi* and the patient's relatives, but more elaborate rituals are conducted by the diyi in performing blessings that have tribal benefit and in which the Gans are called on for support. The most important of these is a girl's puberty rite: which, nowadays, has taken the form of an annual ceremony during which all girls of marriageable age are blessed by the *diyi* and their status acknowledged by the community.

As for ordinary cures, the puberty rite begins when the girl's rel-

atives approach the *diyi* with gifts and mark the *diyi* and the girl with pollen. The gifts on these occasions are of a substantial nature and the ceremony involves the relatives in considerable expense, since the appearance of the *Gans* requires the participation of the entire community whom the relatives will be obliged to feast and provide for over the four-day period of the ritual.

Prior to the ceremony, the relatives build a shelter in which the girl is placed together with an attendant, who possesses shamanic powers, to care for her needs. During this time the girl is dressed in white buckskin which has been painted yellow and is symbolic of pollen, of life, and of the power of procreation. Her costume is said to be the same as the one worn by White Painted Woman and is decorated with symbols of the sun, moon, and stars, with long 'sun-beam' fringes. During the period when the girl is painted with pollen, dancers utter cries said to echo those made by White Painted Woman when the Twin God, Child of Water, returned victorious from his battles with Giant and other monsters.

During the day the sacred enclosure becomes a focus of atten-

ABOVE: *In ancient times the Sangre de Cristo range in the modern state of Colorado formed the natural eastern boundary of the Anasazi area and its highest peak, the Sacred Mountain of the East, was called by the Navaho the Dawn or White Shell Mountain. The Great Sand Dunes seen in the foreground are the highest in North America and are subject to extreme variations in temperature and violent winds. Such dramatic landscapes, although unsuited to permanent settlement, afforded inspiration to shamans of the Southwest.*

123

ABOVE: *The most important ceremony for all Apache groups is the girl's puberty ceremony, when she acts the part of White Painted Woman and is under the care of respected shamans. At this time the village is thought to be filled with the curing power of the shamans and of White Painted Woman. The white deerskin skirt and cape shown here was made especially for the puberty ritual and is said to be the same as the costume worn by White Painted Woman when she first came to the people.*

tion. The power of the *diyi*, the *Gans*, and of White Painted Woman are all concentrated here, and the girl is said to be imbued with the spirit of White Painted Woman herself. Many people come to her during the day to receive her blessing, as it is thought that during this period she is capable of healing the sick by touching them and that her blessing will ensure a long and healthy life.

It is at night, however, that the most spectacular aspects of the ritual occur. A huge fire is built in an open space, and all the women form a large circle around it. By dancing slowly in a clockwise direction they are believed to create a protective ring of female procreative power around the fire which echoes the circular form of the enclosure occupied by the girl, and which, therefore, is also a symbol of the power of White Painted Woman.

The slow, shuffling dance of the women continues from sunset until midnight, and has an amazingly calming and peaceful effect. Then the line is broken in the east, where the *diyi* enters followed by four hooded dancers wearing elaborate 'crowns' of painted boards and carrying painted yucca 'swords'. These are the *Gans*, descended from their mountain homes to help the people. The *diyi* approaches the fire, circles it, then retraces his/her steps back to the east.

Now the *Gans* approach the fire from the east, south, west, and north, while the *diyi* accompanied by a drummer begins the Songs of Emergence and tells the stories of White Painted Woman and the Twin Gods. The dance of the *Gans*, although varying with the songs being used, is totally unlike that of the women. Each performs as an individual, executing rapid, jerky dance steps, and then suddenly and unexpectedly freezing in place, holding difficult postures for long periods and gesturing with the yucca wand, before bursting again into movement. They will reappear each night throughout the four days of the ceremony.

The contrast between the slowly revolving circle of the dancing women and the frenzied staccato movements of the *Gans* is striking, and quite unlike that of the *Kachina* dances of the Pueblo tribes; although it is said that the *Gans* and the Kachinas are related. The relationship is made more apparent when one realises that following the *Gans* is a small boy, dressed in sackcloth, who clumsily and comically mimics the gestures of the *Gans*, almost as a mockery of the awesome power they are believed to possess. Like the *Koyemsi* and *Koshare*, he, too, is a clown, whose function it is to remind the people that even the gods are not infallible.

The Apache's close relatives, the Navaho, share many of the same traits and beliefs, as well as Pueblo influences. For them, too, the pre-

LEFT: *Shamanism and hunting were closely linked in the Apache view, and caps such as this were used both to summon spirit help and to ensure success in the hunt. They are made from deerskin and have eagle (as here) or owl feathers attached to them, as well as being painted or beaded with symbols that represent celestial powers.*

sent world was filled with monsters which had to be defeated so that the people could survive. This was brought about through the agency of a baby girl clothed in light who grew up to become Changing Woman, the Navaho equivalent of White Painted Woman. Changing Woman married Sun and Water and gave birth to twin boys, Monster Slayer and Born of Water. The Twin Gods destroyed all the monsters, with the exception of Old Age, Poverty, Sickness, and Death.

The Navaho world is full of monuments to the achievements of the Twin Gods: isolated rock outcrops, lava flows, and other formations are said to be the severed heads or dried blood of monsters killed by the Twin Gods and turned into stone. To the Navaho the entire world in which they live is a sacred place, and these monuments attest to the sanctity of that world and of the forces embodied in Nature. In addition to the Greater Gods this land is home to the Lesser Gods, or *Yeis*, who, as masked dancers representing powerful supernatural beings, are akin to the Gans of the Apache and the Kachinas of the Pueblos.

Also, like the Gans and Kachinas, the *Yeis* come back each year to help the people. This occurs during the Night Chant, or *Yeibichai*, which is performed as an initiation for both boys and girls into the secrets of the masked gods and is held in late autumn or early winter after the snakes have hibernated and at the time of year 'when Thunder sleeps'. As among the Apache, the children are marked with pollen and corn meal on the feet, hands, shoulders, and heads, following which *Hastseyalti*, the male Talking God, and *Hasttse-baad*, a female *Yei*, remove their masks so the children can see that the dancers are only impersonators.

An interesting insight into Navaho thinking is indicated by the appearance of *Hastseyalti* during the *Yeibichai*. Despite his designation as Talking God, he can communicate only with gestures: to speak while wearing *Hastseyalti's* mask is said to be tantamount to suicide. Talking God appears as a humorous, almost comical, figure during the *Yeibichai*; yet his power is undoubted. He protected Changing Woman while she was a baby and presided over her puberty rituals. He guided and protected the Twin Gods during their battles with the monsters. It was also he who helped the Stricken Twins, one blind and the other lame, when the other gods refused to show compassion, and through this he demonstrated to the people the need to help each other: the Stricken Twins survived because the blind boy carried his lame brother, while the lame boy acted as his brother's eyes.

This is forcefully expressed in a passage from the Crippled Twin Branch of the Night Chant, when the Twins realise that their lament over their misfortunes has turned into song:

> We were crying and crying
> But our crying turned into a song.
> We never knew the song before.
> My blind brother sang it first,
> And this is what we sang:
>
> From the white plain where stands the water,
> From there we come.
> Bereft of eyes, one bears the other,
> From there we come.
> Bereft of limbs, one guides the other,
> From there we come.
>
> Where healing herbs grow by the waters,
> From there we come.
> With these our eyes we will recover,
> From there we come.
> With these our limbs we will recover,
> From there we come.
>
> From meadows green where ponds are scattered,

ABOVE: *The Zuni felt that animals possessed power which could be harnessed, and that it could be concentrated in fetishes carved to represent the animal spirits. Their effectiveness was increased through the addition*

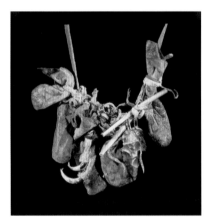

ABOVE: *A Jemez shaman's neckring laden with diverse paraphernalia. Such neckrings typically contained tokens of animals and birds that were considered to be shamanic helpers as well as small buckskin bags containing pigments that were used in ritual painting.*
OPPOSITE: *Four pahos (prayer sticks) of the Zuni and six pahos of the Hopi. The presence of*

From there we come.
Bereft of eyes, one bears the other,
From there we come.
Bereft of limbs, one guides the other,
From there we come.

of other power objects, such as
miniature arrowheads and
feathers. Although sometimes
carried as personal charms,
such fetishes were also placed
on altars or in jars containing
other sacred objects.

Talking God and the Chant of the Stricken Twins exemplify many of the characteristics of the relationship between the *hatali* (Chanter), or shaman, the gods, and the people. In particular they emphasise that compassion and humility are paramount virtues: Talking God never speaks of the power he possesses, and the Stricken Twins blame no one for their unfortunate plight. The nature of Navaho Chants, which are sometimes also called Sings or Ways, does, however, need further explanation, since they are the focus of Navaho religion and it is through them that the curative power of the *hatali* is given fullest expression.

The *hatali* achieves power, or, rather, the potential to exercise

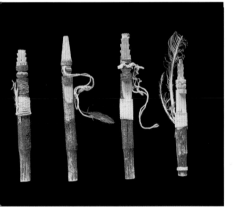

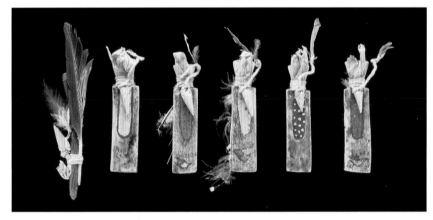

Kachinas was felt to imbue the
pueblos with spiritual power of
a beneficial nature. Pahos were
placed on tracks leading into the
pueblo to ritually seal it, as well
as on or near the altars used
during ceremonies. To protect
itself from malignant forces,
during the ceremonial season
the pueblo is closed even today
to outsiders, including other
Native Americans.

power, through a dream or vision brought about by the agency of a supernatural being. For instance, since the snake is associated with lightning, power to cure snakebite is often vested in Thunder Shamans, and may be acquired by being close to and surviving a lightning strike. Alternatively, someone may acquire power to cure a specific illness after having been cured from that same illness.

The majority of Chants are, in fact, elaborate curing rituals, during which the powers of various deities are invoked through the use of sandpaintings: coloured diagrams made from sand, pollen, charcoal, and so forth, which represent elements and deities in Navaho mythology which have power over the illness being treated. The first stage in curing, however, is to determine the cause of illness, since this dictates which Chant, specific form of a Chant, or combination of Chants, will be used.

Diagnosis can take one of three forms. 'Gazing' involves the diagnostician, or diviner, in standing motionless for hours on end in a secluded place and gazing at the sun, moon, or stars. 'Listening' is similar, except that here the deities will reveal the source of illness through words. The most common form is 'Motion-in-the-Hand', or 'Trembling', in which the diagnostician goes into trance and through uncontrollable movements is able to pinpoint the source from which the illness emanates. None of these procedures is exclusive. A 'Gazer' may, for instance, experience many of the same sensations as a 'Trembler', and the Navaho make little distinction between any of the forms.

The efforts of the diagnostician are, of course, guided by his or her knowledge of the people involved and of any family history of related illness. Even so, few families will embark on a lengthy and expensive curing Chant without assurance that the diagnosis is accurate and that the cure will be effective. Although the diagnostician's sincerity is undoubted, the family may demand a test of his assessment through the performance of a minor Chant before committing themselves to the expense of a full sixteen-day ceremony. A slight improvement in the patient's health indicates that the diagnosis is correct; while regression suggests it has been incorrect.

Lack of improvement need not reflect badly on the diagnostician's competence, since he or she can be misled or deceived: even Turkey Buzzard and his associate, Crow, who were responsible for bringing evil into the world (and, by extension, sickness and death) did not realise the errors of their ways until the Twin Gods defeated them and introduced order and harmony.

Once diagnosis is complete and the minor rituals have been performed, preparations for the Chant are put in place. Sweat-baths, fasting, sexual abstinence, ritual bathing and shampooing in yucca suds, the use of emetics, and so on are all ways of purifying the spaces and persons which are to become involved. They are ways of 'chasing evil', and of making people and locations 'holy'. Similarly, before a *hogan*, the octagonal dwelling place of Navaho families, is used for any ceremonial purpose it must be ritually swept clean and any household goods removed.

In common with Apache practice, a sick person's relatives requesting the help of a *hatali*, or Chanter, send him gifts. The greater the payment, the more elaborate the ceremony that can be sponsored and, consequently, the more efficacious it is expected to be.

ABOVE: *The horned toad was a powerful shamanic figure, due partly to its ability to live in both air and water. This mortar bowl was used for mixing pigments with grease and was found at Snaketown on the Gila River. It dates to the 10th century* AD.

Painted Desert is a spiritual resource for the Hopi as well as the Navaho. Both consider this area as an ancestral homeland which contains many relics of the Anasazi, the Ancient Ones, as well as an abundance of fossil remains, rock paintings, and a varied flora and fauna. The brightly coloured strata in many of the rocks provided some of the pigments used in sandpaintings and created a link between curing rituals and the poweres of both the land and the ancestors.

Small payments do not result in refusal; however, it is believed that the cost involved in the creation of several complex sandpaintings by the *hatali* and his assistants, providing feasts for numerous kin and other affines over a 16-day period, as well the extensive gifting that accompanies ceremonies of this nature, will harness greater power on the patient's behalf than the use of only one or two sandpaintings of simpler design.

While it would be ethically and ritualistically improper for the *hatali* to quote a specific sum as payment, desirable items may nevertheless be included in the ritual instructions he gives to the family. Thus the Male Shooting Chant Holy states that twenty-two items belonging to the Chant must be set out on the sandpainting mound outside the *hogan* entrance during the period the sandpainting itself is being laid down inside. Many of these items, rolls of calico for example, are given away by the *hatali* to those who help in the preparation and singing accompanying the cure.

The cure itself is fairly straightforward in principle, though complex in practice. It consists, essentially, in laying out coloured sands and minerals on the smoothed floor of the hogan in stylised patterns that represent episodes from the stories of the deities to whom the

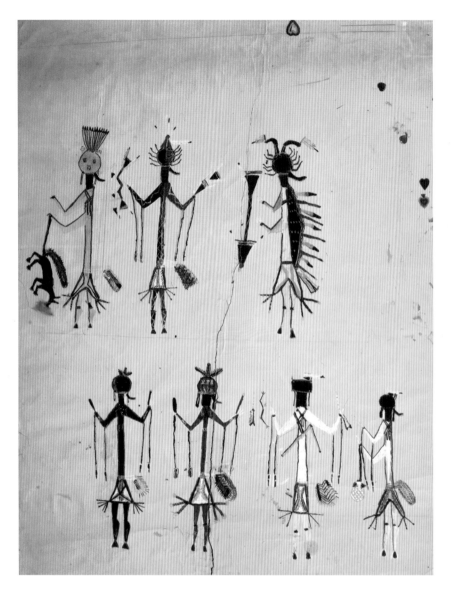

The principal means of curing used by Navaho shamans are sandpaintings. Made from coloured sands, charcoal and pollen, the sandpaintings embody the healing powers enshrined in Navaho mythology and depict the acts of various deities. Sandpaintings are considered extremely sacred and are always destroyed at the end of a curing rite, although representations of parts of the myths they depict are sometimes woven into blankets in simplified form. The more complete scenes shown here are all drawings of various aspects of a healing Chant, or Ceremony, known as the Nightway and were made for the Franciscan friar Berard Haile in the 1940s. They depict the Yei Bichai People (LEFT), the Corn People (BELOW), and the Whirling Logs (OPPOSITE).

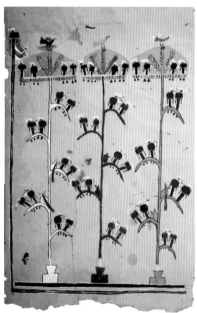

appeal is being made. Colours are symbolic: generally white is east, yellow west, black is north, and blue is south. Red represents the life-giving force of Sun. Colours may, however, acquire additional, or even completely different meanings, dependent on the particular form of the Chant or in variation between one Chant and another.

The patient is seated on the painting, and parts of it at specific moments of the Chant are placed on the patient's body. Sickness is thereby transferred from the patient to the sandpainting, whilst the patient, in turn, absorbs beneficial energy from the painting. When the sandpainting is dismantled and its components safely and ceremonially disposed of, which must be accomplished in a single day

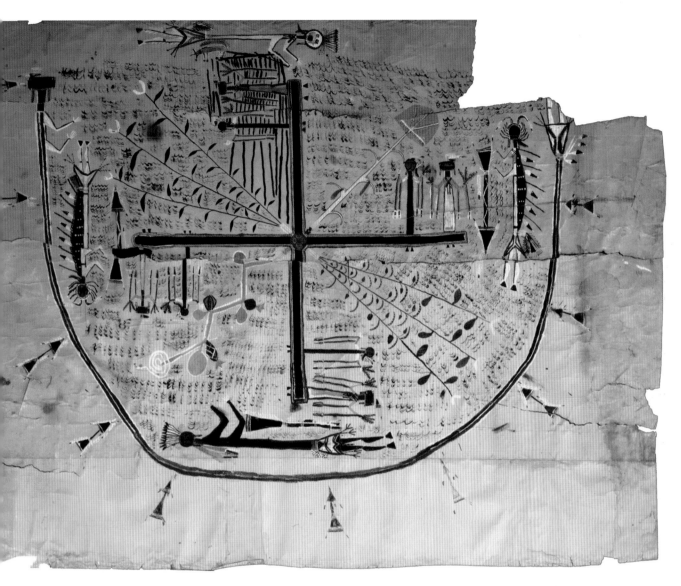

between sunrise and sunset, part of the sickness transferred is buried with it. Consecutive and repeated transferrals detailing different aspects of the deities being invoked enhance the effectiveness of the ceremony as well as exposing the patient to a greater amount of positive energy; hence the Navaho preference for complex and elaborate ritual procedures rather than simple ones.

Even in its simple version, however, a Chant requires the *hatali* to memorise numerous sequences of songs which must be sung in their correct order and without mistake. For the complex Chants, the *hatali* may be expected to accurately recall several hundred songs; a feat of memory that would take a lifetime to learn and which is

ABOVE: *Among the Hopi, the Kachina season was preceded by a group of women's dances given by the Marau, Lakon and Oaqol Societies. The principal function of these dances was weather control, fertility, and curing, and in this respect they echo the major functions of Kachina dances. However, Kachinas can only be impersonated by men; even the Kachin Manas, or Kachina Maidens, are played by men. However, figures similar to Kachinas appear on dance batons, or prayer boards, of the women's societies. The one shown here was used during a Marau ceremony.*

only ever achieved by exceptional individuals. Because of this several *hatali* may combine their efforts in a single ritual, each of them conducting that part of the ritual in which he is proficient. Navaho belief is that the deities, if properly addressed, cannot refuse such supplications; yet it is clear that the complexity of the rituals means that mistakes can, and do, occur. Mistakes may be spotted by the *hatali* conducting the ceremony or by others who are present, and require another series of Chants to counteract any negative influences.

Many Navaho spend a large part of their lives involved directly in Chants or in the preparations for them, particularly so since the network of matrilineal kin who may be called on for support is very wide. Their support is considered by the Navaho to be a binding obligation and is essential in ensuring that the efforts of the hatali will result in supernaturally assured help.

The Chants attempt to persuade the deities to do good rather than inflict harm, but the effectiveness of the rituals is entirely dependent on the degree of control and accuracy the *hatali* is able to exert. Good comes from control; bad comes from lack of control. It is also understood that appeals should be made to those forces which were responsible for causing harm in the first place, since they also have the power to undo it; thus it is not unusual for Snake to be invoked in cases of illness attributable to snakebite or lightning.

Both Navaho and Apache belief, despite an emphasis on the individual power and ability of the *diyi* or *hatali* as the conductors of rituals, address communal concerns similar to those of the more rigidly organised structures of the Pueblo *kiva*-priests. The dance of the solitary *Soyal Kachina*, the blessing of the fire by an Apache *diyi* before the performance of the *Gans*, the placing of a *pahos* prayer stick, or the intonations of a Navaho *hatali* as he directs the gathering of sacred sands and minerals in preparation for a Chant, cannot be considered as isolated acts which are separate from the larger ritual concerns of which they are part. The individual acts build up into minor rituals; the rituals evolve into public ceremonies; and the ceremonies attract the deities, be they *Kachinas*, *Gans*, or *Yeis*, back into the community.

Thus Southwestern belief and shamanic activity are always part of a great cycle of events that reaffirms the people's bond with the land and with the gods. Encircled Mountain, whether considered as the invisible Centre of All or as the Mountain Around which Moving is Done, lies at the heart of Southwestern ceremonialism. Spider Woman, White Painted Woman, and Changing Woman, in turn, testify to the maternal power of the land, of the First, or Earth, Mother, to whom everything ultimately returns to be born anew. When Changing Woman grew old, she rejuvenated herself so the cycle could begin again; and when White Painted Woman returns it is in the guise of a young girl at her puberty ceremony.

Thus the Navaho Twin War Gods, Monster Slayer and Born of Water, although unable to defeat the evil forces of Old Age, Poverty, Sickness, and Death, built on precedents established by the Pueblo peoples to create the conditions for renewal and continuation, expressed in the slow, rhythmic movements of the *Kachinas* just as surely as in the frenzied movements and posturings of the *Gans*.

5   *The First Man*

CALIFORNIAN SHAMANISM

The boundaries of the California culture area correspond approximately to those of the modern State. The area attracted groups of Native Americans from very diverse linguistic and cultural backgrounds, and although the total indigenous population was small by modern comparison, probably never exceeding 300,000 to 500,000, this nevertheless represents about 10% to 15% of all Native peoples living in North America prior to European contact. It was one of the most highly populated areas on the continent, and the tribes living here spoke a bewildering number of different languages and dialects. Even tribes living in close proximity to one another were often unable to understand each other's speech.

The tragic demise of Californian culture, starting with the missionising of the southern and central tribes by the Spanish after 1769 and the virtual extermination of Californian peoples by American gold-seekers and ranchers during the 1840s and 1850s has been noted time and again in both ethnographic and popular literature. In a period of little more than 150 years the Native population of California was reduced to less than 15,000 and many of the smaller tribes had become extinct.

The rapidity with which Californian culture was destroyed has left us with fragmented information. Their original beliefs and customs were of little or no interest to the Spanish missionaries or the American gold-seekers, and few of them kept any records of this rapidly disappearing way of life; thus the spiritual endeavours and highly developed cosmologies and beliefs of the First Californians have usually been underrated or overlooked.

LEFT: *The rocky islands off the Santa Barbara/Ventura coast in southern California were home to the Chumash Indians, where they subsisted from fishing and hunting sea lions and seals. They were the largest Californian tribe and the first to be encountered by the Spanish during their expeditions in the 16th century.*

Yet sufficient remains for us to piece together the clues and understand something about the way the Californian tribes lived prior to contact with Europeans. Diverse beliefs and customs were able to coexist here in a harmonious relationship with each other which is rarely paralleled in other cultures. There is little evidence for social strife, and only rare evidence of intra- or inter-tribal conflict. Whether living in small localised villages or larger multi-village communities, the Californians appear to have enjoyed peaceful and stable relationships with one another.

The reasons for the multiplicity of cultures in indigenous California and the mutual tolerance of what were often very different beliefs and customs needs further consideration. The only common factors here are that the climate is generally mild and natural resources are abundant; but the land varies from mountainous coniferous forest in the north, through oak and deciduous forests and valleys in the central regions, to areas of southern desert, with numerous small and highly localised micro-environments in between.

The resources of each of these areas varied considerably. Some coastal regions were rich in shellfish and seabirds, and gave opportunity for seal-hunting. Northern rivers teemed with salmon, and there was active trade with the tribes of the Northwest Coast. In the central region acorn meal was a staple: once the poisonous tannin had been leached from the acorns, they could be dried and pounded into meal that made a highly nutritious acorn bread. In mountainous areas, small game and deer were abundant. Everywhere were numerous seeds, roots, berries, and fruits that could be gathered in season. What was unavailable in one locality, might be readily traded for from people living only a valley or two distant.

People settled in fertile valleys, along river banks, or established coastal villages with thriving maritime economies, and most of these settlements were so successful that, having arrived, they felt no need to travel further. It is significant that in Californian mythology there is little reference to worlds beyond one's own and inhabited by other races and tribes, or to stories of migrations and great travels. For the Californians home was the village or valley in which one lived, and, with the exception of the Yuman tribes (who were said to travel extensively out of curiosity from their homes in the peripheral regions of the Colorado River system), the people had simply 'always been there'.

When the First Californians arrived is unknown. Some estimates based on linguistic diversity place this at more than 20,000 years ago, in contrast to the conservative claims that Native Americans had no

ABOVE: *Klamath fetish in the form of a pelican. By making the abstract concrete the shamans of California attempted to merge the spiritual with the daily needs of their communities. Fetishes, carved in the likeness of the animals they hunted, were utilised to bring these animals into the public consciousness, and depictions of the animals were thought to establish a link*

between the hunter and the hunted. These fetishes were used in rituals related to hunting or fishing expeditions.
ABOVE: *Klamath fetish in the form of a bear or similar animal bearing a burden on its back, not unlike the Zuni fetish depicted on p. 126.*
RIGHT: *A Klamath fetish in the form of an animal, perhaps a sea lion.*

appreciable presence on the continent until the close of the Pleistocene ice age about 12,000 BC. Regardless of their exact date of arrival, Native people have been living here for a long time in terms of New World populations and of New World archaeology, and this helps to explain the Californian belief of always having been there.

For the sake of convenience, Californian tribes are usually divided into three separate groupings: those of northern, central, and southern California. The peripheral tribes, such as the Yumans, are considered separately. This is the format I have adopted here, although it should be borne in mind that such classifications are aids to reading rather than accurate reflections of Native divisions. It is important to remember, too, that even among groups displaying such preference for isolation as did many of the Californian tribes, there were nevertheless frequent exchanges of ideas and beliefs between them that came about through trade contacts or by inter-marriages.

In their spiritual beliefs each of the three main Californian areas placed a strong emphasis on shamanism, although its exact expression varied widely. In the north, shamans were usually women with healing powers passed on by a female relative who had also been a shaman, and healing was through the formulaic recitation of myths by which the source of the disease was identified and a cure attempted. In the central region, frequently but inaccurately characterised as 'typically' Californian, the shamans were often divided between those who possessed power to diagnose disease and those who possessed the power to cure. Shamans here might be either male or female, and they obtained their power either in a dream (which resulted in ability to cure) or through inheritance (when the Outfit

Shaman inherited a power costume from a former diagnostician). Male shamans predominated in the south, encouraged by dreams induced during initiation rites in the Toloache cult when ingestion of Datura (Jimson-weed) was taken to promote vivid visions, not necessarily all of which were shamanic. The collective nature of the southern cult encouraged a tightly organised fraternity of shamans with shared experiences, rather than the predominantly individual expressions of the central and northern groups.

While bearing in mind the essentially benevolent nature of Californian shamanism and its role as an integrative influence that tended to bind people together, particularly through rituals for public benefit and welfare, as well as for healing, Californian shamanism also had a secondary function in channelling disruptive or negative influences away from the community. This was most highly developed among the northern groups, due primarily to aggressive inroads from the Northwest Coast which were alien to Californian ethos but which forced the people in these areas to develop strata-

ABOVE: *As early as 11,000 years ago the nomads of the Great Basin found refuge in Danger Cave on the edge of the Great Salt Desert. Excavations revealed a series of occupations including evidence of shamanic involvement in day-to-day activities.*

gems for the defence of their villages against hostile incursions and occasional slave-raiding by Northwest Coast tribes.

Northern Californian tribes were not aggressive by nature. Warfare, in fact, was regarded unfavourably - as it was throughout California - and although many northern Californian tribes had both War and Peace Leaders it is significant that each of these was forbidden to engage in any act of violence or aggression. The Peace Leader acted as a spokesman for the tribe who, after consultation with a Council at which everyone's wishes were presented, was responsible for the day-to-day management of tribal affairs. The War Leader took control if disputes arose. His function was to negotiate a peaceful settlement, usually through indemnity payments to the aggrieved parties, rather than to lead war parties or conduct war rituals, and the cessation of hostilities was celebrated as a return to normality rather than a declaration of victory over an enemy.

Shamans were indispensable to the activities of both the War and Peace Leaders, since they strove to promote harmony within the community and to control aggression in its relations with outsiders. The majority of shamans were women who inherited their curative power from a female ancestor, and their role was to identify and dissipate any pernicious influences within the community. They were advisors to the Peace Leader, since their cures and diagnoses prevented harmful influences from affecting the tribe. But there was also a minority of male shamans (the ethnographic literature calls them 'sorcerers' or 'poisoners') who had been influenced in dreams by malevolent spirits and who caused distress.

It is perhaps best to consider the powers inherited by female shamans first and then to compare them with the powers claimed by the male sorcerers. The first distinguishing factor is that the power of female shamans could only be used for good. Such power first became apparent during a girl's youth, often just before puberty, when she began to experience strange feelings and dreams: a sense of aloneness, or of difference, rather than a more specific sense of alienation. At this time she might turn to a female relative, a practising shaman, for guidance and advice and begin to gain some knowledge of the esoteric world of the shamans.

If this relative's help and advice alleviated the girl's worries and fears then it was understood that she was merely experiencing the normal youthful concerns of a girl's adolescence and no further attempt at shamanic training was made. If, however, her concerns persisted, her mentor - who might become the 'donor' of shamanic power - brought her increasingly into situations where such power

ABOVE: *Only 6cm high, these two horned effigies were found at Hogup Cave, not far from Danger Cave, and are about 1500 years old. It is likely they were used by shamans during rituals that appealed to the animal spirits.*

might be encountered or confronted. The experiences of Alice, a Shasta Indian woman who wrote down her life story in the early 1900s, are typical for these northern groups and can be used as an example here.

Under the tutelage of her mentor, Alice began to experience peculiar dreams. She dreamt of narrowly escaping with her life from a grizzly bear, of being at the top of a tall tree or a high cliff and about to fall, or of standing on the banks of a flooded river and about to drown. These were interpreted by her mentor as an indication that the spirits were attempting, at this stage unsuccessfully, to contact her. Her dreams persisted and she was carefully watched, until one day, while engaged in normal activities and without prior warning, she suddenly fainted for no apparent reason.

When this happened, an *Axeki* appeared to her. The *Axeki* are spirit beings, human in form but short in stature and covered with fine, downy hair. They are very numerous, since every mountain, cliff, and rock has its own, and they carry a miniature bow and arrows with which they reluctantly threaten to shoot and kill the initiate unless she learns the songs they are prepared to teach her. The *Axeki* are reluctant because they know that the benevolent power they wish to bestow will benefit the community but might have disastrous consequences for someone who is unprepared to receive it. Alice was confused and fearful. Nothing she had been told had prepared her for this, and she found it difficult to understand the threats of violence and insistent pleadings of the *Axeki*.

Finally she gave in to their demands and permitted the *Axeki* to shoot a 'pain' into her body. This was difficult to bear. She describes the pain as 'like ice', and says this felt like a cold needle-like object about three inches in length which had been placed in her abdomen. When first acquired and consequently not yet under control, such pains can cause severe nausea, vomiting, and fainting. Alice was in agony and tells us she felt 'as if she were dead', describing this as a trance-like state in which she was aware of others around her but unable to communicate or interact with them. Her recovery was slow. She gradually came to her senses, assisted by established shamans, and experienced extreme trembling and incoherent moaning until, finally, she uttered the *Axeki's* name and blood gushed from her mouth.

After she had recovered, Alice was asked to perform the dances and to sing the songs the *Axeki* had given her. This lasted four days, and Alice, exhausted from the trauma of her experience, needed to hold on for support to a rope attached to the ceiling timbers of the

ABOVE: *In common with many Native American tribes, the shamans of the Chemehuevi (one of the Paiute tribes, who inherited a pedestrian nomadic lifestyle from the early occupants of sites such as Danger Cave) used percussive instruments to produce a carefully controlled rhythmic beat that induced a sense of relaxation in a patient through their hypnotic effect. Rattles, such as that shown here, were an important part of almost every shaman's ritual paraphernalia.*

men's house in which the dance took place. Older women gathered closely round to catch her if she fell, for to do so before the dancing was complete would be disastrous, and, from time to time, she was gathered in their arms and swung through the cleansing smoke of a fire. This first experience of shamanic power, despite its very dramatic representation in Alice's recollections, is only a minor manifestation of the *Axeki's* influence.

Throughout her life the northern Californian shaman undergoes further contacts with different *Axeki* and acquires numerous pains of varying degrees of intensity. She learns how to control these and is eventually able to demand the assistance of the *Axeki* during the curing rites she performs. At such times she may make the pains visible to others in a material form they can understand, by, for instance, vomiting a feather said to contain their power. She is believed to be able to extract the pains from and return them to her body as she pleases.

The nature of these pains and the distress they cause the recipient have led some students of Native American cultures to describe the *Axeki* as evil beings who 'try to injure people by shooting pains into them'. This, however, is not the Native understanding. In northern Californian shamanism the healing power of the woman resides in the pains she controls. She possesses no intrinsic power of her own, other than as the agent through which the *Axeki* can become manifest. It is the pains rather than the woman that cure. We should bear in mind, too, that although the pains derive from the *Axeki* they may nevertheless also be those of the woman's mentor, who interprets the girl's dreams and is able to pass on the powers she possesses. At times,

RIGHT: *Highly polished Weather Stones were used by Chumash shamans in rites that were intended to predict future weather patterns. Many Chumash believed that in addition to their ability to foretell the weather, the shamans were also able to influence it.*

control of pains becomes a kind of family heirloom and is referred to as a 'treasure': not only exuding healing power, but also bestowing considerable status and importance on the woman and her family and heirs.

The trauma and distress caused by the pains are proportional to the power that is being conveyed: something powerful is not obtained for nothing. Thus, although the experience of receiving pains is extreme, they should be thought of as gifts from the *Axeki* which are granted to worthy candidates for the exercise of power. It is said that when a shaman dies the pains return to the *Axekis* who gave them, and they might then be given to someone new. Similarly, when pains pass from a donor to a candidate they must first return to the *Axeki* so the power inherent in them can be redirected, and in such cases the donor, having relinquished control, can no longer practice as a shaman.

Fanny Flounder, the last practising shaman of the Yurok in the village of Espen, made it clear when recalling her original trance experience that the power was transferred by the supernatural beings. In her vision she experienced being at the edge where the Sky World touches the Outer Ocean. She describes blood dripping and hanging like icicles from the sky, and recalls the presence of a 'spirit doctor' who broke off one of these blood-icicles and placed it in her mouth. She tells us 'This *telogel* [pain] is of blood. When I hold it in my hands, you can see the blood drip between my fingers. The song when I suck out blood [to effect a cure] says: when the sky moves up and down you are travelling in the air.'

The power of the male sorcerers or poisoners is different from that possessed by the female healing shamans. Although also obtained in dreams, these powers are used perniciously and have no ancestral connections. They cannot be inherited from a previous donor or influenced by other shamans but come directly from a supernatural being, and consist of secret magical practices which are described in the vision by the spirit itself. Such practices involve the mixing of poisons from animals or snakes with the hair or excrement of the intended victim and furtive application by secretly touching him or her, causing sickness or death. The poisoners kept their dark side secret, but anyone suspected of such behaviour was often, curiously, given favourable treatment, because giving offence might result in fearsome retaliation.

The Achomawi neighbours of the Shasta and Yurok also felt that pernicious impulse could be received only by men and had to be kept secret, and that it could not be transferred to anyone else.

The Pomo, Patwin, and Maidu followers of the Kuksu cult practised initiation rituals for boys during which the initiates established relations with the animal spirits and ancestral powers.

OPPOSITE: *Decorative hairpins used in the Kuksu cult. Hair was considered to be the seat of the soul, and lavish attention was placed on the hair and on ornaments associated with it.*

OPPOSITE: *Ear pendants worn during the Kuksu celebrations which included acceptance of young boys into manhood, denoted by the piercing of their ears and the insertion of ear pendants such as those shown here.*

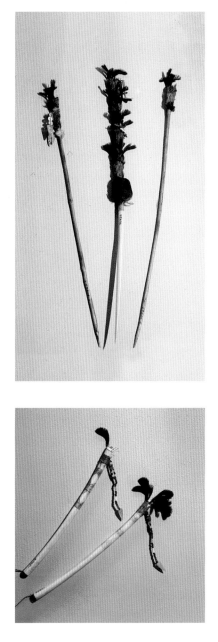

RIGHT: *Shell bead necklaces with stone and abalone shell pendants. These were among the paraphernalia used in Kuksu ritual to establish a relationship between the initiate and the spirit forces.*

Among them, however, such power is obtained via a *QaQu*, a small bunch of feathers which is said be found growing in remote parts of isolated woods. On finding a *QaQu* the shaman-sorcerer attempts to uproot it, but is unsuccessful. Only through persistent searching and endeavour - to which he is driven by the torments of the vision - does he eventually succeed. Even then he is careful to keep the *QaQu* hidden from others: an uprooted *QaQu* is an obvious sign of harmful power and, similarly to Fanny Flounder's *telogel*, is said to continually drip blood. In the past, anyone found in possession of such an ominous symbol of evil intent would have immediately been put to death.

In employing his malignant art, the Achomawi sorcerer 'throws' a pain at someone he wishes to injure. Thus the cause of illness through the throwing of a pain parallels the acquisition of power via the pain inflicted by the *Axeki*, except that one has harmful consequences whereas the other confers good. A thrown pain is said by the Achomawi to always hit at the back of the neck. After some time it crawls up under the hair to the crown of the head, from where it travels beneath the skin to the part of the body the sorcerer wishes to attack. When the person dies, the sorcerer recalls the pain. At this point it is 'bloodthirsty', so the sorcerer places his coat and cap on a stump which the pain strikes on its return, believing it to be the sorcerer whom it now attempts to kill. By subduing the pain the sorcerer is able to recover it from the stump and use it time and again against those he wishes to harm.

The Shasta *Axeki* and the Achomawi *QaQu* represent the extremes of beneficial and pernicious power expressed by the northern Californian groups. These powers are deployed in different ways: benign power openly, harmful power surreptitiously. When malignant power is employed, it is only when it starts to threaten the security of the community that drastic measures might be employed, including the death or banishment of the sorcerer and of the person who had hired him if he was acting on another's behalf.

Beneficent and pernicious powers were also formally acknowledged by the Takelma, living north of the Shasta and Achomawi on the California-Oregon border. Shamanic power among the Takelma was never inherited but always obtained in a vision brought about by one of a host of different spirits. Each of these conferred its own power for either good or evil, and the relationship between 'good' and 'bad' *goyó*, or shamans, was one of open hostility. Although, as among the Shasta, many of the 'bad' *goyó*'s wishes were granted out of fear of retaliation, there was a clearly defined limit beyond which a dangerous shaman was felt to have over-indulged his or her power to 'eat up people'.

Takelma policy was to reintegrate the errant shaman into society, although if intervention failed banishment from the tribe remained an option. In general, however, the services of several 'good' *goyó* were sought, whose duty it was to perform rituals which would drive out the evil spirits from the offender's body. These spirits might be numerous: in one case it was reported that twenty bad spirits

ABOVE: *The majestic redwood forests of northern California provided a focus for the shamans of the Pomo, since their stability and endurance were qualities that the shaman sought and which could be utilised in curing rituals.*

were driven out of one such person, although even this does not appear to have exhausted them all since he was soon back up to his old tricks and further exorcisms had to be performed.

The division between good and evil as expressed in Northern Californian shamanism can be seen as embodying opposing forces: the collective and inherited power for good possessed by women is set against the highly individualised and secretive malignant power of the male poisoners. Both, however, are informed - indeed, made possible - by the northern Californian reliance on power, wealth, and status. Despite assertions that the female shaman works altruistically 'for the community', the acquisition of pains greatly enhances her, and her family's, status. Wealth acquired from curing fees might even give such families standing in the community which exceeds that of the richest members who rely on non-shamanic means such as privileged ownership rights to acorn stands or salmon bearing rivers. Similarly, the poisoner might acquire wealth by being paid to use his power against rival factions in family feuds.

Although dreaming is considered to be a prerequisite for the use of power by either the curing shaman or the poisoner, the actual exercise of power relies almost entirely on the recitation of formulaic stanzas in curing or the carrying out of prescribed actions in sorcery for it to be effective. Herbal remedies are used by lay members of the community in effecting simple cures, but have little place in northern Californian shamanic practice. In theory, the repetition of shamanic formulae or the carrying out of the sorcerer's acts by any member of the community, if correctly done, should bring about the desired result; yet there is a general fear of supernatural retribution for any unapproved use. Use of the *Axeki's* songs and dances by someone not given the right might lead to them being killed by the *Axeki*; the *QaQu* will recognise unauthorised use of their power and strike the sender of the pain rather than the intended victim. Fear of retribution for unapproved usage was sufficient to prevent this happening.

Shamanism in the central California region contains numerous elements which are similar to those of the north. There is a division between benign and malignant power, similar social standing accorded to the successful practitioner, and a belief that pains can be thrown into someone and are the most frequent disease-causing agency. Equivalents to the *Axeki* and the *QaQu* are also apparent

BELOW: *The Maidu shaman wore round his neck this obsidian blade which was credited with supernatural powers ranging from instrument of healing to deadly weapon. The shaman could 'send it out' to counter an approaching menace or as a riposte to an insult.*

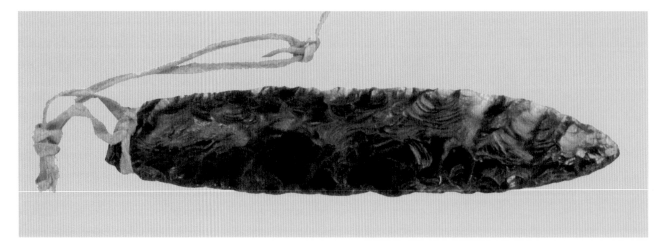

ABOVE: *This painted wooden wand was used by a Diegueño shaman to heal as well as to challenge opponents by 'throwing pains' at them. The pointed stone inset in the wand dates back to 1500 BC. Old objects were sought after because their antiquity invested such objects with the power of the ancestors who once owned them.*

here. A major difference, however, is the importance attached to the shamanic dream, since in the central region there is an unshakeable conviction that dreams are the basis of shamanic knowledge and that power cannot be realised unless it has first been acquired through dreaming.

Once again, there is a division between shamanic roles; although in the central region the division is not so much between the powers of good and evil, although this exists too, but between the shaman who is able to exercise power to cure and one who is qualified in determining the cause of illness. In the former case, the ability to cure received through revelation in a dream is an absolute requirement, and without this the shaman would be powerless. The dream revelation itself follows the pattern already described for the Yurok, when Fanny Flounder was taken to the edge of the Sky World and given a *telogel*, or pain, of blood; but with the exception that it is no longer only females who acquire curing healing power. Women predominate among some central tribes, but elsewhere they may be mostly men, or they could be either.

In all cases, however, the shaman undergoes a period of physical trauma and distress during which he or she acquires the songs and face- and body-paints given by a spirit helper through whom a cure can be effected. The cure is often simply a matter of touching and massaging the patient's body and then sucking out a disease-causing object similar to the pains of the northern groups. The belief that pains can be thrown by someone with evil intent leads to the conviction that disease-causing objects removed by the curing shaman can be made to reveal the identity of the person who caused the sickness, since the pains are said to possess their own will and motivation and are amenable to persuasive techniques employed by the curing shaman.

Specialisation among the central California shamans means that in case of a specific illness it is imperative to find the right healer. Some specialise, for example, only in the cure of snakebites and such healers are known as Rattlesnake Doctors since their power comes from Rattlesnake. Others are Bear Doctors, Thunder Doctors, and so forth, each with his/her own highly focused area of specialisation. Yet others possess more generalised powers, such as the Weather Shamans whose principal function is to ensure good weather during cures and other rituals.

Each of these specialists can cure or be effective only within the area of his or her particular specialism. None of them is able to cure without the help of a shaman who diagnoses the cause of illness or who can identify the source from which any malignant power emanates. They work closely with Diagnostic Shamans who inherit their power from an ancestor. This power is invested in the ritual costumes they wear, passed down through the family, which leads to the diagnosticians being generally known as Outfit Shamans: power resides, allegedly, in the costume or outfit the shaman uses and with the specific ritual acts, songs, facepaints, and so forth associated with it, and which are passed on to succeeding members of the family. At first this appears to negate the requirement of dream sanction, resembling the more common northern concept of formulaic inherited power.

Yet the dream element is essential here too. Shortly before the death of a practising shaman, his relatives - particularly sons and daughters - will begin to dream of the power that resides in the costume. They will have vivid experiences of being visited by the costume's power-helpers: dreams of, say, a spirit-dog who is able to sniff out the causes of various diseases and illnesses. Sometimes the dreams are so vivid that the persons experiencing them begin to feel that the dreams are taking over part of their life. They are unable to sleep, wash, eat, or engage in any normal activity, without feeling the power of the spirit-helper or spirit-animal directing all their movements.

For many of these people such experiences will gradually fade, sometimes with the exorcising assistance of another shaman but often of their own accord. A few people, however, are unable to shake off these constant feelings of being in contact with the former shaman's helpers and will eventually inherit the costume and its associated rituals. There is, therefore, a strong reliance on the power of the dream in enabling the Outfit Doctor to inherit.

The close relationship between the curing shaman and the diagnostician shown in central Californian practice is also reflected in the south. Here, however, there is less reliance on inheritance and a greater concentration on community participation. There is still a strong emphasis on the interpretation of dreams by established

OPPOSITE: *The bear is a potent shamanic animal, not least because of its close association with humans. Of all animals, the bear is the most like human beings in that it can walk upright and is said to share their beliefs and concerns. Pomo shamans frequently referred to the power of the bear and brought its power into their rituals by wearing costumes that established their relationship to this animal.*

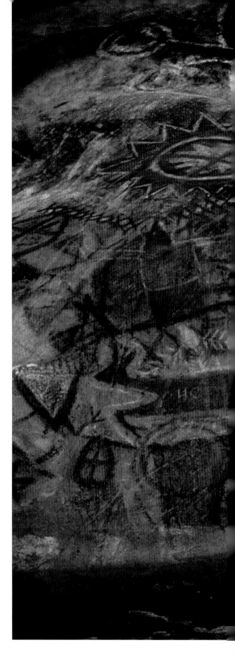

shamans, as well as the encouragement of novices to actively engage with the messages they receive from their spirit guides; but at the same time there emerges an emphasis on ideals of community spirit which is quite different from the more individualistic and status-led privileges of the northern groups. This is especially evident in the Toloache (Datura or Jimson-weed) Cult: a puberty rite undergone by all boys – and some girls – as a part of their initiation into adulthood.

Unfortunately, very little is known of the southern Californian *Toloache* Cult as practised by tribes such as the Diegueño, Luiseño, and Juaneño. All these groups were missionised by the Spanish at an early date: their Native practices were banned by the Spanish, and consequently only fragments of their ceremonies and beliefs have survived. It is nevertheless apparent that the Cult flourished among them, and that they had organised fraternities of shamans who used methods such as maps made from coloured sand as part of their divinatory diagnostic technique, and that there was a very highly developed cosmology which informed the Cult and the activities of its shamans.

We can, nevertheless, look at the beliefs of the Chumash, who live in the coastal Santa Barbara area bordering the southern and central groups, for a clearer understanding of the Cult and of the cosmological beliefs by which it was informed. The Chumash, although also one of the Mission Tribes, had a stronger population than the southern Mission groups, and, consequently, were able to retain more of their traditional lore. They have left many records in the form of rock paintings, made by the Chumash shamans, which help us understand their cosmology more fully. Such paintings are numerous in the Santa Barbara and Ventura areas and contain astrological designs, as well as depictions of spirit animals and shamanic activities.

The importance of the universe in Chumash thinking is apparent from the fact that their shamans are known as alchuklash, a term which includes not only shamanic practice but also defines the shaman's activities as an astrologer-priest. From reading the inscriptions in shamanic rock-art, it is obvious that the Chumash had a clearer concept of the heavens and the heavenly bodies than did the Spanish of the late 1700s when Missions were being established. It is, in fact, becoming increasingly apparent through modern scholarship that everything in the Chumash world, and presumably that of southern California too, was governed by the movements of the stars and planets.

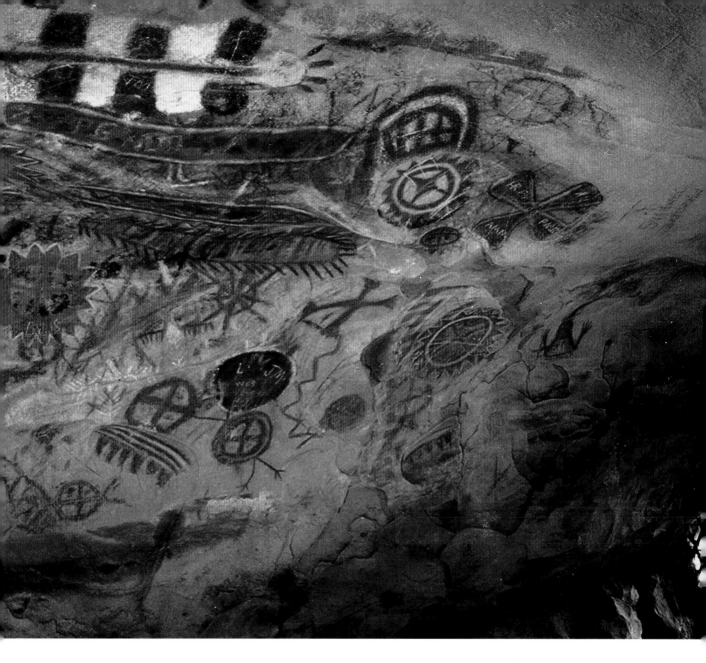

ABOVE: *Painted Cave, near Santa Barbara, is one of the most impressive examples of Chumash cave art. The complex arrangement of figures results from repeated paintings over many years, since the cave was often used as a site of sacred significance. The figures represent numerous elements from Chumash mythology, particularly the celestial powers.*

Unlike the ordinary world of the Chumash, which was orderly and organised, that of the celestial bodies was thought to be unpredictable and dangerous. The principal deity was *Kakunupmawa*, the Sun, who was conceived as a very old man who each day travelled across the sky carrying a torch which gave light and warmth to the people below. His great age reflected his great wisdom; but he was nevertheless a fearsome character. Each night as he travelled home his journey was preceded by fog and gales of wind which concealed his passage from others who might intend him harm, and on entering his house of quartz crystal he first tumbled rocks inside to see if anything unusual awaited him. Inside he fed on human flesh, surrounded by trained but dangerous bears, mountain lions, rattlesnakes, and birds.

Close by the widower Sun lived *Alahtin*, the Moon, whose powers included the ability to cleanse the earth. While not as awesome and frightening as *Kakunupmawa*, *Alahtin's* abilities were formidable. She was protected by a giant condor whose wing movements while eating sometimes hid the Moon and caused eclipses. Instrumental in the daily lives of the people, particularly of women, she also had power to make the seas rise and fall, to control the growth and fertility of trees, plants, and animals, and was even able to influence the movements of the stars and constellations.

Against this background of belief, the Chumash *alchuklash* made nightly observations of the movements of the stars, recording these in elaborately painted and detailed star charts and marking events of a spectacular or unusual nature, such as the arrival of a comet or an eclipse. These events were also recorded in the cave paintings, which are said to be 'full of power' of the deities themselves as well as of that implanted and realised there by the activities of the *alchuklash*. Even today, Chumash visiting these shrines leave small offerings of food, clothing, and other goods as a sign of their belief and respect.

The ability of the *alchuklash* to intervene directly in the lives of the people came, as elsewhere in California, through dreaming for power; but for the Chumash and other southern Californians such dreams or visions were induced through ingestions of Datura during the Toloache. The Chumash rationalise this by linking Datura with Old Woman Momoy: a wealthy mythical widow whose medicine revives the sick and averts death. By drinking the water in which she has bathed the Chumash initiate learns the traditions of the tribe and grows wise. Like other deities in the Chumash pantheon, Old Woman Momoy is said to be of great age and wisdom, since only the wise can survive to great age in a dangerous world.

Chumash initiates experienced Datura induced visions as part of the *Toloache*. Datura, a member of the nightshade family, is a powerful intoxicant and hallucinogen which initially produces feelings of nausea and fainting, and is taken as an infusion: the 'bath water' of Old Woman Momoy. These feelings of sickness are followed by brilliantly coloured ecstatic dreams or visions. After extended periods of fasting and thirsting during which the initiate is taught what to expect, the cultural pattern of the dreams is always similar. The initiate experiences a sense of rebirth, of a new beginning, and is taken from mountain-top to mountain-top by the animal spirits who teach him or her the 'right way' to live. It is said that the entire life

OPPOSITE: *Whistles made from deer shinbone enabled the shamans to produce a piercing sound calculated to impress the uninitiated as much as their spirit helpers. The shell beads are placed to suggest the night sky at the winter solstice.*

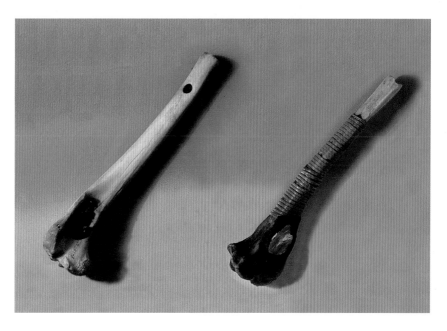

of a Chumash is decided by the dreams he experiences at *Toloache*.

It is the responsibility of the *alchuklash* not only to administer the Datura infusion, but also to stay by the initiate throughout the trance, to interpret the dream on his awakening, and then to become his instructor for a period of at least a year following the vision. During this period the initiate learns Chumash lore and is introduced to the subtler aspects of Chumash cosmology. It is said that anyone who follows the principles set out by the *alchuklash* will experience only good in his life; but to ignore this advice will result in the deities withdrawing their power and leave the initiate susceptible to danger in his contacts with them.

For a few of the boys the experience will lead to contact with powers that exude shamanic ability. Such powers might include Rainbow, Thunder, or Frog, and exposure to them may lead the ini-titate to believe that he can charm the weather, cure the sick, and direct performances which aid other individuals to obtain power. However, given the capricious nature of Chumash deities, such revelations are not to be trusted. Only after lengthy training and instruction, intended to determine both the extent of power and its 'truth', might the initiate be admitted inside the *siliyik*, a sacred enclosure containing the *chwashtiwi'l* shrine of a feather pole surrounded by beads, seeds, feathers, and other tokens of the deities.

Here he is gradually taught the esoteric language used by the *alchuklash* in preparation for becoming a member of a social elite known as the *antap*. In many ways the *antap* are the pivot of

ABOVE AND BELOW: *Polished stones with holes drilled through their centres are referred to by the popular name of 'Doughnut Stones'. They were used in rituals by shamans in a similar manner to the Weather Stones, but had a more practical function as weights on atlatl (spear thrower) shafts.*

Chumash ceremonial, political, and economic life. Although stemming from the experiences of the *Toloache* initiations, the *antap* form a privileged exclusive body whose activities control Chumash relations within the community, with other tribal groups, and with the deities. Every Chumash village of any size or influence has its own council of *antap* members which includes, in addition to the *alchuklash*, the family members of the village leaders and those who, through the beneficent intervention of the deities, have gained wealth and social standing.

The *antap* can in many senses be considered the vanguard of Chumash spiritual thought and endeavour. Each of its members, both male and female, requires sanction from the deities which brings them into direct contact with the spirit-beings of the *Itiashup*, or Middle World. This world, supported by giant serpents, is the abode of supernatural beings, the First People, whose culture is much like that of the Chumash themselves. They form a link between the malign, deformed and misshapen *Nunashish* creatures of *C'oyinashup*, the Lower World, and the celestial beings of *Alapay*, the Upper World.

Antap activities are expressly intended to maintain the harmony and balance of *Itiashup* through the performance of rites conducted by the *alchuklash* astrologer-priests, . For the Chumash this Middle World is the geographical centre of the Universe, and hence significant sources of power have to be channelled through here to be of benefit to the people. It is within this region of supernatural interactions that the Chumash shamans carry out their observations of the stars and make their lunar and solar calendars, where they inscribe events of great mythological and spiritual significance on the walls of sacred caves, and where the *antap* officials meet in the sacred *siliyik* enclosure to compose the songs and poems which use secret words to convey messages to the deities.

Antap activity is nevertheless carried even further than this. Among the officials are specialist ranks such as the Weather Shamans, Bear Shamans, and Rattlesnake Shamans, which parallel the specialisations found elsewhere in the California area. Each of these might be called upon to exercise appropriate power as and when it is needed, and there is little ranking order of authority between them. Thus in addition to their collective duties as *antap* officials, each member also possesses power of a more specific nature.

Among the *antap* elite some individuals do, however, possess greater power than others. These form a group of twelve who are responsible for the conduct of regular monthly rituals which are

RIGHT: *This winged creature may represent either the condor or the eagle, both of whom the Indians in southern California regarded as sacred. It may be a spirit in flight, or conceivably the shaman who painted here an image of himself in the state of transformation. This is one of the paintings in the Painted Cave at Santa Barbara.*

held in accordance with the movements of the sun, moon, planets, and stars; thereby officiating over an annual cycle of events through which the people's world is synchronised with that of the deities. Most important is a high official known as the Sun Priest through whom the power of the *antap* itself and of the twelve shamans responsible for the annual cycle can be concentrated in one single event which coincides with the Winter Solstice. This event, the erection of the feathered pole shrine in the *siliyik*, is held to represent the completion of the annual rituals and to renew the Chumash world.

Throughout California, the purpose of rituals was to promote harmony in the tribe, and the beliefs of tribes living in adjacent areas reflected those of California. Principal among these tribes were the Yuman-speaking groups, such as the Mojave of the Lower Colorado River. Broader in outlook than some of the Californian peoples who spent their entire lives in very restricted localities, the Yumans travelled widely and, in the process of doing so, adopted many ideas and beliefs of neighbouring peoples which they added to the prevailing ethos of their Californian outlook.

Thus we find among them the occasional use of Datura, although this is not a usual Yuman trait, as well as specialisation in weather control, some inherited power, a belief in intrusive power objects causing sickness, and so forth. Most characteristic of the Yuman peoples, however, is the even more intense attention paid to the significance of dreams. For the Yumans life itself was conducted almost as a dream, and every activity was informed and influenced by what a person dreamt.

In some senses, of course, dreams merely served as a means of breaking through the restrictive boundaries of everyday life. In dreams a man was free to travel wherever and whenever he wished, and among the Yumans these travels took him on journeys of truly cosmic breadth. A great shaman was one who had gained his knowledge and experience, not through practice or instruction but through dreaming. Similarly, despite a belief in intrusive illness, most diseases and misfortunes occurred because one dreamt about them and they could, similarly, be dreamt away by a capable shaman. Bad dreams might affect not only the dreamer: children could become sick because of the dreams of their parents or of a visitor, and it was a generally held belief that there was a primal stock of illness afloat in the world with which one came in contact through the dreams of one's own or of others.

In many ways, the Yuman belief in the all-pervasive effect of dreams has its parallel in their love of travelling 'for pleasure'. This broadened their horizons compared with other Californian tribes, and was reflected both in dream content and in perception of the world at large. The closely integrated Middle World of the Chumash as the centre of the universe is, for instance, alien to Yuman thinking. For them the world is wide-open, not without dangers and difficulties, but also full of excitement and adventure.

In this world each individual's experience is unique, since each dream is an adventure into realms that have not been experienced by others. Thus there are no organised associations of shamans among the Yumans, and no sense of a collective responsibility such as that shouldered by the *antap* elite of the Chumash. The dream is

the personal property of the dreamer, and it follows from this that an ideological shift in the nature of dreams should also occur.

As we have already seen, much Californian dreaming links the dreamer with the world of mythical beings who have acquired their wisdom and knowledge through the experience of past events. Old Woman Momoy, for instance, is a classic example of wisdom related to age. For the Yumans, however, every experience was new, and dreams were conducted in a contemporary spirit world rather than in the mythical past. Thus the nature of the spirit-helpers shifts from that of the powerful deities, and relies more heavily instead on the intervention of animals, birds, and anthropomorphic beings which become personal spirit-helpers. Shamans simply acquire a greater number of more effective helpers than ordinary people.

Among the Yumans the forces of good and evil are not clearly differentiated. There is no class of spirits that is intrinsically harmful neither is there one that is solely beneficial. Power can manifest itself in any number of ways at any time. The shaman's intervention is one in which he or she sets off undifferentiated forces against each other in a juggling act which can result in an effective cure but is also potentially disastrous.

RIGHT: *Steatite bowl found near Triunfo Canyon in Chumash territory. Stone bowls of this type were used in the central and southern Californian areas as mortars for grinding pigments. The ground pigment was mixed with grease to make a viscous substance used by shamans in body painting and for applying colour to rock surfaces in sacred localities.*

There is a tendency among the Yumans as elsewhere in California to believe that shamans are capable of deliberately manipulating power to suit their own ends, but this is somewhat different from ideas concerning manipulation held by the Californian tribes. The Shasta shaman who fails to cure, for instance, does so from greed rather than malice, or to ensure that intervention will be required again, earning her a further curing fee. The Yuman doctor who fails to cure, however, may do so because of the spiteful or malicious character of his spirit-helpers, or he may contrive to cause illness which is beyond another shaman's power to cure simply to prove that his dreams are more powerful than those of a rival.

Whatever the divergences, it is clear that throughout the region the shamans intervene in ways that are intended to harness power and, in general, to bring it to bear in a communal setting. Even the Yuman doctor, despite his greater freedom and independence, is subject to similar inhibitions and beliefs as those that govern the strictly regulated activities of the Chumash *antap* or the manipulation of shamanic pains by the Shasta.

Despite great regional variations and discrepancies in the manner in which dreams are interpreted, California presents us with a unified vision of complementary powers in which good and bad are seen as opposing forces, and this, in turn, results in a division in the exercise of shamanic power for either benign or malignant purposes. In contrast with areas such as the Subarctic, where an individual shaman can be seen to act in both helpful and harmful ways, these functions are often separated in California and ascribed to different individuals.

Californian shamanism, while reflecting the many cultures, languages, and environmental aspects of the region, as well as diverse influences reaching the area through local trade and from regions such as the Northwest Coast and the Southwest, presents us with a unified concept of power based on dream revelation. This often relies on observation of the movements and interactions between the celestial bodies in their roles as controlling deities, and this, in turn, governs the thoughts and actions of individuals. Chumash star charts provide not only a 'record of time', but also specify what is permissible in relations between individual members of the community.

In many ways the Californians looked outside their immediate environments, to the stars and planets, for confirmation of the forces that could be applied within relatively small localised communities that were frequently isolated from one another. Few Californians travelled far from their homelands, and only peripheral groups such as the Yumans attempted to express their beliefs in broader terms. Even among the Yumans, however, the focus of power is centred on the individual and expressed through personal dream experiences that validate any possible course of action.

6   *The Sacred Hoop*

PLAINS SHAMANISM

The Great Plains are the heartland of North America. This vast region, comprising some one million square miles of almost unbroken grasslands, was one of the richest game areas of the world: buffalo herds numbering millions of animals roamed here, as did huge numbers of white-tailed antelope and numerous smaller game animals. The grasslands were broken in part by rivers along whose banks stands of cottonwoods, considered as a sacred Tree of Life, supported extensive animal life and birds, and where there were also abundant stretches of dense thickets of bushes bearing fruits and berries.

Most characteristic of the grasslands, however, is the sense of infinite space. For hundreds of miles this 'sea of grass' is unbroken. Constant winds ripple the surface, unhindered by any natural obstacles, and set the grass stems in continual motion. In the western regions this is largely the short stemmed but highly nutritious Buffalo Grass, while in the eastern Prairie regions the long-stemmed Prairie Grass could reach three feet or more in height. The line of sight, like the sea of grass, is unbroken too, and this creates a deceptive sense of distance and perspective, as if the eye could 'see forever'.

This region, with its infinite spaces and huge resources, attracted numerous bands of nomadic hunters: among them were the Blackfoot in the north, Siouan tribes in the central regions, and the Comanche and Kiowa in the south. Along the Mississippi-Missouri, which marks the eastern boundary of the Great Plains area, were

LEFT: *Chief Mountain in northern Montana is sacred to the Blackfoot tribes. According to Blackfoot mythology, Chief Mountain was the only peak left above water at the time of the great flood. Napi, the Trickster/ Transformer, sent various animals to dive for mud with which he could recreate the earth. Otter, Beaver, and Muskrat all failed in their attempts, but finally Duck was successful.*

161

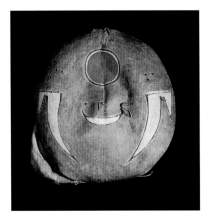

ABOVE: *The visionary elements painted on this Plains Cree buffalo hide shield represent celestial forces, with depictions of the Sun and Moon as the central figures. The shield granted supernatural aid to its bearer by guaranteeing him a long life.*

semi-nomadic hunter-farmers, such as the Pawnee, Oto, and Osage, who spent part of their year in permanent earth-lodge villages where they planted corn and part following the buffalo herds during their seasonal migrations, when they lived in hide-covered tipis identical to those used year round by the nomadic tribes.

The lives of all the people living here, whether nomadic or semi-nomadic, were closely attuned to the idea of space and movement. Practical considerations, such as the use of the portable tipi, as well as fringed skin clothing and flowing eagle feather headdresses, were reflections of this sense of continual motion. So, too, were the religious and ritual concepts involved in tribal ceremonies and in the individual acts of their shamans. Ceremony, on the Great Plains, is never static: all ritual involves motion, a moving forward with temporary halts until the sacred journey is completed and can be recommenced.

In Plains ideology, this sacred journey is likened to a hoop and everything in nature and in man is conceived as circular in motion and in form. The tipi is round and is, therefore, a sacred dwelling just as surely as it provides shelter and accommodation. A shield, too, is circular and sacred and offers its bearer spiritual as well as physical protection. Even life is considered as a sacred cyclic journey, from birth, through youth and maturity, to old age and death, thence to rebirth so the cycle can begin anew.

The same concept of circular motion is reflected in Plains shamanism. In Blackfoot belief, the first shaman, *Napi*, or Old Man, was a Trickster-Transformer. He did not create the world, but he shaped it into the form we know today. As *Napi* travelled he altered everything he came into contact with, raising parts of the earth to form mountains, turning tears into rivers, and placing people and animals everywhere. It is significant that *Napi* is restless and unable to settle, and even in death he continues to travel in realms beyond those of the present world, to which he will ultimately return when his travels elsewhere are completed.

This concept of cyclic motion is also clearly expressed by the Wahpeton Dakota (Sioux) who claim that their *wicasa wakan*, holy men or shamans, have a pre-natal existence among the Thunderers, from whom they gain experience and prior knowledge of all that will befall them during life. Such men are *wakan*, mysterious or sacred, and are predestined for their roles as shamans, although they do not generally begin to practice until they reach maturity and once their power has been publicly demonstrated, or proven. At death their *nagi*, the 'breath of life' or spirit which is believed to live

RIGHT: *An Assiniboine hand drum painted with an image of a mystical figure seen in a vision. Although the spirits often appeared in visions in either human or animal form, they could sometimes appear in strange forms that are more difficult to interpret. Each vision was a highly personal experience, and although it was explained and interpreted by a shaman its full significance might only ever be known to the visionary.*
The composite figure shown here exhibits human, bird, and animal characteristics, but its exact meaning is unknown.

independently from the body, returns to the Thunderers. Thus the cycle of shamanic power is founded in movement from the spirit world to the world of the people and back to that of the spirits, from which it is reborn.

The concept of motion applies equally to the acquisition of shamanic power or, rather, to the granting of authority to practise as a shaman. All Plains men, and some women, seek power via the vision quest. This in itself requires a journey, since the seeker after power must travel away from the abode of the people to a lonely spot in order to receive a revelation. Such places are often on isolated bluffs or hills or in places where danger threatens, such as a path frequented by bears or, in the past, on trails travelled by war parties.

The emotional state of the seeker and his receptivity to a 'power dream' are heightened by prolonged periods of thirsting and fasting and by sleep deprivation. Throughout the vigil he beseeches the spirits to appear, taking no food but making regular smoke offerings from the pipe he carries with him. Such smoke is said to 'make the breath visible'; thus enabling the person's *nagi* to travel in visible

LEFT:
This Medicine bundle of the Crow Tobacco Society belonged to its Weasel Chapter. It was opened during a fertility ritual when a woman danced with the weasel skins to gain supernatural power in keeping with the promise made by the Weasels in a vision. This ensured the fertility not only of the sacred Tobacco species, distinct from ordinary smoking tobacco, but also of the whole Crow tribe.

form. Physically weakened by lack of food, water, and sleep the individual hopes to experience a dramatic dream in which a power-animal appears.

Typically, the power-animal discloses its presence in successive stages. Appearing first as an ordinary animal which reveals itself by a call or a rustle in the grass, it gradually changes in shape and manner to assume human form. In this form it may take the *nagi* of the seeker on a spiritual voyage, during which he is shown some of the secrets of the spirit world and given a power-song and face- and body-paint through which this initial encounter with the spirits can be reactivated at a later date. Generally he is instructed in certain rules he must respect and follow in order to ensure that his power remains effective. Prominent among these are taboos on certain foods, such as refraining from eating the flesh of the power-animal appearing in the vision, and instructions in making up a Medicine Bundle containing tokens representative of specific aspects of the vision. By utilising the songs and paints and through the ritual blessing of objects taken from the Medicine Bundle, the animal spirits of the vision are invoked and will give assistance to the Bundle Owner.

Vision seeking is not necessarily successful or all-embracing, and many men seek visions on a number of occasions to achieve success or to increase their contact with spirit power. Without power the individual is thought of as being at a disadvantage. When a power-animal appears it usually grants very specific benefits which, previously, included invulnerability in warfare or the ability to elude one's enemies. Today, visions more generally grant success, happiness, or a long life. Such visions, although clearly related to the general practice of shamanism, are not in themselves shamanic. Occasionally, however, the spirits will recognise that the *nagi* of the seeker has been instructed by the Thunderers in the life before birth, and then a spirit animal with exceptional shamanic power, such as Toad, Buffalo, or Bear, will appear.

Each shamanic vision, although conforming to the cultural patterning and expectations of the Plains tribes, is highly individual, and though there are fraternities of, for instance, Bear Shamans, each individual shaman will have specific rites and paraphernalia that are exclusive to himself. The different shamanic power-animals nevertheless possess particular characteristics peculiar to their species. Toad, for example, usually imparts power to suck out illness, whereas Bear Shamans are said to have the ability to cure serious wounds.

Black Elk, a Lakota Sioux shaman, vividly described the shamanic

BELOW: *Hole-in-the-Mountain Prairie near Lake Benton in southwestern Minnesota. The open spaces of the Plains grasslands convey a sense of perpetual motion, since even on a still day the land is never quiet. A constant wind, its flow unimpeded by any natural barriers, is typical of the tall grass regions. The idea of the shamanic journey, as envisaged by Plains shamans, is one of a continual quest for sources of power.*

ABOVE: *Rock carvings and paintings have been used on the Plains since prehistoric times to mark places of sacred and mystical significance. The petroglyph shown here is in the Bighorn Basin in Wyoming and has been described as a warrior wearing a feathered headdress. It could, however, just as readily be a depiction of a shaman in elaborate costume; this interpretation is supported by the fact that the figure appears to be carrying a shaman's rattle rather than a warrior's weapons.*

OPPOSITE: *The Blackfoot shaman's headdress has a form that is characteristic of the Buffalo Horn Society, and suggests that the wearer possessed virtues of stamina and endurance which*

vision and the power journey of the *nagi* to the spirit world when, as an old man in the 1920s, he dictated his life story to the ethnologist John Neihardt. Black Elk tells of the time when, as a child, he was seriously ill and in coma and expected to die. During this traumatic period he experienced a vivid dream that was to affect the rest of his life. In it he saw two men descending from the clouds carrying spears that flashed lightning. They urged Black Elk to follow them to the clouds, to the home of the Thunderers, where he was instructed by the Black, White, Sorrel, and Buckskin Horses of the West, North, East, and South.

He was then taken to the Flaming Rainbow Tipi, which was built from Cloud and sewn with Lightning, that was the home of the Six Grandfathers representing the powers of the West, North, East, South, Sky, and Earth. Each of the Grandfathers, whom Black Elk believed to be as old as Creation, gave him a token: a cup containing 'living water' from the West, a healing herb from the North, a sacred pipe from the East, a hoop symbolic of the unity of people and nature from the South. The Grandfather of the Sky, the oldest of them all, gave Black Elk the power to bring all these things together to help his people, but it was through the Grandfather of the Earth that his power was to be made real.

In this initial vision Black Elk's *nagi* is taken first to the Sacred Horses, then to the Flaming Rainbow Tipi, and from there to a mountain peak identified in the vision as the Centre of the World, before, finally, travelling back to his comatose body in the tipi of his family. These four successive stages in the spiritual journey are very significant in Great Plains symbolism, and the circular journey through life as well as the annual cycle of renewal are frequently conceptualised in similar ways, which are equated with the four stages of life as well as with the annual passing of the four seasons.

Black Elk's vision, although complex and considered to be very powerful, is not extraordinary in terms of Plains patterning and symbolism: it is expected that power will reveal itself through motion, that such motion will relate directly to the Four Quarters, and that from the Four Quarters power can then be transferred or transmitted to everything else.

The Oglala Sioux shamans formalise this, using an esoteric language different from the everyday speech of the people, by saying that there is one great power which in ordinary language is called *Wakan Tanka* and which White observers have translated as Great Mystery or Great Spirit. Christian missionaries have identified this with God, as a benevolent presence which is manifested in every

were comparable with those of the buffalo. The Blackfoot consider such headdresses to be sacred objects and classify them as Medicine Bundles.

part of the Creation. The shamans, however, know that the power of *Wakan Tanka* governs and controls everything and benevolence is relative to the humility of the people and their correct observation of ritual and ceremony. The Plains deities are neither good nor bad, but capable of expressing their power either benevolently or malevolently in response to human actions and respect for, or neglect of,

167

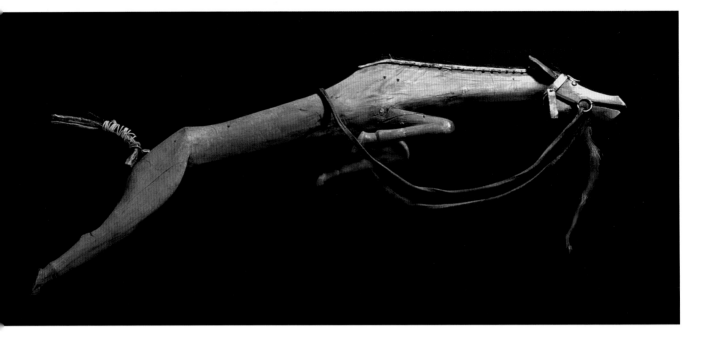

ABOVE: *The war pony was an integral part of Plains warfare after the introduction of the horse in the early 18th century, and horses wounded in battle were highly regarded as having given proof of their bravery. This wooden effigy was made by the Sioux and was carried during celebratory dances at which the horse was honoured. The holes marked with red paint represent the pony's wounds.*

their sacred duties.

In the shaman's language, *Wakan Tanka* is referred to as *Tobtob Kin*. A direct translation of this is Four-times-Four Gods, reminiscent of the four successive stages already encountered in Black Elk's vision. The Four Gods are *Wakan* (mysterious, or beyond normal comprehension) and each is only a part of *Wakan Tanka* whose presence is everywhere. The *Tobtob Kin*, to whom we can refer as the Superior Gods, are *Wikan* (Sun), *Hanwikan* (Moon), *Taku Skanskan* (Sky), and *Tatekan* (Wind). Each of these has Four Helpers, the Secondary or Associate Gods, which include *Yumnikan* (Whirlwind), *Makakan* (Earth), *Wohpe* (Beautiful Woman), *Inyankan* (Rock), *Wakinyan* (Thunder), *Tatankakan* (Buffalo), *Hunonpakan* (Grizzly Bear), *Wanagi* (Human Spirit), *Woniya* (Human Life), *Nagila* (Non-human Spirit), and *Wasicunpi* (Guardian Spirits). The *Tob Kin*, or Four Winds, are the Messengers or *Akicita* which enable communication between the people and the deities to take place.

The shamans say that the association of four Secondary Gods with each of the four Superior Gods is the reason they refer to *Wakan Tanka* as *Tobtob Kin*, or Four-times-Four, or as 16 different gods; but that each of these represents only one aspect of Creation. Some of these gods are visible, others are invisible, yet each of them has the power to do supernatural things. Only the shamans understand this, since through their prenatal connection with the Thunderers they have an insight denied to others and through their power visions they alone are given the sacred songs and face- and body-paints by which this initial shamanic contact can be re-established and made evident in the world of the people.

Ordinary visions, or 'power dreams', enable others to connect with this world of the spirits in a peripheral sense, through gaining long life, health, invulnerability, and so forth in accordance with the specific revelations and instructions given to them as individuals. However, with their greater visions the shamans are able to go back to the source of power: to the essence of *Wakan Tanka*. Black Elk, we should remember, was taken to the Centre of the World in his dream through the successive journeys his *nagi* had to undertake.

A definition of the Centre of the World is crucial to an understanding of Plains shamanism. Although Black Elk referred to this as Harney Peak in the Dakota Badlands, which he identified as the specific mountain he visited during his great vision, he also commented that the centre could be anywhere. He meant no contradiction by this. Just as the power of *Wakan Tanka* is a part of every-

ABOVE: *This canvas altar, which would formerly have been made of buckskin, was used by a Blackfoot Horse Doctor in rituals intended to increase wealth in horses. Such rites were extremely sacred and only the Horse Doctors and their wives were admitted to them; the right, or guest, side of the tipi remaining vacant during the ceremony.*
LEFT: *The buffalo-runner, or war and hunting pony, played a significant part in ceremonies in recognition of the importance that horses had in safeguarding their riders safety. Elaborate horse masks, such as this one from the Sioux, reflect this importance as well as serving as indicators that the pony was linked with the supernatural power of the spirit-animals. This mask portrays a buffalo.*

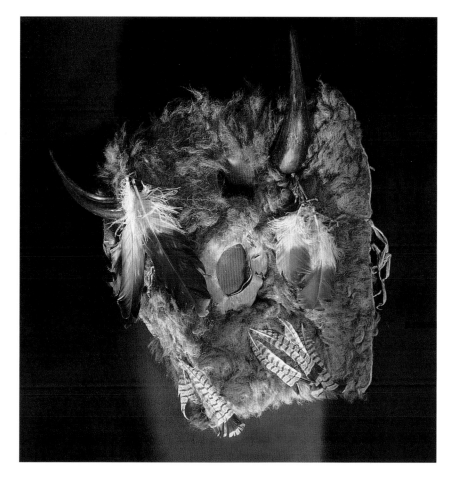

thing, so each thing also functions as a symbolic representation of this power and contains within itself all the potential forces of the cosmos. The Centre of the World can, therefore, be invested in a grain of sand just as readily as in such a dramatic and impressive representation as Harney Peak.

The shamans understand this concept of centredness as a focus of power rather than a physical place, but for ordinary people, lacking shamanic insight, it is necessary to recreate this centre by localising it or through the use of sacred objects and altars during rituals and ceremonies. Thus the sacred painted buffalo skull altar used during tribal renewal ceremonies becomes a symbolic representation of the Centre of the World and an expression of the life-giving power of Buffalo made manifest in the skull by the ritual activities of the shamans.

The shamans themselves do not require this specific identification of power with a particular object. In their knowledge that power is everywhere and that they are capable of travelling to its source, the shamans hold that power must in some way be held within them-selves as surely as it is manifested in the world about them. Through trance or meditation they can thus travel 'within themselves' to this internalised centre of power, force, or energy. At such times their

Stone is a symbol of permanence for Native American communities, and is considered to have existed before the creation of the present world.

TOP LEFT: *Quartzite charm in the form of a buffalo. Carried as a personal talisman, the charm established a connection between the bearer and the animal spirits.*

ABOVE LEFT: *The Crow had many Rock Medicines. They were kept in Medicine Bundles that were opened at the first sound of thunder in spring. The elaborate bead decoration on this example indicates that it was used for tribal, rather than individual, benefit.*

ABOVE: *The Blackfoot iniskim, or Buffalo Stone, was used during*

Calling the Buffalo rituals at times of scarcity. Most iniskim *are fossil forms, and when not in use are wrapped in buffalo hair and stored inside a Medicine Bundle.*

ABOVE: *Birds of prey featured prominently in warriors' vision quests, linking the warrior with the bird's ability to strike its prey swiftly and successfully.*
Such visions were interpreted by a shaman, who instructed the visionary to obtain tokens of the bird for use as a War Medicine. The eagle talon shown here is decorated with downy feathers, trade cloth, beads, and small bells, and was the personal talisman of a Crow warrior.

physical self and the spiritual force of the *nagi*, which has its own independent existence, become merged. In other words, the shaman's physical shell 'becomes spirit'.

In this spiritual form, achievable only by shamans, the *nagi* and the body are synchronised with all the forces present in the spiritual world, and particularly with the spirit or spirits that gave the shaman his various power dreams and visions, and via them with the greater powers for whom they act as the *akicita*, or messengers. Because of this focusing of power inside the self and the merging of the *nagi* and the body, the shaman during curing rites becomes 'possessed' or 'taken over' by the spirit. It is the spirit, or power-animal, that effects the cure, rather than the shaman himself. Many Plains shamans describe this state by saying that they act only as a means whereby spirit power can be realised in the world of the people: they are like a 'channel' through which power can pass from one realm to another.

George Catlin, who travelled along the Upper Missouri in the 1830s and recorded many Plains customs, witnessed a cure performed by a Blackfoot shaman influenced by Grizzly Bear. During the cure the shaman seemed to have taken on all the characteristics of the grizzly. Wearing a complete grizzly bear skin, the shaman prowled around the tipi in which the patient lay. His shuffling gait, pauses, the sounds he made, even the tentative way in which he touched the patient and rolled him over, made the shaman seem to be more bear than human. Catlin, in fact, was astonished at the accuracy and realism with which the bear was portrayed. To the Blackfoot, of course, the shaman was bear and not merely a human impersonation of the animal.

It would also be clear to a Blackfoot audience that this was not any ordinary bear but the specific supernatural Grizzly Bear that had appeared to the shaman in his dreams and which had returned at the shaman's call. Catlin noted that attached to the bear skin were the furs, beaks or claws of numerous other animals - what he called 'the odds and ends, and fag ends, of every imaginable creature' - each of which was a minor assistant to the Grizzly Bear shaman in the performance of the cure.

The practice of the shamanic vision thus varies considerably from the manner in which power derived from non-shamanic visions is expressed. In the non-shamanic vision the owner of power calls on the spirit animals to assist and in this way obtains some of the qualities of the power animal, but he does not become that animal. A hunter inspired by Hawk, for example, will gain ability to strike swiftly; yet it is clear that Hawk is functioning here only as a helper

171

In the 1830s the Swiss artist Karl Bodmer accompanied Prince Maximilian zu Wied during his travels among the tribes of the Upper Missouri, making numerous watercolours and drawings of the people and scenes that he witnessed.

LEFT: *The hide-wrapped poles in this shrine are effigies of the Sun and Moon, two of the most powerful deities in Mandan belief. Sun, the Lord of Life, was seen as a creator; Moon was associated with the life-giving properties of buffalo and corn.*

RIGHT: *Maximilian described this Assiniboine shrine as a 'magical device' that was intended to attract buffalo; although it was more probably used as a place of homage where small personal articles were left as a sacrifice to the buffalo gods. Bodmer painted this shrine in the summer of 1833 in the vicinity of Fort Union.*

and that although there is an association between the spirit and the hunter there is not an identification of one with the other as expressed by shamans in their relationship to the spirits by which they are influenced.

The distinction between shamanic and non-shamanic visions and spirit helpers is nevertheless not as clear-cut as implied above. The Crow Indians of the Bighorn Basin in Montana say that all power is *maxpé*, sacred, but that maxpé power may become manifest in numerous forms and degrees as well as that the granting of power by one animal spirit may result in the acquisition of power from another animal spirit with which the first is associated. Dreaming of Snake, for instance, which is a power of the Earth, automatically includes Otter, Chief of the Water Animals, since Snake and Otter complement each other and both are essential in the curing rites of the shamans. As far as the Crow are concerned, to invoke either of these powers independently of the other would be ineffective.

Robert H Lowie, an eminent anthropologist and the foremost student of the Crow Indians in the early 20th century, spent many years talking with prominent shamans and Elders of the tribe about their religious beliefs and practices. All of them explained that *maxpé* power derived ultimately from a single source, identified as *Bahkoore-Mahishtsedah* (He Above With Eyes Yellow) and who is equivalent to the Siouan concept of *Wakan Tanka*. Although some confusion exists about the identity of this creative power - due, in part, to the

ABOVE: *Cycles of renewal and permanence hold a core position within Plains Indian shamanism and ritual belief, and are frequently symbolised through naturally occurring phenomena. This photograph shows a cliff face in Red Rock Canyon State Park, Oklahoma, which is used as a breeding site by cliff swallows. The swallows return each year, adding new mud nests to the canyon walls and reusing the nests built in previous years. The return of the swallows is heralded as a sign of both renewal and of continuation.*

attempts of Christian missionaries to equate the Crow ideal with the Christian concept of God as an all-embracing deity named *Akba-tekdia* (He Who Does Everything) – it is generally thought of as a nebulous source of energy that is imparted to everything, and from which it can be spread and disseminated.

An early identification was given in 1862 to Robert Meldrum, a fur trader who lived among the Crow for 35 years and probably knew more about their traditional beliefs than any other White man before him. The Crow told Meldrum that all power came from a Great Spirit called Who Made It, which was deemed to mean that 'he is composed of all the vapory elements that existed before the world was formed'. He is equivalent to the contemporary Crow deity *Eehtrashhohedish*, whose name is usually translated as First Worker. It was First Worker, according to these reports, who gave power and purpose to everything and who enabled the birds, rocks, plants, trees, and so forth to bestow this power, in their role as supernatural helpers, on human beings.

Whether *Bahkoore-Mahishtsedah* or *Eehtrashhohedish* is the original creative force is, nevertheless, of little import in the actual practice of Crow shamanism. Power undoubtedly derives from some vague, perhaps unidentifiable energy source, and can be passed in varying degrees from this source to people. The man or woman who receives a limited amount of *maxpé* power in the settlement of a domestic matter receives this, essentially, from the same source as the spirit helpers that inspire the most famous and effective shamans. There is thus a continuum of power which is undifferentiated in origin.

It is nevertheless clear that the shamans function in ways that are different from those of other people: their power is greater, since they can return to the source which is inaccessible to others, but so, too, are their obligations and responsibilities as the spiritual guardians of the people. Lowie tried, unsuccessfully, to categorise Crow beliefs in terms of similarity in function and correspondences in the contents of Medicine Bundles. He found many Bundles containing virtually identical objects which were used for a variety of purposes while others that were very different from each other shared a similarity of function.

It is clear that the Crow, in common with the Sioux, Blackfoot, and other occupants of the western Great Plains, feel that the content of the vision – or of a succession of different visions – will determine the exact nature of the power that any individual can call on, and that some individuals are more favoured than others. Thus the appearance of Morning Star, a guardian of warriors, to two different

individuals might in the past have resulted in one simply gaining the right to join a war party and return safely, while the other might be offered a Medicine Pipe as an indication of his role as War Leader (status equivalent to that of Chief).

Shamans, too, display this great diversity in the amount of power they claim: from a simple healing ritual to power that theoretically throws a protective ring around the entire tribe. Shamans are also more likely than others to have a series of successive visions which serve to increase the power at their command and, at the same time, tends to differentiate them even more. No two Bear Shamans, who are always powerful, will have the same subsidiary helpers since their individual vision experiences by which additional power was granted will have been different. Even the original vision of Bear, who grants power to cure serious wounds and illnesses, may differ, with one individual granted, say, the power to heal deep cuts while another's skills might lie in the treatment of complex fractures.

Even so there is a sense of commonality or association between different shamans inspired by the same supernatural visitant. Thus all Oglala Sioux shamans who have dreamed of Bear are members of the Bear Dreamer Society and act as leaders during the curing rites. This power to lead is granted by the vision. At the same time, the

ABOVE: *The Redbud tree was adopted as the symbol of Oklahoma, the 46th state of the Union, when it was said to be emblematic of the eternal renewal of all life and to act as a symbol of red earth. The State Tree Resolution was, however, founded on earlier Native American beliefs held by tribes who had moved into what was then called Indian Territory as part of the forced relocation of Native peoples by the authorities. The Osage, in particular, held that the magenta blossoms of the Redbud contained the life-force of the tree and used ash from Redbud wood as a sacred paint.*

Bear Dreamer Society includes among its members all those who have been healed by the Bear Doctors, forming a kind of lay membership who act in support of the shamans but who possess no shamanic power of their own.

Similar ideals are found among the Crow in the Tobacco Society, although here the Society is divided into a number of different chapters as a consequence of the varying sanctioning visions of its shaman-leaders. The rites of the Society, although ostensibly concerned with the spring planting of sacred tobacco seeds (*nicotiana multivalvis*, rather than the commonly smoked *nicotiana quadrivalvis* which was obtained in trade from the Hidatsa), are a complex amalgam of individual vision experiences combined with a general blessing for tribal welfare, growth, and prosperity.

Tobacco Society rituals also reflect the Plains tendency to think of sacred actions as taking place in a succession of four movements. On each day of the four-day planting ceremony the entire camp moves to a new location, where collective and individual rites and minor ceremonies take place. Later, at the time 'When the Wild Cherries are Ripe', the crop is harvested with a similar set of four camp movements, following which the leaves are stripped from the tobacco stems and the entire crop is sacrificed to a nearby river. The rites of the Tobacco Society - gathering of seeds, planting, growth, and harvest - are thought of as a reflection of the four sacred movements, or the four phases of life. Sacred tobacco is used only for this purpose and is never smoked; thereby reinforcing its sacred function.

Links between individuals might also be reinforced by the actual vision itself. Many visions, especially among the Blackfoot and

Hair was considered to be the seat of the 'soul' or 'spirit', and Plains shamans formed the hair into a characteristic top-knot style as insignia of their calling. Karl Bodmer painted a number of shamans with this hairstyle.
ABOVE LEFT: *The Atsina chief and shaman Niätóhsä, who travelled on the keelboat* Flora *with Maximilian and Bodmer. His hair is painted with red ochre as a sign that he was the owner of a sacred Medicine Pipe.*
ABOVE CENTRE AND RIGHT: *Neither of these shamans is identified by name in Maximilian's Journal, and Bodmer inscribed both sketches as 'Piegan medicine man'. However, the facial painting on the left figure is remarkably similar to that shown on the portrait of the Atsina shaman Niätóhsä, and it is more than likely that this is a representation of the same individual.*

Crow, specify that a Medicine Bundle, or an object from the Bundle, has to be replicated a certain number of times, and the individuals to whom these copies are distributed are then thought of as having shared in the original vision. The Arrow Medicine of the Crow is a case in point. According to its origin myth, the Arrow Medicine was given to a man named Bear-in-the-Water by Morning Star, and in the vision he was told that power had been granted by the Seven Stars (the Pleiades) and, consequently, he was to make seven Medicine Bundles each containing a different colour arrow and was to distribute these to other members of the tribe whose own visions qualified them to become owners. Although the owners of the Arrow Bundles do not form a shamanic fraternity, each of them is

LEFT: *Pioch-Kiäiu was among the Blackfoot at Fort McKenzie when their camp was attacked by a force of Assiniboine and Cree warriors. Pioch-Kiäiu survived the attack and later told Bodmer that, although his own shamanic spirits had failed to predict the event, the portrait that Bodmer had painted of him had saved him from the bullets of his enemies.*

thought of as related through the original vision of Bear-in-the-Water.

The Blackfoot have taken this concept of transferable power a stage further by introducing the idea that the privileges associated with major Medicine Bundles, or *saam*, are purchasable rights; which generally involve considerable expense on the part of the purchaser. While it is still believed that the original, or sanctioning, right had to be secured in a vision, it is possible through a ritual re-enactment of this vision to pass full- or part-ownership of the Bundle on to someone else.

In Blackfoot Bundle transfers, the owner of the Bundle becomes 'ceremonial father' to the 'ceremonial son' who is its recipient. This, in fact, re-enacts the original relationship between the vision-seeker and the spirit animal who adopted him in the original transfer of power. Shamanic power may similarly be transferred through the adoption of an initiate, and this power may later be elaborated if the shaman receives further visions enabling him to add elements to the original Bundle received from his adoptive 'ceremonial father'. We are reminded here of the Blackfoot Bear Shaman observed by Catlin who, in addition to the use of a bear skin costume, employed tokens representing spirit animals which had appeared to him in a number of different visions.

The principles of transferable privileges introduce another aspect to the practice of shamanism, since it is clear that later initiates are thought to share in the original vision but do not necessarily require a sanctioning vision of their own. They are, in fact, taught the rituals and the accompanying face- and body-paints by the 'ceremonial father' acting in lieu of the spirit animals. In some senses this takes us away from pure shamanism, since the right to practice is removed from the realm of the spirits and paid for in the realm of the mundane.

Such secondary acquisition of power tends to create a group of people, related through sharing in a common Bundle ceremony, who function as ritualists: they can bring desired results by learning about and then correctly performing the rituals, but do not enter ecstatic trances and do not become possessed by the spirit animals in the manner of the curing shamans. These ritualists or Bundle Owners, especially among the Blackfoot but also among other western Plains tribes, form an elite of wealthy and often elderly men who, with the assistance of their wives, are responsible for maintaining the ritual integrity of the tribe and thereby gain positions of social prominence.

OPPOSITE: *Mexkemauastan, or Stirring Iron, was an Atsina chief and shaman who the year prior to Bodmer's visit had threatened to kill the superintendent at Fort McKenzie. Although his attitude towards the visitors was tolerant, his standing as a warrior is indicated by the fact that he is armed with both a gun and bow and arrows.*

RIGHT: *George Catlin was the most prolific recorder of Native American life in the 1830s. He produced several hundred sketches and paintings of the people he met. The paintings shown here were both made in 1832 during a visit of Sioux chiefs, warriors, and shamans to Fort Pierre. Little Bear* (RIGHT) *was a member of the Hunkpapa Sioux.*

There is thus a distinction between the role of the ecstatic shaman as a doctor and seer and that of the taught ritualist who officiates at Bundle ceremonies. The distinction is not completely clear-cut, since any individual may be both a shaman and ritualist, and, as we have seen, the ritualistic performances are, essentially, re-enactments of the original visions through which power is given to the people. It is not unusual for the purchaser of ritual privileges to pledge to do so only at a period of personal crisis, which echoes in some respects the near-death experiences that often lead to shamanic insight.

A case in point is the well-known Sun Dance of the Blackfoot, which today has come to take on the appearance of an annual trib-al renewal ceremony. This appearance is, however, misleading, since

Tchan-dee (Tobacco) belonged to the Oglala band. Catlin described Tchan-dee as 'one of the most respectable and famous chiefs of the tribe'; however, both Little Bear's and Tchan-dee's hairstyles indicate that they were active shamans.

the Sun Dance is pledged in fulfilment of an individual vow made during a period of personal crisis. The name itself is a misnomer - stemming from the generic application of the word for a Sioux ceremony called Gazing at the Sun - and the Blackfoot Sun Dance is more properly known as the Medicine Lodge. Like many Plains rituals its form is a composite one, but in myth it is said to have originated with a girl who promised to marry a Star and it is from her that it takes its characteristic form.

In the originating myth a girl and a girlfriend of hers idly speculated about what it would be like to marry a star and, pointing to a bright star low on the horizon, she said, 'That is the one I will marry.' A few days later, while she was again lost in her dreams, a handsome young man appeared and claimed her as his wife, saying

181

that he, Morning Star, had come for her to fulfil her promise. He took her to the home of his parents, Sun and Moon, where she was given every freedom but warned never to dig up a sacred turnip that grew near their house. Her curiosity, however, overcame her and with the help of Crane Woman she dug the turnip. Through the hole left by the removal of the turnip she could see the camp of her people far below, and, longing to visit her parents, she persuaded Morning Star to let her return to earth.

Morning Star assented and gave her a ceremony, the Medicine Lodge, to take back to her people, as well as a Medicine Bundle called the *Natoas* (Sacred Turnip Headdress). He also promised her that if her people were ever in danger or distress that they could call on him for assistance by asking a virtuous woman to make a pledge on their behalf. This woman, known as the Sacred Woman, plays the role of the girl who married a star, and the Medicine Lodge is, in essence, a re-enactment of the transfer of the Natoas by Morning Star. Although the *Natoas* transfer is so vital in the Medicine Lodge, the actual transfer takes place secretly when the former Sacred Woman and her husband transfer their rights in the *Natoas* to the incoming Sacred Woman who has made the pledge and her husband.

The complex nature of the ceremony means, however, that numerous other elements have been added to the Natoas to give the impression of a tribal ritual. Scar-Face, a culture hero who travelled to the Sun and helped defeat the monster birds that threatened Morning Star, has given elements; as has Elk-Woman and the Owners of the oldest and most sacred Medicine Bundles, in particular those of the Beaver Medicines. In addition there are numerous rituals associated with other Bundles, the fulfilment of personal pledges, as well as a great deal of social dancing and feasting. In fact, the entire tribe is involved either as direct participants or as witnesses.

The shamans play a major role here as well. The Sacred Woman's pledge and the transfer of the *Natoas* are under the control of a respected shaman, as are all the other major rites that take place. In addition, Weather Shamans attempt to ensure good days for the four-day period during which the main ceremonies take place, and other individuals who have made pledges each seek the advice of shamans in their devotions. The roles of the shamans who have received sanction in highly personal visions and those of the ritualists who gain their experience through having been taught, overlap and interact in complex ways in major rituals such as the *Natoas* of the Blackfoot or the Tobacco Society of the Crow.

OPPOSITE: *This photograph of Bear Bull, a Blackfoot, was taken in 1899 by Edward Curtis. Bear Bull's hairstyle indicates that he was a shaman and Medicine Pipe owner. Curtis was an intrepid traveller throughout the remote regions of North America, and was driven by what he felt was a need to record a comprehensive visual history of the tribes before they succumbed totally to white influence.*

THE SACRED HOOP: PLAINS SHAMANISM

It is nevertheless in the eastern Prairies, among the semi-nomadic groups, that this blending of the ecstatic and the learned is given its fullest expression, since here there are clear indications that personal visions open a path into shamanism that is expressed through apprenticeship to highly structured shamanic organisations and fraternities in which membership may also be dependent on hereditary rights. Although at first this appears to be a contradiction, it is worth looking more closely to see how such disparate ideals have become so intimately connected.

A clue is given in the lifestyles of the semi-nomadic tribes. For six months of the year they live in permanent villages, close to which are extensive fields of corn, beans, and squash. Houses are often massive structures. The former earth-lodges of the Pawnee, for instance, were large enough to house several generations of an extended family and, in winter, also served as stabling for the prized hunting ponies, or buffalo-runners. Part of the crop gathered each autumn was dried and stored in massive underground storage pits located in various parts of each village, and this often served as a staple food during the winter months when hunting was less productive.

For the remaining six months of the year, however, these large permanent villages were virtually abandoned. The entire tribe, men, women, and children, packed up its belongings after the spring plantings and engaged in seasonal buffalo hunts. During this period they followed the migrating herds and lived in skin-covered portable tipis, adopting a lifestyle identical to that of their western nomadic neighbours and returning to the permanent villages only in autumn in time for harvesting. The tribes thus spent half the year as sedentary agriculturalists, and half as nomadic hunters.

Some students of Plains culture have attempted to interpret this as a blending of two cultures, known as the Northern Hunting Tradition with an emphasis on individual shamanism and the Southern Agrarian with its emphasis on collective priesthoods. In this view, hunting traditions of northern tribes migrating on to the Plains from areas at too high a latitude to support farming have mixed with those of other groups migrating from southern areas where corn was a staple. Although this has the advantage of creating a neat and logical explanation, it goes only part way to explaining the unique cultural features of Plains semi-nomadism.

The Northern Hunting Tradition is, in fact, unlikely to have had such an influential impact on the semi-nomadic Plains tribes, simply because there is little evidence to suggest major migrations from the far north except for those of the Apache and Navaho to the south-

ABOVE: *Hell's Half Acre, Wyoming. This is the site of a prehistoric buffalo jump, or piskun; a method of hunting*

184

in which a shaman disguised as a buffalo lured the animals to the edge of a cliff, where the herd was stampeded over the edge. Such tactics were an essential strategy in the pre-horse period, when pedestrian hunters were at a disadvantage in killing highly mobile game in order to supply the camp. It was felt that the shaman's success in ensuring adequate food supplies was due to the intervention of helpful animal spirits.

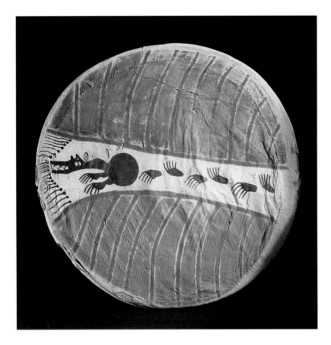

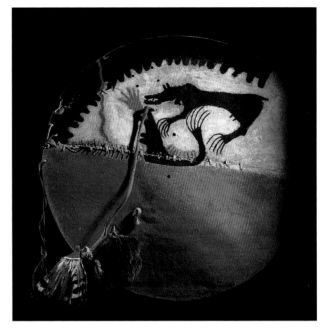

ern Plains or of the Sarcee alliance with the Blackfoot in Alberta. Indeed, large Plains tribes such as the Sioux and Blackfoot actually migrated from eastern farming areas onto the Plains but abandoned any attempts at agriculture after their arrival, as did the Cheyenne whose well-documented movement onto the Plains from the east at the beginning of the nineteenth century shows a rapid abandonment of farming in favour of nomadic hunting. Even the Crow, who separated from the village-farming Hidatsa of the Upper Missouri relatively recently, retained only a token element of farming in their Tobacco Society rituals but grew no staple crops.

Southern Agrarian, perhaps, has a stronger claim to influence. Caddoan groups, such as the Pawnee and Wichita, and Siouan groups, including the Oto, Omaha, and Osage, moved on to the Plains from the south/southwest and east, bringing with them traditions relating to the structured hierarchies of crop-growing societies. Yet even here there is no precedent for the wholesale abandonment of permanent villages for half the year nor of nomadic pursuit of game herds.

We should, instead, look to the Plains themselves: to these vast expanses of grass and the sense of movement integral to them, and to the habits of the animals that occupy these regions. All herd animals such as the buffalo, the mainstay of Plains hunting economies, white-tail deer, and the wild horse (mustang), are range animals. They do not stay long in any one place, but are constantly on the

Prior to the introduction of the breech-loading rifle, Plains shields offered their bearers physical protection. Made from the heat-shrunk neck skin of a buffalo bull they were strong enough to stop arrows or to deflect bullets from muzzle-loaders. Their efficacy was however thought to reside in the power vested in them through the animal spirits painted on their surfaces. The Crow shields shown here rely on the power of Bear or Buffalo to protect the owner.
ABOVE LEFT: *This shield depicts a bear that has been flushed from its den. It is charging forward to face a hail of bullets indicated by the 'tadpole' figures near the edge*
ABOVE: *The bears on this shield are inspired by a vision of a ferocious female bear with another bear emerging from the red field.*

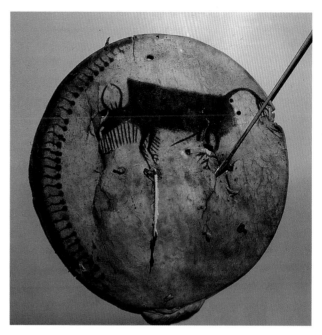

The red hand coming from the bear's mouth is a symbol of war. Bear's ears attached to the shield provide a link between the real animal and its spiritual counterpart.

ABOVE: *The bear paw in the centre of this shield shows the principal spirit animal that safeguarded the shield owner. The attachment of hawk feathers suggests, however, that the shield owner had more than one spirit helper and could call on the power of both Bear and Hawk.*

ABOVE RIGHT: *The buffalo was a symbol of the life-giver or life-sustainer, and was therefore a potent helper to the warrior since it guaranteed the preservation of the shield bearer's own life.*

move. Even territorial animals, such as wolves and coyotes, range over vast territories of hundreds of square miles. There is little that is static or localised in Plains animal life.

Combined with this is the fact that farming, even in the fertile river floodlands of the eastern regions, is always uncertain without the introduction of complex irrigation systems. The semi-nomadic tribes simply responded to these environmental concerns, growing corn and hunting buffalo as complementary aspects of their economies, and, consequently, combining the individual powers and animistic beliefs of the shamans as the Masters of Animals with those of the priestly hierarchies attuned to the repetitive cycles of the growing season.

The most elaborate organisation occurs among the Pawnee, whose shamans combine the individual skills of the vision inspired shaman with those of the structured learning of a partially hereditary priesthood. This is explained in Skidi Pawnee cosmology. *Tirawa*, the Supreme Being or Creator, was wedded to *Atira* (Born From Corn, or Vault of Heaven). *Tirawa* placed all the deities, the Stars, in position in the Sky, and it was at his will that Morning Star married Evening Star, and that Sun married Moon. The child of Morning Star and Evening Star, a girl, married the child of Sun and Moon, a boy, and *Tirawa* placed these on the Earth. Each of the thirteen Skidi villages was given a Medicine Bundle which had to be opened at the first sound of Thunder in spring; but four of these

ABOVE: *A warrior's shield was his most valued possession. It was considered sacred and thought to be invested with the supernatural power of the animal depicted on it, in this case a bear. Its power could however be dissipated through contact with the earth, and for this reason shields were never allowed to touch the ground. When not in use they might be displayed outside the tipi on a special tripod, as shown here. They were frequently moved during the day so that they would always face towards the life-giving power of Sun.*

Bundles were pre-eminent, and a fifth, the Evening Star Bundle, took precedence over all others. The Evening Star Priest is said to be the only person who had the knowledge to bring the power of all the other Medicine Bundles together and, as such, his position was superior to that even of the titular chiefs. All of this was pre-ordained by *Tirawa*, and in recognition of this every earth-lodge in a Skidi village was a representation of the star patterns and the village layout itself was a cosmological map of the heavens.

In this system we can already see the structure of an agricultural community: everything is set in place and has an immutable role in the repetitive annual cycle that is so closely linked with planting and harvest. Yet, at the same time, each Bundle Owner, through whom *Tirawa's* power was manifested, had to obtain a sanctioning vision from the animal spirits and ultimate power resided in the Evening Star Priest whose principal function in times of scarcity was to perform the Calling The Buffalo ceremony.

Inevitably, the close cooperation of the Bundle Priests in the political and religious organisation of the Pawnee led to the formation of shamanic fraternities or societies, some of which are closely paralleled by similar societies among other semi-nomadic groups such as the Osage, or among the nomadic Sioux or Crow. These societies functioned both to pass on the knowledge of the older shamans to their protégés, since an experienced and famous shaman often had a number of disciples, but they also served as public forums through which shamanic power could be demonstrated and validated.

The most elaborate public demonstrations of shamanic power are, again, to be found among the Skidi, whose shamans gather together each year in early autumn in a special earth-lodge, with the initiates, to give performances witnessed by large numbers of spectators. On these occasions the earth-lodge is ceremonially prepared as a representation of the spiritual universe. The fireplace is cleared and a Turtle effigy is modelled in its place, so that new fire can be built on Turtle's back. Surrounding the fireplace is the mythical Water Monster, with a clay figure of a woman at the south and a rawhide male effigy placed above the lodge. By these means the power of Sun (new fire), Moon (the woman), and the Morning Star (the male effigy) are all brought into symbolic existence.

The shamans' performances are preceded by a parade through the village, each shaman wearing a costume and carrying paraphernalia dedicated to the animal spirit by which he is inspired. Then, after a secret dedication ceremony, the earth-lodge is opened to the public.

RIGHT: *The Pawnee are said to have had the most complex cosmology of all the Plains tribes, and relied heavily on interpretations of the movements and positions of the stars. This buckskin map, or Star Chart, is a representation of the night sky. The clustered stars through the centre represent the Milky Way.*

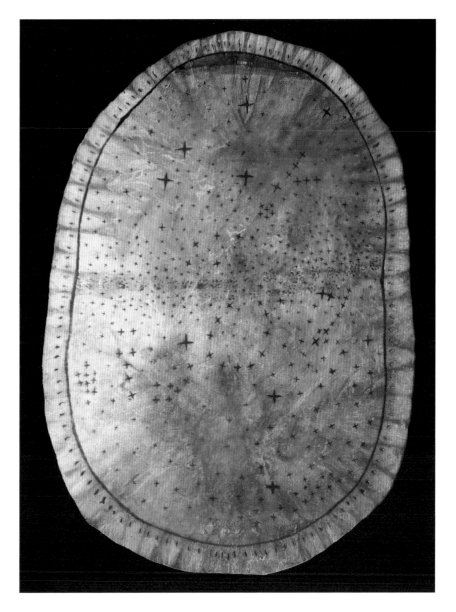

During the public parts of the performance the *Iruska* shamans demonstrate their ability in controlling the supernatural: some make their animal spirits appear or disappear at will, others demonstrate their power over their rivals by forcing them to act in involuntary ways, while others demonstrate their immunity to pain by handling burning corn cobs or taking meat out of a kettle of boiling water with their bare hands.

Similar feats, particularly of fire-handling ability, have frequently been described for other tribes as well, as in the skill of the Sioux *Heyoka* shamans to walk or stand on red hot coals or to stir the kettles of ritually prepared dog meat with their bare arms prior to using their hands to ladle out meat from the pot to the assembled guests. Other miraculous feats are reported for Crow shamans, who are said to be able to make the entire audience fall over to one side simply by gesturing at them or to make a seed of corn sprout, grow, and mature within the space of a few minutes. Bear Shamans might tear a man to pieces, rip out and devour his raw liver, and then restore him to life unharmed; or they will ask someone to cut them open with a knife, fall dead, and then after some time rise up with no visible trace of any wound.

Numerous, but unconvincing, attempts have been made to explain these demonstrations of shamanic power: they have been described as a form of mass delusion or hypnosis, or as clever sleight-of-hand or magical tricks performed with the aid of chosen accomplices hidden in the audience. Fire-handling has been mundanely described as made possible through ritual preparation in which the shamans smear their hands and arms with bear's grease so they will not feel the heat. Whatever the explanation, whether due to trickery on the shamans' part or attributable to some inexplicable power the shamans possess, all observers are unanimous in declaring how spectacular and realistic these performances appear to be.

This, however, introduces another peculiar aspect of Plains shamanism, since is is often the case that the more sacred and significant a shaman's actions are then the less spectacular and the more secretive they appear to be. A case in point is the Blackfoot Medicine Lodge, where the defining aspect of the ceremony - the transfer of the sacred Natoas headdress - takes place in a closed tipi with only the immediate participants as witness. The Arapaho Sacred Pipe ceremony, their single most important ritual, similarly consists simply of the shaman unwrapping the sacred flat-stemmed pipe, purifying it in a smudge of sage, and then replacing it in its container, all performed before an audience of only four or five people: the Pipe Keeper and his wife, the pledger of the ceremony, and the shaman's assistant.

Indeed, the larger part of any Plains shaman's activities is conducted away from the public gaze. Acquisition of power, and its reinforcement and increase through successive additions, is via lonely vigil in an isolated spot distant from other people; and much of the shaman's time is spent in silent contemplation of the forces by which he is surrounded and in personal communion with his guiding spirits. It is only in relatively rare public demonstrations that the spirit manifests itself openly and that the shaman becomes ecstatically possessed; most of the time the power is simply, and quietly, carried

OPPOSITE: *Pawnee belief was based on a deep understanding of the movements and positions of the stars and planets, and that these combined in the form of Tirawahut (the Universe and Everything Within).*
The ceremonial cycle began with the first thunder in spring, and Thunder was conceived as the Voice of Heaven. On this hand drum Thunder is shown in the form of a giant bird, which hurls lightning bolts at a group of darting swallows.

within himself.

Yet in everything the shaman does, the concept of movement takes precedence. Sacred objects, such as the Medicine Bundles, are moved continuously throughout the day so that they always face the Sun. The shaman's contemplations are thought of as part of his journey towards understanding and enlightenment. Ceremonies are only effective if they follow a sacred path, with ritual stops on the jour-

ney. Everything is carried by and expressed in movement. The movements of the buffalo herds that were so essential to Plains survival are clear indicators of the ways in which the deities impart motion to the world, but even the agricultural year is tied to the gradual growth of crops, which echo the seasonal movements and

OPPOSITE: *This Crow shield decorated with the head of a crane and eagle feathers represents a vision given by Moon to its bearer. Such shields were used by shamans to predict the fate of war parties. The shield was rolled along the ground, and if it fell face up then the war party was assured of success.*

which, in turn, repeat the cycle of life in both the human and spiritual realms.

According to the Sioux shamans, the concept of movement is an essential aspect of creation itself. When the world was formed and its individual constituent parts given their roles in maintaining its balance, each of them was given charge of a part of the motivating spiritual force that pervades all things: through this they achieve their individual identity, but they also function as inseparable elements and each contains the entire cosmos within itself. This motivating force, without which existence is unthinkable, is called simply That Which Moves.

7 *Werowances and Soothsayers*

SOUTHEAST SHAMANISM

When the Spanish entered the Southeast in the sixteenth century they encountered numerous tribes whose leaders claimed direct descent from an omnipotent Sun God. Although their religion depended on paying homage to a host of minor deities, or Servant Spirits, who controlled and directed many facets of everyday life, the myths explained the belief that at some time in the distant past the son of the Supreme Deity had descended to earth, when he had given the people their laws, ceremonies, and social customs, and had also decreed that his word would thereafter be vested in his descendants - the Sun caste or clan - and that through them he would be honoured and revered.

The Sun thereby gave these families the right to represent his interests on earth, and all the Servant Spirits were subservient to his whims and wishes. As a token of his presence he left the people a remarkable stone, said to be of clear crystal and too heavy for a man to lift but through which the grain of a man's hand could be clearly seen, which was to be preserved in perpetuity. Loss of this stone would result in the destruction of the tribes, and great care was therefore taken to preserve and safeguard it for future generations.

The care of this stone was in the hands of a caste of priests, over whom the Great Sun was both Chief and High Priest. It was preserved in a temple built on top of a great earth mound, where there were also relics of the minor deities and within which the priests maintained a perpetual fire that symbolised the life-giving energy force of the Sun himself. The Spanish remarked on these massive

LEFT: *When the Spanish arrived in the southern parts of the Southeast in the early 16th century they called the area Florida, the Flourishing Land, reflecting the abundant sub-tropical growth and teeming wildlife of the region. The Florida swamps offered a benign environment for tribes such as the Calusa, enabling them to devote plenty of time to developing a complex mythology and elaborate ritual life.*

195

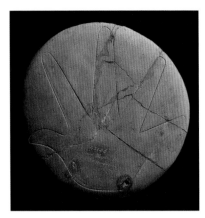

ABOVE: *The hand was a powerful and enduring shamanic symbol throughout the Southeast and the Eastern Woodlands. It symbolised personal contact between the spirits and the individual and functioned as a signifier of possession or power. This fine-grained stone disc marked with an engraved hand is from the Hopewell culture and is about 2,000 years old.*

temple mounds, noting that they were also places in which the bones of previous Great Suns and their families were interred. Tonti, who travelled with the De Soto expedition of 1540, wrote of the Taensa village on the Lower Mississippi that:

> there is a temple opposite the house of the chief, and similar to it, except that three [carved] eagles are placed on this temple, who look toward the rising sun. The temple is surrounded with strong mud walls, in which are fixed spikes, on which they place the heads of their enemies whom they sacrifice to the sun.

Despite the extreme reverence in which these temples were held – the Great Sun of the Natchez Indians and his wife coming every evening, for example, 'to worship their idols' – the Spanish, searching for gold, invaded some of them and put the guardian priests to the sword. But instead of the gold and other precious materials they expected to find, they discovered only skeletons bedecked with shell beads, broken fragments of pottery, mica carvings, and stone pipes and other implements. The English also noted that in some temples were small niches, covered with woven mats, in which were kept idols, variously described as Kiwasa or Oké dependent on the local dialect, and which were said to 'shew terrible' and to be 'evill favouredly carved', and which were the most revered of objects. European disappointment at not finding the wealth they sought led to bitter persecution in which they attempted to force the chiefs to reveal their 'hidden' caches, and equally bitter response from the tribes who led the Europeans in bewildering circuits for this non-existent treasure and almost succeeded in exterminating them in the process.

By accident, the Europeans had stumbled across the last remaining vestiges of the once-flourishing Mississippian Culture. These people, perhaps by association through trade with the Aztec Empire of Meso-America, believed that the deities resided on earth and made their presence known among the people through the reincarnation of a supreme god whose powers were limitless. By all accounts, common people would sacrifice their lives to this demi-god rather than cause any offence by impious behaviour, and the Great Sun was carried everywhere in a litter lined with swansdown, goose feathers, and bearskins so that his feet would not be contaminated by touching the earth on which ordinary people trod.

The Great Sun was an extraordinary individual; someone who had been touched by the hand of the Supreme Deity and who was thereafter separate from common people. He was woken in the morning by a shaman/priest who whispered gently in his ear so as not to startle him, and every morsel of food he ate was first tasted by one of the priests to ensure it would suit his taste and would be acceptable. At his death, the entire nation went into mourning: mothers sacrificed their first-born at the feet of the priests leading his funeral procession, and his closest relatives begged to be strangled so that they might accompany him to the other world.

There was an emphasis on death and reincarnation, since the rebirth of the Sun each day was crucial to the continuation of life, and the most complete early description of the appearance of the shamans is consequently from a detailed account of the funeral of a Natchez named Tattooed Serpent, who is variously described as the Great Sun or as the First War Leader, which was written by Du Pratz in 1758. In this description the shaman is described as the 'master of

BELOW: *The German publisher Theodore De Bry made this engraving after a watercolour by John White, who accompanied Sir Walter Raleigh in 1585 when he founded the first English colony on Roanoke Island (North Carolina). White describes this as a wooden effigy of an idol named Kiwasa. It was kept in a temple at the town of Secotan. White notes that the idol had a 'terrible aspect', although this is not apparent from De Bry's engraving.*

ceremonies', wearing

> a red-feathered crown, which half encircled his head, having a red
> staff in his hand in the form of a cross, at the end of which hung
> a garland of black feathers. All the upper part of his body was
> painted red, excepting his arms, and from his girdle to his knees
> hung a fringe of feathers, the rows of which were alternately
> white and red.

From other descriptions we know that the shamans habitually cut their hair in distinctive patterns, wore cloaks and other clothing different from ordinary garments, and often fastened insignia of their rank – such as a stuffed bird skin or other animal charm – in their hair. By these means they distinguished themselves from ordinary people and claimed an exclusiveness that extended only to the shamans and the werowance, or chief, who, in his dual function as Chief Priest, shared with them the distinction of supernatural sanction and direct contact or descent from the denizens of the other world.

This other world, too, was often exclusive. Among some of the Algonquian-speaking tribes, for instance, it was reserved only for the werowances and their families and for the priests, who would reside there for a short time before being reincarnated, but was forbidden to the common people. Such a world was described to the English colonists as being

> beyond the mountaynes . . . where the sun setts into most pleasant
> fields, growndes, and pastures, where yt shall doe no labour; but,
> stuck finely with feathers, and painted with oyle and pocones, rest
> in all quiet and peace, and eat delicious fruicts, and have store of
> copper, beades, and hatchetts; sing, daunce, and have all variety
> of delights and merryments.

Even among tribes who believed that the souls of all deceased travelled to another world, this notion of division still prevailed. Thus, among the Siouan-speaking tribes of the area, it was felt that the crystal gate to the other world was guarded by an old man who sat in judgement on all who appeared before him. Only the righteous and good could pass his scrutiny and enter this Land of Delights, but the wicked – that is, those who had failed in some way to show the deepest respect and reverence during their lives – were condemned to a dark and barren country where winter prevailed

OPPOSITE: *The Indians of the Southeast, especially those of the so-called Mississippian Culture and of Florida and the Everglades, believed that the Sun was the supreme Life-Giver. His representative on earth, who functioned both as a secular leader and as high priest, held status as a semi-divine being whose rule was absolute but who was nevertheless under strict obligation to perform ritual procedures that guaranteed the continuation of the tribe. Among these was the observation of the sun at both its rising and setting, when it was addressed in prayer and spoken to as the 'father' of the tribe.*

198

RIGHT: *John White referred to the 'Flyer' he painted here as a 'conjuror' or 'juggler', a 16th century reference to the fact he was a shaman. The small black bird attached to the shaman's hair was said to be the shaman's 'badge of office' and was most certainly a form of Medicine through which the shaman claimed to derive power. Although White was generally very suspicious of the shamans, whom he believed to consort with devils, he nevertheless made the interesting comment that many of the events they predicted were later found to come true.*

The flyer.

and where they were forced to reside for a number of years appropriate to the transgressions they had committed on earth.

In this world they became old, lost their teeth, and suffered per-

ABOVE: *A 1585 watercolour by John White, showing Algonquian Indians during a ritual dance at the village of Secotan. White noted that this was a 'grand and solemn occasion' and commented on the carved posts that marked out the sacred enclosure within which the dancing took place. Such effigies almost certainly represented guardian deities intended to prevent malign forces from entering the dance circle.*

petual hunger. Their only companions were haggard old women with 'Claws like a Panther, with which they fly upon the Men that Slight their Passion' and who were said to 'talk much and exceedingly Shrill, giving exquisite Pain to the Drum of the Ear, which in [this] Place of the Torment is so tender, that every Sharp Note wounds it to the Quick'. For many people death was not a release from this life and a pleasant interlude before they could be reborn, as it was for the chiefs and shamans, but was, instead, a punishment for any wrongs they had committed while living.

Although the Spanish, as well as the French and English, quickly realised the exclusiveness and authority that the werowances and shamans held over their people, and played up to this in attempting to form political alliances that would serve their own purposes, they

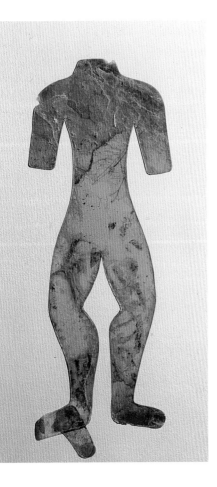

ABOVE: *The focus of Hopewell culture was the Scioto Valley in Ohio, c. 100 BC – 600 AD. Many of the larger earthworks include burial mounds which contained elaborate burial goods made from precious materials that were often traded over vast distances. This partial human figure is made from sheet mica imported from the Appalachian Mountains. The exact function of the figure is not known, although, like other goods that have been recovered, it clearly had no practical use and served purely as a ritual burial offering.*

were nevertheless dismissive of the powers that the shamans claimed. To them the shamans were 'quacks, magicians, and coniurors' whose only intent was to fool and deceive the general population. Indeed, in the early texts, the word 'coniuror' (conjuror) is synonymous with shaman: it was used to imply magic and trickery on the shaman's part, and his activities are invariably described as deliberately fraudulent.

Yet we need to look a little more closely at these societies and at the social conditions that prevailed within them to understand the shamanic role more clearly. Southeastern economies were based on agriculture and the cultivation of a 'Holy Trinity' of corn, beans, and squash, known as the Three Mothers. Fertile land was restricted to floodwater plains along the major rivers, and, with the establishment of large ceremonial and population centres, competition for such land was intense. The temple described by Tonti which was surrounded with spikes on which the heads of enemies were displayed is an indicator of the necessity to secure tribal territories by deterring or subjugating neighbouring groups.

Under these conditions warfare was endemic, and captured enemies were enslaved to till the extensive fields that surrounded major religious centres, some of which had population in excess of 15,000 or 20,000 people. Thus it was essential for the tribes to establish centralised administration, which was effected through the offices of the hereditary chiefs and the shaman/priests, as well as by a class system of Nobles and Honoured People supported by elite warrior societies. These people, who were usually full tribal members rather than the members of subject tribes, were distinguished by their elaborate tattooing, striking hairstyles, and distinctive clothing; yet in many tribes the commoners - people without status, adoptees, and slaves - greatly outnumbered the ruling elite, and sanction to rule therefore had to be granted by unquestioned right which they were forced to accept.

Although this right was exercised by the chiefs, it was nevertheless maintained and perpetuated by the shamans who, despite the European perception of them as frauds, were the pivot around which society revolved. We have already seen that the chiefs functioned equally as High Priests: that is, their power was both secular and religious. Far from being the despotic autocrats the Europeans took them for, they were subject to the dictates of both the secular and religious hierarchies. Simply because their power to govern came from their supposed divine birthright as the sons of the Sun, this did not absolve them from duties and responsibilities, since even the

BELOW: *The Great Serpent Mound in Ohio is the most spectacular of the great earth monuments erected by the early Adena-Hopewell peoples. It winds along a hilltop and encloses a circular burial mound within the serpent's jaws. It was not, however, built primarily as a burial site and has yielded few archaeological finds or grave goods. Its specific function is unknown, although it appears to have acted as a sacred clan marker and to have served important ceremonial purposes.*

deities had specific roles in safeguarding the welfare of the people. As political and religious leaders, they were both *werowances*, or Chiefs, and *quioughcosughes*, or Holy Men.

The temples in which the sacred remains of the previous *werowances* were interred thus functioned as a focus of secular and religious authority. The perpetual fire maintained in these temples was a symbol of the Sun and also a symbol of the *werowance's* divine right to rule, and thus was a symbol of the integrity and stability of the nation itself. If the fire died out through the negligence of one of the priests he would be immediately put to death, but the status of the *werowance* would thereby suffer since his symbol on earth has been extinguished, revealing his mortality.

The *werowance* was therefore totally dependent on the support of the *quioughcosughes*. Without them his rule was meaningless, and a *werowance* who was able to rely on the services and devotions of a number of powerful *quioughcosughes* was elevated in status and position above that of other *werowances* with lesser support. Thus they legitimised his authority and standing in the community. However, their role could not be dependent on the sanctioning visions and dreams of individuals we have encountered elsewhere, since they had to receive instruction in the precise enactment of the esoteric rituals it was their duty to perform.

Southeastern shamans had to be born into families whose lineage was unquestioned, given that outsiders or adoptees were unaccept-

ABOVE: *Figures with bird-like headdresses or costumes are commonly depicted on artefacts from the Southeast, and are said to represent 'flying shamans'. Birds and flying shamans have an ancient history in the area, as seen in White's drawing on page 200. The gorgets (LEFT & CENTRE) shown here also feature the characteristic forked-eye motif associated with the Mississippian Southern (or Death) Cult and said to represent a hawk.*
LEFT: *Gorget from Tennessee in which the shaman is carrying a death's head and ceremonial mace.*
CENTRE: *This gorget from Etowah, Georgia, depicts the shaman in a winged costume and with the talons of a bird of prey.*
RIGHT: *Winged shamans also appear on other objects, such as this incised conch shell dipper from the Mississippian site of Spiro in Oklahoma. Southern Cult insignia here include the sun-disc earrings that the shaman is wearing.*

able, and had to demonstrate a facility for learning and devotion in addition to any divine right to practise they might claim. Thus they acquired their skills through apprenticeship and instruction in the mysteries of the other world, but their ability to acquire these skills was nevertheless held as being passed down to them from the deities.

Exactly how these men came to hold their positions is unclear, and although there is little direct evidence to suggest the priests had an hereditary right it is equally obvious that such privileges were carefully guarded and protected within certain families. Social conditions may, of course, have been such that there was a predilection for particular individuals to follow in the footsteps of their predecessors: by living close to a practising shaman, children would have heard and been involved in many of the esoteric aspects of shamanic practice, and through encouragement of these interests became further involved; ultimately taking up the profession themselves.

Shamanism thus tended to run in certain families and the instruction of an initiate was often the responsibility of close relatives. Part of this instruction was in learning the shamanic language; since the shamans spoke in tongues that had long been forgotten. Their archaic words linked them to the mythical past, a world in which animals and humans had spoken a common language that was no longer understood by ordinary people. In this world, using the language of the shamans, deities such as Rattlesnake and Turkey Buzzard could impart their infinite wisdom, and also give guidance to the people on the manner in which they should conduct themselves in the present world.

Southeastern mythology details a number of such animal-gods who were able to pass on shamanic power. Among the most powerful of these, for the Algonquian-speaking tribes, was Hare. Although

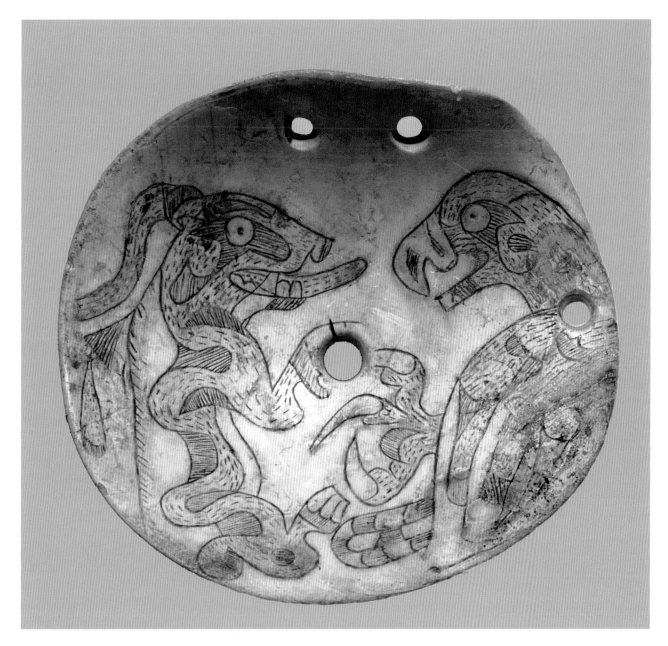

ABOVE: *The eagle confronting a panther on this conch shell gorget may represent the mythical conflict between the deities of the Upper World represented by the Thunderbird and those of the Lower World, represented by the Underwater Panther.*

the real hare was a relatively insignificant animal, the Great Hare was said to have created the world, the water, the fishes, the land, and the deer, as well as men and women. He was opposed by evil spirits, who are in some of the tales represented by Hare's own twin brother, symbolising the evil aspects of the personality that need to be suppressed. Hare overcame these and told the shamans they could invoke his power in the future to subdue evil and to ensure plentiful supplies of game and fresh fruits, and that, by him, they would

205

ABOVE: *Deer mask carved from cedar and inlaid with shell. This mask was recovered from the Southern Cult site of Spiro in Oklahoma, and was probably used by shamans during Deer Dance rituals held to ensure success in hunting. Similar rituals persisted in the area until the historic period.*

OPPOSITE: *The Southeastern connection between shamanic power, death, and the afterlife is chillingly brought to life in this shaman's mask from Mound City, Ohio. Mound City was a walled necropolis of burial mounds that also served as a ritual centre. This mask incorporates half a human skull and is trimmed with human hair.*

enable the Chiefs, the Nobles, the Honoured People, and the warrior societies, to keep the world in order.

The *quioughcosughes* were thereby charged with responsibility for maintaining the status quo: not only in respect of the duties and position of the *werowances*, but for the entire society and for the relationship that was thought to exist between people and the animal patrons. By the correct performance of rituals and observance of tribal dogma, they alone could ensure that the dictates of the deities and the benign expression of their power were brought to fruition on earth, and they alone could conduct the rituals and observances that established the right of the *werowance* to rule and which, at his death, secured the lineage for his heirs.

Southeastern shamans therefore controlled the reins of power overtly exercised by the Chiefs. Everyone, including the Great Sun himself, was subject to their ultimate authority, and it was through them that punishment was demanded for the breach of any rules of behaviour on ritual occasions, since it was to the Spirit World with which the shamans were in communication that people had to atone for deviations affecting the community, the clan, and the individual.

We do not need to rely entirely on European observations to understand something of shamanic practice in the Southeast. Excavations of Mississippian sites indicate these were great metropolises surrounded by defensive palisades, in which were contained the earthen mounds supporting the houses of the chiefs, the priests, and the temples themselves. People came to these centres from miles around to pay homage to the gods and deities enshrined in such sacred precincts, and also to avail themselves of the physical protection offered by the warrior societies in the present world as well as the divine protection secured by the priests for their future.

They were places of pilgrimage, but also strongholds where the people could demonstrate their allegiance to the *werowance* of any particular territory. Such gatherings for ritual and social purposes were called *Pow-Wows* by the Algonquian tribes, and this word has come into modern parlance to mean any tribal meetings at which dances and celebrations are held. The importance of the ceremonial centres was that they offered a focus for ritual and social activity, and also acted as places through which tribal cohesion could be actively expressed. The shamans had a key role to play, since it was through them that the tribal identity was stated, and it was by their power that the relationship between the sacred and the secular was established and maintained.

The effectiveness of the shamans was, in turn, subject to public

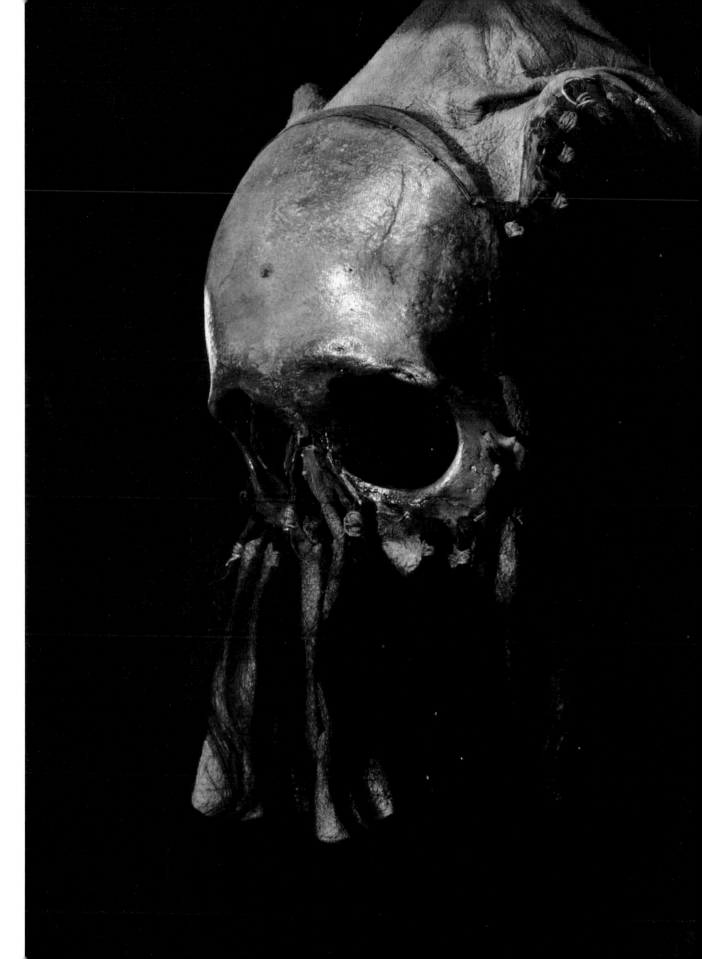

acknowledgement of the powers they claimed to possess and recognition of their responsibility to carry out their sacred duties. If they failed, whether in individual cures or in their higher capacity as guardians of the sacred fires, they would be put to death. The identity of the tribe – of the people – was dependent on shamans acting responsibly in everything they did, and they had no recourse to excuse for any laxity or lack of diligence.

It is therefore apparent that the powers of the *werowances* and the *quioughcosughes* could not have been as absolute as the early European reports suggest. Even the deities whom they represented on earth never had absolute power, and it is important to remember that when the Sun God delegated responsibility for the control of matters affecting the people he did so through a host of Servant Spirits. Their name alone suggests that they served the needs for which he had created them. Even the Great Sun was only a representative of this power: a medium via which the power of the Sun could be brought to the people, but he was still only the son of the Sun and therefore subservient to the wishes of the omnipotent Sun God himself.

When Europeans first came to the Southeast they witnessed only the dying vestiges of the Mississippian Culture. By that time many of the temple precincts had been abandoned, and the large numbers of people who had previously inhabited these centres were already dispersed. We don't clearly know the reasons why this had happened. Prolonged droughts were a contributory factor, since it had become impossible to produce the huge annual harvests of corn required to support so many people; but warfare and competition for resources may also have diminished populations and forced refugee groups to seek shelter elsewhere.

European incursions accelerated this decline, and in the process undermined the power of the shamans. Some of it was accidental: shamans had little control over introduced European diseases such as measles, smallpox, and syphilis. Some was deliberate: missionaries derided the shamans as superstitious pagans and sought to impose their own God and their own forms of worship. The two combined to weaken the power the shamans formerly claimed. Christianised Indians in Florida, for example, were inoculated against smallpox and their recovery rates were far higher than those treated by shamans in more remote areas by traditional methods that could not deal with diseases which were previously unknown. The missionaries played on this, and claimed that their God protected his children whereas the deities invoked by the shamans were powerless.

ABOVE: *Most of the pre-Columbian archaeological finds from the Southeast region are made from non-perishable materials such as stone, mica, or shell. However, conditions at the swampland site of Key Marco in Collier County, Florida, were such that a number of remarkable wood carvings dating to the late prehistoric Calusa have been found. The exact function of such carvings can no longer be determined, although it is clear that they provided a link between the world of the people and that of the spirit animals.*

ABOVE: *Carving of a wolf with gaping jaws. It has been suggested that the menacing appearance of this wolf was intended to safeguard a sacred site by warning off any interlopers.*

Yet even at this late date the shamans demonstrated powers which even the Europeans sometimes found quite remarkable. For instance, they were often able to heal deep wounds that the European ships' surgeons had declared untreatable, or they were able to effect other 'miraculous' cures. In one instance, an English settler who suffered from a bowel complaint that had been treated unsuccessfully for many years by European physicians, was persuaded by his half-Indian wife to consult a shaman. The settler had already sold all his livestock and leased his lands in payments for the treatments given to him previously. The shaman expressed regret that the settler had not come to him earlier and agreed to treat him in exchange for a blanket to keep himself warm in winter.

Believing in the superiority of his own physicians, the settler at first refused the shaman's help; but his wife pointed out that their situation was desperate, that without help he would die within a few months and leave her destitute, and that one blanket was a small

ABOVE: *This carving is a depiction of a pelican. Pelicans were revered in the area for their expertise in fishing. Cloaks made from pelican feathers were used during the historic period to indicate status as a chief or shaman and may have served a similar function among the early Calusa.*

RIGHT: *Deer head. The carving of this head is particularly fine, and it is also noteworthy for the articulated ears attached by rawhide bindings. Although the Calusa were primarily seafarers and fishermen, they also relied on game animals and plant produce. This mask, by capturing the deer's likeness, creates an affinity between the hunter and the hunted.*

ABOVE: *Figure of a kneeling shaman from an Ohio burial. The characteristic top-knot hairstyle was a distinguishing feature of shamans throughout the Southeast, Woodlands, and in the Great Plains. The antiquity of this symbol is indicated here by its appearance on a Hopewell figure that dates back to about 2000 years.*

price to pay for the chance, at least, of some hope for the future. He reluctantly agreed to accept the shaman's help and was given potions that caused him to break out into a 'terrible sweat'. For several days he lay in a comatose state; but on the seventh day – seven being a sacred number in Southeastern ritual and unrelated to the Christian concept of Sunday – he rose from his bed, donned his working clothes, and went out to work his fields.

In such individual cures the shaman was always approached by the family and his help was requested by them. This was partly because it was a breach of social and religious code for the shamans to volunteer their views and opinions in any matters of a personal nature. In the example given above it is significant that the shaman, despite being described as a close friend of the settler and having witnessed him over a period of years selling his livestock and possessions to pay European physicians for ineffective treatment, made no offer of help until the settler requested it himself. Even in their judicial functions as mediators in public disputes, the judgements of the shamans were never imposed but always came at the request of the injured party. Thus in the case of, say, a theft the shaman, although knowing who had committed the crime and where exactly the stolen articles were located, would reveal this information only if formally requested to do so.

The extraordinary powers of the shamans were demonstrated on another occasion when a European trader who had tolerated petty pilfering for some time finally asked a shaman to identify the culprit. All the people gathered and the shaman, after invoking various powers, and already having prior knowledge as to who was responsible, identified the thief, but while the people gathered to hear these revelations the situation was taken advantage of by someone else who ransacked several houses in the village: bushels of corn, bundles of dressed skins, personal possessions, and various other items that had been collected for trading went missing.

This was reported to the shaman, who was asked by a member of one of the families who had lost goods to find out who was responsible. He told the people to form a great circle, with openings at the north, east, south, and west, and then requested that his head be bound with several deerskins so that he was unable to see and could focus on his 'inner vision'. When this was done, and after a half hour of mumbled prayers in the shamanic language, he, still blindfolded, walked unerringly through the gap at the north of the circle, squatted on the ground at some distance from the group, and drew two lines on the ground to form a cross. He then asked for the blindfold to be removed, and pointing to a man in the audience said that if they removed his shirt they would find a cross on his back and that this was the person who had stolen property. Although the man protested, his shirt was removed and the cross was found, and after being interrogated he admitted his offence and showed the people where he had hidden the things he had taken.

In the latter case the shaman could not have known who the thief might be and was unaware that any thefts were taking place. Indeed, thefts from fellow members of the tribe – rather than the 'legitimate' theft of European property – were, in fact, so unusual that it is unlikely the shaman would have been the instigator. The accused man is also unlikely to have collaborated: as punishment the tribe offered him in slavery to the trader, who refused, and he was then banished from the tribe, a judgement equivalent to a death sentence.

Although Europeans were sceptical of the shamans' powers, the shamans were often vindicated in their predictions. On another occasion, in the Florida village of the Timucua chief Outina, their 'sorcerer' singled out the shield carried by the page of Captain D'Ottigny, one of several French visitors. He laid this on the ground, and drew about it a circle in chalk which he marked with various figures. He then sat on the shield in such a manner that no part of his body touched the earth, and, in this position, went into violent contortions. The French noted that his 'appearance [was] so frightful that he was hardly like a human being; for he twisted his limbs so that the bones could be heard to snap out of place'.

After several hours of this 'unnatural conjuring', which D'Ottigny stayed to watch, the shaman came to his senses, exhausted from his exertions and apparently astonished to be back in the presence of his fellow beings. Once recovered he began to relate, in a calm voice, the disposition of the enemy, their numbers, and the weapons they had available. Outina, acting on this advice, was able to surprise and defeat his foes; the shaman's predictions having proved correct in every detail.

Numerous other instances could be cited to show the formidable powers the shamans claimed to possess: power over illness, the power of clairvoyance, and ability to locate missing objects or persons, to see into the future, or to influence the weather and favourably influence the course of events. Most important was their ability to communicate directly with the animal-spirits of the supernatural world which European priests dismissed as 'conversations with the devil'.

Conflict between Europeans and Native tribes therefore developed on two fronts. The first of these was military and depended on

ABOVE: *Also found in Ohio, at the Turner Mound site, this clay figurine of a woman demonstrates the Hopewell artisan's skill in capturing the human likeness. Such figures were placed in tombs, either as a means of representing and preserving the physical aspects of the deceased or as a way of providing companionship by representing a spouse or relative.*

BELOW: *Tobacco was used in rituals intended to secure peace and friendship, as well as being a means whereby a prayer or vow could be solemnised. There was little recreational use of tobacco, and the Native varieties had a powerful narcotic effect useful as an aid in attaining trance states through which the spirits could be reached. Hopewell pipe bowls were often carved in the form of animals, such as the frog shown here. Typically the animal faced towards the smoker, with a hole in its back to receive the tobacco. A reed pipe stem was inserted in the hole in the base of the bowl.*

forming alliances with friendly tribes, since although European technology was superior and the Indians' bows and arrows, blowguns, and spears were no match even for early muskets, the European presence was tiny compared with the Native populations of the area. Settlement also meant the appropriation of Native lands and hunting territories which could be turned over to agriculture. The support of powerful werowances was therefore crucial to the survival of European settlements; but this support was often denied by the *quioughcosughes* simply because the priests condemned their 'devilment'.

Thus the second front on which conflict developed was a religious one, fought over by Native shamans and European priests. Curiously, this battle was fought by means that are more shamanic than Christian. The European priests invoked the powers of various saints and hurled exorcisms at the shamans, while the shamans invoked the powers of their own animal-spirits and uttered incantations that set their deities against the saints. This battle therefore took place on ground that was as familiar to the European priests as it was

to the Native shamans, and this tended to exacerbate the rivalry between them.

While the European priests made converts and attempted to turn them against the shamans, who were deemed to be beyond redemption, the shamans retaliated by condemning converts to the eternal torments of an afterlife in which they would be hungry and surrounded by plenty but unable to eat because their teeth had rotted, where the pleasures of the flesh could only be satisfied by haggard witches who demanded more than they could give, and where their bodies would grow old and weak but without any possibility of release through death or rejuvenation. They would suffer forever in this World of Disorder.

Meanwhile the Christian priests condemned the shamans themselves to an eternal Hell from which there could be no escape. The shamans' response was to throw the beliefs of the Christians back against them. The Calusa, a Florida tribe, claimed, for instance, that annual sacrifice was essential to bring things into order and to offset the diseases introduced by Europeans. They threatened the Spanish, who claimed their territory, by declaring that only the sacrifice of a Spaniard would appease their deities. Since the Spanish had introduced the diseases it was logical that the Spanish should suffer and make recompense. In consequence the Calusa captured shipwrecked Spanish sailors and threatened to sacrifice them in retaliation for Spanish incursions in Florida and to counteract the disastrous effects of introduced epidemics and diseases.

Other tribes developed their own shamanic methods of using vestiges of European power in influencing the supernatural world. When Laudonnière visited the Timucua in northern Florida in 1564 he found that they worshipped a column bearing the Royal Arms of the King of France which had been erected the previous year by Ribaud. He tells us that

> before the monument there lay various offerings of the fruits, and edible or medicinal roots, growing thereabouts; vessels of perfumed oils; a bow, and arrows; and it was wreathed around from top to bottom with flowers of all sorts, and boughs of trees esteemed choicest.

The Timucua, although no less warlike or feared than their southern Calusa neighbours, with whom they had engaged in intermittent warfare for centuries, chose to placate rather than oppose the French by adopting Christian saints as deities; although their reasons for this may have been political rather than shamanic. The French were intruders in a country that had already been claimed by Spain, and had arrived in an impoverished state. If the Timucua chief, Athore, had not given them access to his store-houses of grain, meat, and fish it is unlikely the French would have survived. Athore, in turn, was well aware of Spanish intrigues in the area, and was therefore keen to enlist the help of the French arquebusiers in shows of strength against his enemies.

The Calusa and Timucua examples show the extreme reactions to European intrusion. Spanish attempts at supremacy met with resistance from the shamans; French dependence encouraged the shamans to capitalise on their weaknesses. Ultimately Spanish rule prevailed. The French Fort Caroline was burned and its inhabitants massacred; the Calusa were enslaved and deported to Cuba; the Timucua disappeared without trace. Later, the English and their Indian allies would drive the Spanish out of Florida, and finally the whole area was ceded to the United States.

Shamanic beliefs nevertheless persisted. Although Natchez culture foundered, and the Timucua, Calusa, and other tribes of the region were annihilated or deported, the shamans of the area continued to exercise influence and much tribal lore was interpreted in terms of what the shamans held important and was determined by their acceptance or rejection of views imposed by outside agencies. These tribes, whose strategic significance became apparent in the 18th century when Europeans enlisted their help as 'buffer nations' in their own struggles for supremacy in the area, are referred to today as the Five Civilised Tribes: the Choctaw, Chickasaw, Cherokee, Creek, and Seminole.

With the possible exceptions of the Creek and Seminole, they continued many of the practices of the earlier Mississippians, especially their congregation in large villages and a dependence on corn, bean, and squash farming. Their chiefs and shamans were not, however, as authoritarian as their predecessors. Among the Cherokee, for instance, the position of shaman was held by a single representative of each of their seven clans. These seven men - since women were forbidden to enter their ranks, although they did work as physicians and midwives - formed a Council of Beloved Men and oversaw the entire conduct of society and the enforcement of social rules. Any wrong committed was passed to them for their decision, and only they could determine what attitude the tribe would adopt towards the outside world. Although the Cherokee had both Red and White Towns, the Red Towns being responsible for managing Cherokee affairs during times of war and the White Towns in peace, the

OPPOSITE: *A bowl with alternating effigies of frogs and human heads around its rim. In Southeast belief, the frog or toad was the bringer of rain as well as being a powerful shamanic figure. The bowl shown here was probably used by a shaman during rituals that were intended to appeal to the spirits of rain and thunder. The human heads refer to the connection between people and spirits, rather than expressing any warlike activity.*

RIGHT: *The exact significance of the hands and bones that decorate this Hopewell bowl is unknown, although, as a funerary object, it is likely they are intended to suggest the connection between life and death. The hand was a symbol of possession or ownership, and in this instance may therefore be representative of spiritual ownership, perhaps over the ancestral forces associated with he soul of the deceased.*

Council of Beloved Men rather than the War and Peace Chiefs had final jurisdiction. In inter-tribal relationships it was only the Council of Beloved Men that could declare war, and only they could bring hostilities to a close.

In everyday matters all disputes were brought before this Council, which met on a regular basis and couched its decisions in mythological terms by reference to the Servant Spirits by whom they were guided. They were renowned not only as the magicians and conjurors of the European texts, but as adjudicators they were the nation's court of justice, and their collective word was law. In effect, the Council of Beloved Men acted like a modern judiciary and the most important building in a Cherokee town was, instead of a temple for the interred bones of deceased chiefs, a form of council house which functioned as a courtroom and where the Council sat in judgement. Their deliberations, however, were shamanic in both intent and practice, and were based on the Council's interpretations of the ancient laws handed down by their ancestors in the esoteric language of the shamans.

Furthermore, each shaman was believed to carry within him a number of animal spirits - most commonly in the form of lizards and snakes - which directed and guided his judgements. Decisions were made on the basis of advice supposedly received from such supernatural animal helpers. In addition, every shaman boasted specific skills in the curing of certain types of illness and wore appropriate insignia to proclaim this fact. Thus among the Creeks a

ABOVE: *Birds of prey feature prominently in shamanic belief, since they are swift, courageous, noiseless, and deadly efficient. All these qualities are those sought by shamans in their contacts with adversarial spirit powers, as well as being essential to a warrior ethos; although the shaman's war, unlike that of the warrior, was fought on a spiritual plane. This mica cut-out is a stylised representation of a bird's talon, and is notable for its beauty and craftsmanship.*

shaman who was able to heal gunshot wounds wore a buzzard feather, a fox skin was worn by one who could treat snake bite, and an owl feather was the badge of a shaman capable of trailing the enemy at night.

Here, too, we find the old Mississippian belief in the sanctity of fire. The Creeks and the Chickasaws held that there was a supreme Sky God who was connected with both sky and sun and whose symbol on earth was a fire kept burning in their sacred grounds and tended by the shamans. In Cherokee ritual, all the old fires in the houses were extinguished in March and a new fire was kindled through friction by drilling in a dried grape vine. Embers of this new fire were then carried to every house in the village so that the cooking fires could be relit, and we know this had been a practice also of the Natchez and of the Mississippians before them.

It is significant that many ceremonies conducted by the shamans, whether as private cures or in public rituals, were preceded by token sacrifices to fire. Even in a major ceremony such as the so-called Green Corn Dance, when the entire tribe celebrated the ripening of the first corn of the year, the shamans took the grains of seven ears of corn and 'fed' the fire before anyone was allowed to roast the new ears or to prepare a ceremonial tea made from wild horehound.

There are also reports that, at least on some occasions, the shamans had recourse to fire in their treatments of the sick. Platforms are described on which a patient was laid above the glowing embers of a fire made from herbs said to be effective in treating various kinds of illness. The smoke from the herbs was thought to enter the body of the patient and to purge him/her of the illness. The purifying effects of smoke were used as well in fumigating buildings to rid them of harmful influences and thus render them safe for the performance of any sacred rituals within their boundaries.

The Creeks are even reported to have conducted an annual ceremony in which they gathered all the worn clothes of the previous year, swept and cleansed their houses as well as the streets of their towns, and collected all the rubbish and detritus to cast together into a purifying fire. The event was officiated over by the shamans and is reminiscent of the ritual burning out of the old year so the new can begin afresh or of the annual relighting of the village fires in the Natchez and Mississippian towns.

Although the shamans of the Five Civilised Tribes did not claim direct descent from the deities, their beliefs had their origins in the earlier Mississippian patterns, in the worship of the deified Great Suns of the temple complexes, and in their association with the

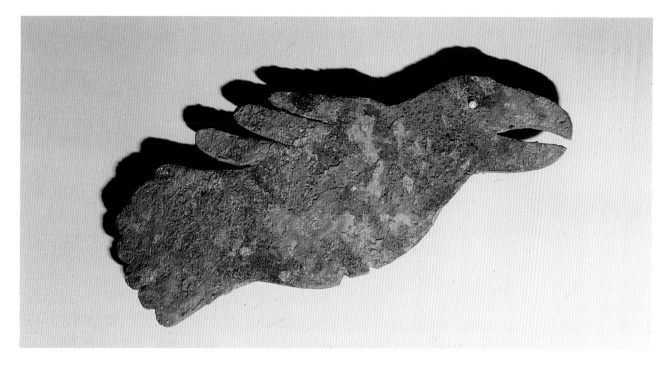

ABOVE: *The raucous raven is an inquisitive, and in some respects comical, bird; but it is noted for its fearlessness. In many myths Raven appears as a Trickster/Transformer, and in this role was an invaluable helper to shamans. This image of Raven is made from a nugget of Native copper that has been hammered out to form a thin sheet, and has a freshwater pearl inserted for the eye.*
It is Hopewell and dates to between 100 BC and 200 AD.

sacred fires maintained by the shaman-priests in their fortified towns.

Partly because of the formality of their roles and the obvious links with a Mississippian heritage, the shamans of the historic Southeastern tribes, despite their reliance on mythological explanations for their actions, enjoyed a reputation for successful cures and were believed, by both Native and settler populations, to possess ancient knowledge. Although the priests continued to denounce shamanic practices, they were aiming more at the shamans' beliefs and their insistence on invoking the assistance of animal deities than at the efficacy of their cures and predictions.

In many areas, particularly those remote from large population centres, the shaman was, in fact, often the only skilled medical practitioner for hundreds of miles and his methods of treatment were sometimes superior to those used by the barber-surgeons and quack doctors of the frontier settlements. Early reports are rife with comments that the surgeon, together with the priest and the lawyer, was the 'scourge' of civilisation, driven too often by pecuniary interest and, more often than not, responsible for a greater number of deaths through inappropriate intervention than for successful recovery from illness.

Against this background the shaman, with an extensive knowledge of innumerable herbal remedies and with the skill to set broken bones and heal other wounds, was often successful in his treatments - even in cases considered hopeless by white practitioners. The frontier farmer, a rugged practical man, paid little heed to the mumblings of the shamans and was more concerned that his treatment, in whatever language it was couched, should produce the desired effect. He judged things by result rather than theory, and by all accounts shamanic results were often spectacularly successful in the treatment of illnesses and diseases with which the shamans were familiar.

Yet, despite the effectiveness of his herbs and remedies - many of which were to be incorporated in the materia medica of the United States - the prevailing belief among Southeastern shamans was that all illness, unless caused by an obvious external factor such as a gunshot wound, had a supernatural origin. Even as late as 1935, William Corlett, writing about disease-origin beliefs in the Southeast, noted:

> the most important are the spirits of the animals, who thus gain revenge for slights and abuses. Disrespect toward fire, such as urinating on the ashes, or throwing offal on it, or spitting on it, will bring disaster. Insults of like nature to the river have their penalty. Human ghosts who naturally feel lonesome for their friends and relatives cause a disease . . . while an animal ghost will cause trouble if respect has not been shown to its body after it has been killed. A powerful disease-bringer is the magic used by witches to cause sickness. Other causes of disease are dreams, omens, neglected taboos.

We must, however, make a distinction between the explanatory language used by the shamans and the effectiveness of their cures and predictions, while bearing in mind that the nature of shamanic belief allows for the influence of malignant forces which are only partly under the control of the shamans. Throughout the Southeast there was a belief in a race of spirit beings, usually pygmies but occasionally giants, such as the *lofa* of the Chickasaw, whose sole interest appears to have been to cause harm to humans. They would carry off women and sometimes waylay and flay solitary hunters. Although these were only limited powers, they were nevertheless thought to pose a very real threat to the people.

Linked with the pygmies and giants were witches and wizards, although they more usually appeared in human form. Shamans themselves might be thought to act as witches if they lost control over the animal-spirits by whom they were inspired, and failure to cure a patient or a wrong prediction could lead to deep suspicion

ABOVE: *West of the Cumberland Gap the Big South Fork River flows freely among the forests that were once the hunting ground of the Cherokee. The floodwater plains of rivers also provided a rich fertile soil for Cherokee crops of corn and beans. Although mainly dependent on farming, which enabled them to form large permanent communities, the Cherokee were also skilled hunters. Shamanic rituals frequently combined elements of both farming and hunting.*

that the shaman might be acting with malice.

Using power for witchcraft was formerly a frequent accusation, and witchcraft accusations were used by missionaries as a practical way of fomenting dissent and undermining the authority of the shamans. By discrediting the shamans the priests hoped to attract converts, and were often quite successful in doing so. Among the Five Civilised Tribes many people converted to Christianity, aided by the high incidence of mixed marriages and the fact that tribal lore made no ethnic distinction. In fact the parentage of the most famous leader of the Cherokees in the early 1800s, John Ross, was less than half Cherokee. The Southeastern heritage of divinely inspired *werowances* and *quioughcosughes* also came to the aid of Christian missionaries, who described themselves as God's representatives on earth and quite often claimed divine inspiration.

Despite these inroads the shamans continued, and continue, to enjoy considerable power. Notwithstanding the Christian concept of a separation between good and evil compared with the Native view that all forces have a capacity for benign or malicious action, many Native peoples see little real difference between indigenous and imposed beliefs. Details differ, but the concept that malevolent forces oppose benevolent ones and that these have to be brought into balance via the intercession of a divine intermediary is remarkably similar. The two beliefs were readily assimilated within Native communities.

In addition, the widespread acceptance of shamanic curing techniques in the 1800s allied with later romanticism centred on the image of the Noble Savage, resulted in a peculiar kind of compliment being paid to the shamans in the form of the 'Indian Doctor': itinerant white and half-breed salesmen peddling so-called 'Native' remedies for virtually every ailment. These, prior to government regulation of drugs and medicines, led to companies such as the Kickapoo Indian Medicine Company being formed in the late 1800s to manufacture patent medicines said to derive from the ancient remedies of the tribes and which carried advertising slogans such as 'Take and Be Healed - the Great Spirit Planted It'.

Although the patent medicines generally bore little relationship to Native cures - the main ingredient being distilled alcohol (which was unknown prior to its introduction by Europeans), mixed with various dubious ingredients purchased from pharmaceutical companies - they nevertheless served to reinforce the notion of the Indian as a curer possessed of ancient wisdom, and led, ultimately, to the formation of the touring Medicine Shows which, like the circuses, broke the monotony of small-town existence and established the concept of shamanism as a commercial activity.

Many erroneous notions about shamanism stem from its romanticisation and commercialisation, which had little to do with Native practice although it claimed Native inspiration mainly from the Southeastern tribes. Today, in more enlightened times, the shamans are reasserting their authority as the traditional keepers of the ancient laws, and, despite centuries of derision, persecution, and misrepresentation, these laws - based as they are on the natural principles understood and acted upon by the forefathers - are again significant in the reinstatement and maintenance of traditional tribal identity, beliefs and customs.

Although the Mississippians, the Natchez and Taensa of the lower Mississippi, the Timucua, Calusa, and Apalachee of Florida are all gone, and the Creek, Choctaw, Chickasaw, Cherokee, and most of

ABOVE: *This ornate Seminole turban is decorated with flamingo feathers and a silver band and would have been worn by a shaman during ceremonies as a symbol of his power. Elaborate headdresses almost always included feathers in recognition of the desirable qualities possessed by birds and as an expression of the shaman's putative ability to transform himself and fly into the spirit world.*

the Seminole have been forcibly removed from their Southeastern homelands to Oklahoma, the spirit of the Southeast - the spirit of fire - lives on in their descendants. The ancient laws, set in place when the world was created, have survived generations of neglect and discord, and centuries of political intrigue and systematic undermining of shamanic authority. Nowadays, shamans are once again playing a prominent role and are called upon to bless the grounds for the annual harvest festivals, or busks, celebrated by the descendants of the Creeks and other Southeastern tribes, rightful inheritors of the ancient laws.

Conclusion

Shamanism is a world-wide phenomenon that has ancient roots and which has influenced all the major religions. It stems from the beliefs of early hunting cultures, but has been adapted to fit the needs of more settled agricultural communities where the role of the shaman has been integrated with that of the priest. In a contemporary world, with its concern for materialistic ends, the shaman appears as an anomaly: concerned with contact with spirits and with an animistic world that is defined in myths, shamanic activity seems at times to be distant from and to have little relevance to modern life.

But to dismiss the shamans as archaic vestiges of a long-forgotten past would be unwise. Their beliefs stem from a personal calling rather than the more highly organised rituals of a formal priesthood, and through this they affirm the importance of the individual in a world where individualism has come to be seen as idiosyncratic or eccentric. Despite persecution by Church authorities and through government legislation devised to curtail their activity the shamans continue to be important. As the holders of ancient wisdom which is enshrined in the myths and traditions of the people they are at the forefront of worldwide revivalist movements; in North America they are vital to religious and political efforts to assert a Native American identity.

This identity is partly expressed through the rituals of the Native American Church, which combines Native beliefs with Christianity and teaches a strict moral code of brotherly love, care of the family, self-reliance, and the avoidance of alcohol. The Native American Church uses peyote as a sacrament, and peyote-induced visions are

Indians believed that certain conspicuous features of the landscape they lived in were particularly propitious for establishing contact with the forces which governed the natural world. Medicine Mountain in Wyoming was one such place as evidenced by the sacred Medicine Wheel outlined with stones on top of this mountain's high plateau.

223

defined as the Peyote Road through which the moral codes the people must follow on their journey throught life are revealed. Although some conservative shamans claim that the use of peyote is a 'false' route to to a vision, the importance of the vision itself is shamanistic in origin. Incorporated in Oklahoma in 1918, the Native American Church now has a membership comprising about half of the Native population of the United States.

Shamans today also support a Native American identity by serving on Tribal Councils and acting as advisors to the tribes as well as to the Federal and Canadian governments, and are increasingly working in close association and cooperation with medical teams in modern hospitals. The analytical skill and support they offer complements conventional tratments and surgery and has been shown to aid recovery times in both Native and non-Native patients.

The problems that face the shamans in a modern world are often different from those they were concerned with in the traditional contexts that are primarily discussed in this text. History has seen to it that the tribes have come under influences and pressures from outside that have forced them into situations where they need to accommodate other views. The shamans readily accept that times have changed, but also assert that their traditional ways continue to have validity. The *angakok* of the Eskimo recognise that the world is never quite what it seems and that change is inevitable, but point to the fact that this was also the belief of their ancestors.

The shamans of today regard themselves as the protectors of tradition and ethnic identity, but also see their activities as essential safeguards of the people's future. They do so not from a sense of confusion or uncertainty but from a position of strength. The *diyi* who invokes the sacred healing powers of the *Gans* during an Apache girl's puberty rite but who makes his living as the employee of a lumber company, or the Pueblo *kiva*-priest who attends Catholic mass and then officiates over the arrival of the *Kachinas* in the Pueblo plaza, sees no contradiction in these diverse activities.

Looking back into the past and forward into the future, they point out that the shamanic view has always been an all-embracing one: that spiritual power cannot be confined or focused within spatial or theoretical limits, and that although the power of the old-time shamans may have been different in application it was not dissimilar in intent. By providing leadership and setting an example both the old-time shamans and their modern counterparts are responsible for the spiritual guidance of their people.

The history and identity of the people resides in the myths the shamans recite and the rituals they conduct. In the Blackfoot stories *Napi*, the first shaman, was a wanderer who introduced the elements that defined Blackfoot culture until his presence was made permanent by the Woman Chief who transformed him into a pine tree. The Blackfoot say that this pine tree still stands on the banks of a river near Calgary, in Alberta, and it is through this that *Napi* has become rooted to the earth. His spirit, however, is expressed through the actions of the people.

Shamanism is similarly rooted both in the earth and in its mythical origins, yet continues to have a permanent presence and significance today and through the activities and stories of the shamans it is being preserved and passed on to future generations.

Bibliography

Bancroft Hunt, Norman. *Warriors*, Salamander Books, London, 1995
    'Tricksters, Heroes, Shamans and Ritualists: A Cultural Analysis of Blackfoot Story-Telling', Ph.D. Thesis, Goldsmiths' College, University of London, 1999
Bancroft Hunt, Norman and Forman, Werner. *People of the Totem*, Orbis, London, 1979
    The Indians of the Great Plains, Orbis, London, 1981
Benedict, Ruth F. 'The Concept of the Guardian Spirit in North America' in *Memoir* No. 9, American Anthropological Association, 1923
    Patterns of Culture, Houghton Mifflin, Boston, MA, 1924
Bierhorst, John. *The Sacred Path: Spells, Prayers and Power Songs of the American Indians*, Quill, New York, NY, 1984
Boas, Franz. *The Social Organization and Secret Societies of the Kwakiutl Indians*, Annual Report, Bureau of American Ethnology, Smithsonian Institution, Washington, DC, 1897
Boas, Franz and Hunt, George. 'Kwakiutl Texts' in *Jesup North Pacific Expedition*, Vol 3, Brill, Leiden & Stechert, New York, NY, 1905
Bourke, John G. 'Apache Medicine Men' in *Annual Report*, Bureau of American Ethnology, Smithsonian Institution, Washington, DC, 1887-1888
    On the Border with Crook, Scribner, 1892
Brasser, Ted J. 'The Creative Visions of a Blackfoot Shaman' in *Alberta History*, Vol. 23, No 2, Alberta, 1975
Brown, Joseph E. *The Question of Mysticism Within Native American Traditions*. Image, New York, NY, 1980
Brown, Vinson. *Voices of Earth and Sky: The Vision Life of the Native Americans and their Culture Heroes*, Stackpole Books, Harrisburg, PA, 1974
Burch, Ernest and Forman, Werner. *The Eskimo*, Macdonald Orbis, London, 1988
Burns, Louis F. *Osago Indian Customs and Myths*, Ciga Press, Fallbrook, CA, 1984
Burt, Benjamin W. 'Power in the World of the Blackfoot Indians', M. Phil. Thesis, University College, London, 1976
Cartier, Jacques. *Bref Récit et Succincte Narration de la Navigation*, Paris, 1863
Catlin, George. *Letters and Notes on the Manners, Customs, and Condition of the North American Indians*, 2 vols., London, 1841
Charles, Lucille Hoerr. 'Drama in Shaman Exorcism' in *Journal of American Folklore*, 66, 1953
Clark, Laverne Harrell. *They Sang for Horses*, University of Arizona Press, Tucson, AZ, 1966
Clayton, Lawrence A., Knight, Jr., Vernon, Moore, Edward (Eds.). *The De Soto Chronicles: The Esxpedition of Hernando De Soto to North America in 1539–1543*, University of Alabama Press, 1996 (reprint)
Cloutier, David. *Spirit, Spirit: Shamans' Songs*, Copper Beech Press, Brown University, Providence, RI, 1980
Codere, Helen. *Fighting with Property*, Monograph XVIII, American Ethnological Society, 1950
Corlett, W. T. *The Medicine-Man of the American Indians and his Cultural Background*, Thomas, Springfield, IL, 1935
Cremony, John C. *Life among the Apache*. Roman & Co., San Francisco, CA, 1868
de Laguna, Friederica. *Under Mount St Elias: The History and Culture of the Yakutat Tlingit*, Smithsonian Institution Press, Washington, DC, 1972
de Laudonnière, René. *L'Histoire notable de la Floride, contenant les trois voyages faits in icelles par des capitaines et pilotes français, Paris, 1586*
Dixon, Roland B. 'Some Aspects of the American Shaman', Presidential Address, American Folk-Lore Society, Chicago, IL, January 1st, 1908.
Dorsey, George A. 'Traditions of the Skidi Pawnee, Memoir', American Folk-Lore Society, Vol. VIII, Boston, MA, 1904
Durkheim, Emile. *The Elementary Forms of the Religious Life*, Allen & Unwin, London, 1915
Eliade, Mircea. *Le chamanisme et les techniques archaïques de l'extase*. Payot, Paris, 1951
    'Recent Works on Shamanism' in *History of Religions*, I, 1961
Feest, Christian. 'The Indians of Northeastern North America', Institute of Religious Iconography, State University, Groningen, Section X, Fascicle 7, Leiden, 1980
Fewkes, Jesse Walter. *Hopi Snake Ceremonies: An Eye-witness Account*, Avanyu Publishing, Albuquerque, NM, 1986
Fitzhugh, William W. and Caplan, Susan A. *Inua: Spirit World of the Bering Sea Eskimo*, Smithsonian Institution, Washington D.C., 1982

Halifax, Joan. *Shamanic Voices: a Survey of Visionary Narratives*, Dutton, New York, NY, 1979
  The Wounded Healer, Thames & Hudson, London, 1991
Hallowell, A. I. 'Bear Ceremonialism in the Northern Hemisphere' in *American Anthropologist*, Vol. XXVIII, 1926
Hartmann, Horst. *Kachina Figuren der Hopi Indianer*, Berlin, 1978
Hill-Tout, Charles. *The Salish People*, 4 Vols., Talonbooks, Vancouver, BC, 1978
Hudson, Travis and Underhay, Ernest. *Crystals in the Sky: an Intellectual Odyssey involving Chumash Astronomy, Cosmology and Rock Art*, Santa Barbara Museum of Natural History, CA, 1978
Hultkrantz, A. *Conceptions of the Soul among North American Indians: a Study in Religious Ethnology,* Statens Etnografiska Museet, Stockholm, 1953
  The Religions of the American Indians, University of California Press, Berkeley, 1979
  Belief and Worship in Native North America, ed. by C. Vecsey, Syracuse University Press, New York, 1981
  Shamanic Healing and Ritual Drama: Health and Medicine in Native North America, Crossroad, New York, 1992
Irwin, Lee. *The Dream Seekers: Native American Visionary Traditions of the Great Plains*, University of Oklahoma Press, Norman, OK, 1994
Kalweit, Holger. *Shamans, Healers, and Medicine Men*, Shambhala, Boston, MA, 1992
Kroeber, Theodora and Heizer, Robert F. *Almost Ancestors: the First Californians*, Sierra-Ballantine, New York, NY, 1968
Landes, R. *Ojibwa Religion and the Midéwiwin*, University of Wisconsin Press, Madison, 1968
Leh, L. L. 'The Shaman in Aboriginal American Society' in *University of Colorado Studies* 20, Boulder, CO, 1934
Lévi-Strauss, C. *The Way of the Masks*, University of Washington Press, Seattle, 1982
Lewis, I. M. *Ecstatic Religion: a Study of Shamanism and Spirit Possession*, Penguin Books, London, 1971
Lowie, Robert H. 'Myths and Traditions of the Crow Indians' in *Anthropological Papers*, Vol. XXV, Part I, American Museum of Natural History, New York, NY, 1918
  'Notes on Shoshonean Ethnography' in *Anthropological Papers*, American Museum of Natural History, Vol. XX Part III, New York, NY, 1924
  'Shamans and Priests among the Plains Indians' in *Reader on Comparative Religion*, New York, NY, 1979
Michael, Henry N. (ed.). *Lieutenant Zagoskin's Travels in Russian America 1842–1844,* University of Toronto Press, 1967
Neihardt, John G. *Black Elk Speaks*, Morrow, New York, NY, 1932
Nicholson, Shirley. *Shamanism: an Expanded View of Reality*, Quest Books, Wheaton, IL, 1987
Park, Willard Z. 'Shamanism in Western North America' in *Northwestern University Studies in the Social Sciences*, Evanston, IL, 1938
Parsons, Elsie Clews. 'Hopi and Zuni Ceremonialism' in *Memoir 39*, American Anthropological Association, 1933
Radin, Paul. *Primitive Religion: its Nature and Origin*, Viking Press, New York, NY, 1937
Rasmussen, K. *Across Arctic America: Narrative of the Fifth Thule Expedition*, Putnam, New York, 1927
  Report of the Fifth Thule Expedition, Gyldendal, Copenhagen, 1931
Reichard, Gladys A. *Navaho Religion*, Bollingen Foundation, New York, NY, 1950
Riches, David. 'Shamanism: the Key to Religion' in *Man*, Vol. 29, No 2, Royal Anthropological Institute, London, 1994
Ripinsky, Naxon M. *The Nature of Shamanism: Substance and Function of a Religious Metaphor*, State University of New York, Albany, NY, 1993
Rogers, Stephen L. *The Shaman: his Symbols and his Healing Power*. Springfield, IL, 1982
Rothenberg, Jerome. *Technicians of the Sacred*. University of California Press, Berkeley, CA, 1968
Shirokogoroff, S. M. *What is Shamanism?* Quest Society, 1924
Spier, Leslie. *Klamath Ethnography*, University of California Publications in American Archeology and Ethnography, Vol. 30, Berkeley, CA, 1930
Spier, Leslie. *Cultural Relations of the Gila River and Lower Colorado Tribes*, Yale University Publications in Anthropology, No. 3, New Haven, CT, 1936
Stewart, K. 'Spirit Possession in Native America' in *South western Journal of Anthropology* 2, Albuquerque, NM, 1946
Strickland, Rennard. *Fire and the Spirits: Cherokee Law from Clan to Court*, University of Oklahoma Press, Norman, OK, 1975
Swanton, John R. *The Indians of the Southeastern United States*, Bulletin 137, Bureau of American Ethnology, Smithsonian Institution, US Government Printing Office, Washington, DC, 1946
Vogel, Virgil. *American Indian Medicine*, University of Oklahoma Press, Norman, OK, 1970
Walker, James R. *Lakota Belief and Ritual*, University of Nebraska Press, Lincoln, NE, 1980
Waters, Frank. *Book of the Hopi*, Viking Press, New York, NY, 1963
Wissler, Clark. 'Ceremonial Bundles of the Blackfoot Indians' in *Anthropological Papers*, Vol. VII, Part II, American Museum of Natural History, New York, NY, 1912
Wissler, Clark. 'General Discussion of Shamanistic and Dancing Societies' in *Anthropological Papers*, Vol. XII, Part II, American Museum of Natural History, New York, NY, 1916
Wolf, Fred. *The Eagle's Quest; A Physicist's Search for Truth in the Heart of the Shamanic World*, HarperCollins, London 1991

Acknowledgments

The publisher gratefully acknowledges the permission of the following to reproduce illustrations:

Alaska Gallery of Eskimo Art 19a, 23; American Museum of Natural History 47, 80, 146, 147; Anchorage Museum 41; Arizona Historical Society 120; Arizona State Museum 109, 111a, 111c, 113b, 124, 128; Norman Bancroft Hunt 174, 175; David Bernstein Gallery 85; Claude Bouchard 44, 49; British Museum 30, 31, 39, 96, 162, 200, 201; Burke Museum of Natural History and Culture 99; Canadian Museum of Civilization 51b, 57a, 81, 82, 86b, 86c, 87b, 87c, 87d; William Channing Collection 17; Eugene Chesrow Trust 42; Corbis/Tom Bean 165; Detroit Institute of Arts 66, 68; Ethnologisches Museum Berlin 61a, 61b, 62, 119a, 122, 126a, 126b, 127a, 127b, 127c, 187a; Field Museum of Natural History 12, 40, 60, 64, 65, 77, 90b, 104, 143a, 143b, 143c, 186a, 186b, 187b, 189, 191, 192, 202, 216, 217; George Fischer 56–7; Peter Furst 155; Glenbow Museum 169b (altar), 170a, 170b; Phoebe Anderson Hearst Museum of Anthropology 24, 78b, 136, 137a, 137b; Sheldon Jackson Museum 16, 21, 32; Joslyn Art Museum 53, 172, 173, 176a–c, 177, 179; Landesmuseum Natur und Mensch Oldenburg 27, 36; Frank McClung Museum 215a; Maxwell Museum of Anthropology 113a; Milwaukee Public Museum 59a; Museum für Völkerkunde Hamburg/B. Saal 25, 46; Museum of Northern Arizona 9; Jeffrey R. Myers Collection 11, 19b; National Anthropological Archives 59b; National Museum of the American Indian 37, 38, 57b, 67, 69, 119, 121, 125, 140, 145, 220, Heye Foundation 78, 103, 169a (mask), 204a, 205, 206; National Parks Service 6, 106, 123, 129, 134, 157, 194, 99, 219; New York Public Library 183; Ohio Historical Society 203; Ohio State Museum 56, 207, 212; Robert S. Peabody Foundation for Archaeology 204b; Peabody Museum of Anthropology 108b, 149, 210, 211; Peter the Great Museum of Anthropology and Ethnology 26, 79, 83, 91a, 97a, 97b, 101a, 101b; Plains Indian Museum, Buffalo Bill History Center 16, 163, 164, 166, 188, Chandler Pohrt Collection 163, A. Spohr Collection 171, Willoughby & Howard Collection 170c; Provincial Museum of British Columbia 74, 86a, 88, 89, 92, 93; Robinson Museum 168; Royal Ontario Museum 51a; Santa Barbara Museum of Natural History 151; Schindler Collection 116a; Smithsonian American Art Museum 180, 181; Smithsonian Institution 58, 118, 196, 204c, 215b; George Terasaki Collection 35; Übersee Museum Bremen 84, 87a; Special Collections, The University of Arizona Library 130a, 130b, 131; University Museum, University of Alaska 18; University of Pennsylvania Museum 208, 209a, 209b; University of Washington 33; Utah Museum of Natural History 111b, 139; Ventura County Museum of History & Art 141, 153a–c, 154a, 154b, 158; Werner Forman Archive 2, 9, 11, 12, 14, 16, 17, 18, 19a, b, 20, 21, 22, 23, 24, 26, 28-9, 30, 31, 32, 34, 35, 37, 38, 40, 41, 42, 52, 56, 57a, 60, 61b, 63, 64, 65, 70, 72, 74, 77, 76, 77, 78a, 79, 81, 82, 83, 85, 86a, b, c, 87b, c, d, 88, 89, 91a, b, 92, 93, 94-5, 96, 97a, b, 101a, b, 103, 104, 108a, b, 110, 111a, b, c, 113a, b, 114a, b, 115, 116a, b, c, 117a, b, c, d, 128, 132, 138, 139, 143a, b, c, 145, 160, 162, 163, 164, 167, 168, 169a, b, 170a, b, c, 171, 185, 186a, b, 187a, b, 188, 189, 191, 192, 196, 202, 204a, b, c, 205, 206, 207, 208, 209a, 209b, 210, 211, 212, 215b, 216, 217, 222

Index

INDEX

INDEX